1113 7014

KEEPING CHRISTMAS

KEEPING CHRISTMAS

The Celebration of an American Holiday

Philip Reed Rulon

ARCHON BOOKS 1990

First published 1990 as an Archon Book, an imprint of
The Shoe String Press, Inc., Hamden, Connecticut 06514

Printed in the United States of America

Library of Congress Cataloging-in-Publication Data

Rulon, Philip Reed.
Keeping Christmas : the celebration
of an American holiday / Philip Reed Rulon
p.   cm.
Includes bibliographical references.
1. Christmas stories, American.
I. Title.
PS648.C45R85   1990
813'.010833—dc20   90-43295
ISBN 0-208-02278-3

Designed by Abigail Johnston

The paper used in this publication meets the minimum requirement of
American National Standard for Information Sciences—
Permanence of Paper for Printed Library Materials.
ANSI Z39.48-1984⊗

To Annette

and Yvonne (and Gary)
Ann Marie (and Philip)
Bill
Scott
and Douglas

Contents

A Word from the Editor

The Christmas holiday that Europeans brought to the New World had a fifteen-hundred-year history, beginning with the birth of Jesus Christ as described in the gospels of the New Testament. The precise date of this momentous event is and perhaps always will be shrouded in mystery. Nevertheless, the birth of the Bethlehem infant had an enduring effect on how the world marks time. Dionysius Exiguus, in the early sixth century, rejected both the birthday of Abraham and the founding of Rome as the basal point of the calendar and substituted the phrase Anno Domini or "in the year of our Lord" behind the numeral. Modern time thus dates from approximately 750 years after the founding of Rome.[1]

Time and place also do indeed shape and color the lives of all of us, opening a door here and closing one there, having more effect than is sometimes acknowledged on choices that we believe are based on free will. The hour, the day, and the season help to determine where we go, how we dress, and what we eat. The place where we live—or more to the point, where we lived as children—is often a vital spirit within us, making our deci-sions—how to act, how to spend time, even how to feel. Human actions and feelings are scarcely ever more programmed than they are during holidays. We are—the majority of us anyway—conditioned to behave differently at Mardi Gras than in the Lenten days that follow. For Americans with familial and cultural roots in Christianity, Christmas is undoubtedly the most celebrated festival of the year. We look forward to it most, and our memories of it last longest. The old adage has remained true, that "A Christmas gambol oft would cheer/ The poor man's heart through half the year."

In our own times, too, a reunion or gift may have meaning far beyond the moment. Moreover, the Christmas holiday touches all ages of mankind, from the infant to the old and infirm. Even Americans who are not religious or who belong to non-Christian faiths are often caught up in the spirit of Christmas.

Peering back into history, we see that most people did not at once follow the path of the scholars in identifying Christmas as an occurrence of great importance. Common Christians of the Middle Ages were more interested in the crucifixion and the resurrection (surely extraordinary events) than in the rude manger birth. Nevertheless, the missionaries who exported Christianity to distant lands took with them, along with many other trappings of the early Church, the idea of a special mass to celebrate Christ's nativity.

In fact, the precise month and day of the anniversary did not become an issue until the Roman Catholic and Eastern Orthodox churches found themselves at sharp variance. Though records and documents are scarce, it is known that the Roman Catholics used December 25, and the Eastern Orthodox, January 6 (a date also referred to as the Epiphany). By the fourth century, when heads of the Church in Rome decreed that Christ was born on December 25, for most of the world the controversy was ended.

From the very start of Christendom, the celebration of Christmas was not practiced consistently. Indeed, practices have often tended to vary within a given land as well as from country to country. The clergy, for example, have most often seen the day as an important religious event while laymen have consistently opted for the festive observation, commingling it with pagan traditions whose origins may be lost in antiquity. There is some evidence, especially in the writings of St. Chrysostom, Bishop of Constantinople, that the Roman Church purposefully placed the keeping of Christmas between two popular folk festivals, Saturnalia and the Kalends of January, in order to give Christians something to celebrate while others were engaged in secular merrymaking. The good bishop explained: "On this day

2

also the Birthday of Christmas was *lately* fixed at Rome in order that while the heathen were busy with their profane ceremonies the Christians might perform their sacred rites undisturbed. They call this (Dec. 25, or viii. Kal. Jan, as the Romans wrote it), the Birthday of the Invincible One (Mithras); but who so invincible as the Lord? They call it the Birthday of the Solar Disc; but Christ is the Sun of Righteousness."[2]

By the tenth century, the British Isles, Germany, and Norway had joined Rome in recognizing December 25 as the birthday of Christ. As the observation of the holiday moved from land to land, each place contributed something unique. The Romans brought Christianity to Italy, created the church structure that institutionalized the celebration of Christmas, and, during the reigns of Popes Sixtus II, Gregory III, and Gregory IV, developed the concept of the Madonna and Child. The French may not have invented the carol, but France's musicians transformed it into art. The Christmas tree, from Germany, may be traced back to the days before Martin Luther. The followers of Odin in Scandinavia originated the idea of a Yule log. Ferdinand and Isabella of Spain financed the voyages of Christopher Columbus, Admiral of the Ocean Sea, and it was he who named La Navidad in the coastal waters of the Caribbean. It is, however, to the Brits of England that Americans can trace their largest debt for the festival.

Christmas has been important in the history of England since the days of William the Conqueror, who was crowned on the holiday and reigned from 1066 to 1087. (It is speculated that he chose Christmas for the solemnities in order that his anointing might coincide with the most popular and widely celebrated holiday in the land).

All of the following customs predate, some by hundreds of years, the kingship of Henry VIII and the English Reformation. The use of holly and ivy, and to a lesser extent bay, rosemary, and laurel, is probably an inheritance from the Druid priests, although there are similar reports from the Hebrew culture. The Christmas dinner, complete with boar's head and mince pies, is as much English as Scandinavian in origin. The sacred mystery play and mumming were elaborately performed as early as A.D. 1415. "Barring out the schoolmaster" (Christmas vacations from school) definitely has English antecedents; so does the Christmas Box (tips saved by servants to donate as church alms). And finally, the colorful antics of the Lord of Misrule or the "Abbot of Unreason" were at the height of popularity in the days of Edward VI, who reigned from 1547 to 1553.

All good things come to an end, however; the English Reformation made Christmas a controversial event, casting on the celebration clouds that still occasionally appear on religious horizons. In 1536 Hugh Latimer sounded the alarm, writing of Christmastide as several weeks of drunkenness, strife, dancing, dicing, idleness, and gluttony. In *Anatomie of Abuses,* the old Puritan Philip Stubbs described a march of the Lords of Misrule. He wrote that as they approached

> the church and the churchyard, their pipes piping, their drums thundering, their stumps dancing, their bels jyngling, their handkerchiefs swinging about their heads like madmen, their hobbie horses and other monsters skirmishing amonst the route; and in this sorte they go to the (I say),—into the church (though the minister be at praier or preaching), dancing and swinging their handkerchiefs over their heads in the church, like devils incarnate, with such a confused noise, that no man can hear his own voice.[3]

It is no wonder, then, that when the Puritans took power in England, Christmas-keeping was not ever to be the same again.

Following the lead of Swiss Protestant reformers Calvin and Zwingli, the Puritans in England sought to ban among other things the celebration of Christmas. In the first year of the protectorate, the holiday was not celebrated because Parliament traditionally fasted on the last Wednesday of each month, and Christmas happened to fall on this day. Two years later, in 1647, Parliament abolished officially the observance of Christmas.

This was the situation in 1660 when Charles II came back

to the throne. Thereafter, Episcopalians, Roman Catholics, Lutherans, members of the Reformed sect, and Moravians kept Christmas and took the holiday with them when they left England and Europe for the New World. Quakers, Scotch-Irish, Methodists, Baptists, and the "Plain Dutch" (Mennonites, Brethren, and Amish) objected to restoration of the festival and joined Congregationalists and Presbyterians in continuing the ban. The quarrel over Christmas came to Virginia and Massachusetts in the early 1600s, and there are those who believe that the matter is not yet completely resolved.[4]

Although Washington Irving, in his *Knickerbocker History of New York* (1809), and Clement Moore ("A Visit From St. Nicholas," 1822) strongly cultivated popular acceptance, the taproots of Christmas in America were established by the mighty pen of Charles Dickens. The English journalist wrote *A Christmas Carol* in 1843. Later he was shocked to find the book had sold out in one day, and the story had become as familiar in America as in England. On subsequent trips to the United States, Dickens was almost always asked to read from his manuscript (now housed in New York's Pierpoint Morgan Library). Scrooge's name is in our vocabulary. And so is Tiny Tim's Christmas, complete with family around the table, dining on fowl and drinking spirits; mistletoe over the door; exchange of gifts; alms for the poor; chestnuts on the hearth; holly at the window; and greeting cards with snowy streets and carriages. In fact, Dickens had resurrected Catholic traditions blurred by the Protestant Reformation. The celebration was so old that it seemed new.

But there is more to American Christmas than the legacy of England's famed Victorian, and it is the purpose of this book to trace the development of the holiday and to show the impact of the festival on people of many persuasions and stations of life in the successive historical periods of the nation.

The narrative and readings in *Keeping Christmas* are derived from a long search. Background for the project came from standard references, like the *Book of Days* and William DeLoss Love's *The Fast and Thanksgiving Days of New England*, as well as Tristram Coffin's *The Book of Christmas Folklore* and James H. Barnett's *The American Christmas: A Study in National Culture*, all classics. The essay and story citations listed in the *Readers' Guide to Periodical Literature* proved the biggest disappointment. Most of these selections were sentimental stock productions of a few Christmas writers. The same held true for nineteenth-century publications, such as *Godey's*, *Harper's*, *Lippencott's*, and others. By and large, the two areas that produced the best yield were libraries in and around Boston (the Massachusetts Historical Society, the Boston Public Library, the Athenaeum, the Houghton Library, the American Antiquarian Society) and Colonial Williamsburg (the Rare Book Room of William and Mary and the Institute in the restored district). There one may find old newspaper articles, broadsides, diaries, and manuscript letters as well as copies of rare, published works seldom seen elsewhere. In the end, however, Christmas customs and practices, except for the middle class, are largely an uncharted social and cultural frontier. This book is a sampler compiled to whet the taste as well as entertain.

Notes

1. For a deeper discussion of this matter, including why some scholars believe that Dionysius was wrong by at least three years, see William Muir Auld, *Christmas Traditions* (New York: Macmillan Co., 1931), 19–33.
2. Ibid., 33.
3. Quoted from Katherine Lambert Richards, *How Christmas Came to Sunday Schools* (New York: Dodd, Mead and Co., 1934), 44–45.
4. Michael Harrison, *The Story of Christmas: Its Growth and Development from Ancient Times* (Long Acre, London: Odhams Press, n.d.)

Prologue

Tuesday, December 25, Christmas Day. From the logbook of the flagship, *Santa Maria*.

Navigating with little wind yesterday from the Sea of Saint Thomas to Punta Sancta, and covering only one league every watch, and as it was eleven at night, he [Columbus] decided to sleep because it had been two days and a night that he had not slept. Since it was so calm, the sailor at the helm decided that he too would sleep and left the steering to the ship's boy despite the admiral's warning: whether the sea is calm or rough, they should not let a ship's boy steer the ship. The admiral was well aware of nearby sandbars and reefs because on Sunday he sent the launches to shore, and they had sailed east of said Punta Sancta a good three-and-a-half leagues, and the sailors had seen the shoreline that extends from Punta Sancta east southeast a good three leagues, and they saw where they could pass, although they had not tried to on this journey.

It was God's will that at midnight, as they had seen the admiral in sound sleep, and that it was dead calm and the ocean was like water in a bowl, everyone also went to sleep, leaving the steering in the hands of the ship's boy. The current carried the ship into a sandbank [a sound] which in the dead of night should have been heard for at least a league. But the prow moved so slowly into the sandbank that it could hardly be felt. The boy, however, felt it in the helm and heard the sound the ocean had hollered out, whereupon the admiral came on deck. Everything happened so fast that no one realized the ship was already aground. Then the captain, who should have been at the helm, came on deck. The admiral told him and the others to lower the lifeboat that they carried on the poopdeck and to pick up the anchor and drop it off stern; the captain and a few others jumped into the lifeboats, and the admiral thought that they would do as he had commanded. But they thought of nothing but fleeing to the other boat that was windward a half league away. The other crew refused to receive the men, behaving honorably, and because of this the men returned to their ship, but not before the other ship sent its own lifeboat over. When the admiral saw that his own men were running away, and that the tide was going out, and the prow was crosswise in the water, not seeing any other remedy, he ordered that the mast be cut and the prow be lightened as much as possible to free the ship. The tide was still going out, and there was no solution yet. By now the ship was almost sideways in the choppy although shallow water; they had tried everything but the prow remained stuck. The admiral went to the other boat to arrange for the evacuation of his crew. Since there was now a light shorewind blowing and still much of the night remaining, and they did not know how extensive were the sandbars, they tied up the ship until daylight, and then the prow went even deeper into the sandbank. The admiral had already sent the launch to shore with Diego de Arrana of Cordova, an army officer, and Pero Gutierrez, chef of the royal house, to let the chief know that the admiral had sent them to greet the chief and to beg him to let the ship dock there on Holy Saturday. The chief's village was a little more than a league and a half away from the stranded ship, and when the chief heard, they say that he wept and sent all of his people with very large canoes to unload the ship.

And that's what happened, they unloaded everything from the ship very quickly; so great was the help and diligence that the chief gave. He himself, with his brothers and other relatives, carefully guarded the cargo on board and on shore. From time to time, the chief sent a relative to console the weeping admiral, with words urging him to be neither angry nor sad and assurances that the chief would give him any help he needed. The admiral certifies to His Majesties that nowhere in Castilla could be found such careful guarding of the cargo that not even a needle was lost. The chief put all the cargo under shelter and ordered warriors to surround it and remain throughout the night. "He cried, with all of his people, so much," said the admiral. "The people are loving, not greedy, and ready to help with anything, I swear to Your Highnesses that in all the world there is no better people and no better land. They love their neighbors as themselves and they have the sweetest speech in the world, they are peaceful and always smiling. They walk naked, men and women, just as they were born from their mothers, but Your Highnesses must believe that among them the customs are good, and the king has such great presence, and such a regal manner that it is a pleasure to behold, and the intelligence they have; they wish to see everything, and they ask what it is for." All this spoke the admiral.[1]

When did Christmas begin in America? Samuel Eliot Morison, the best known of Christopher Columbus's biographers, suggests in his interpretive translations of the *Journals* that the explorer's mind was on the miracle in ancient Bethlehem when the *Santa Maria* struck sand on Tuesday evening, December 25, 1492, in the Caribbean. On the other hand, it is just as likely that Columbus and his men were far too busy salvaging cargo to pay attention to the calendar. If they were, then, it may have been an English sea dog or a member of one of the plantations who first thought of Christmas in the New World. In any event, the previous excerpt reveals to us the activities of the crew of the *Santa Maria* on the night of one of the most famous shipwrecks in American history.

Perhaps the common bond of those men and women who came to the New World some 500 to 1,000 years ago is that they were all in search of something. "God, gold and glory" is the traditional phrase used to describe the motivations of the Portuguese and the Spanish as sailors left their homeland in the fifteenth century. Their nations were on the downside of high civilization and it was believed that the Golden Age could be restored. In addition, however, men like Christopher Columbus were also seeking spices and cotton, new medicines, tall timber for ships' masts, and slaves. Those nations such as England, whose stars were ascending in the late 1400s and early 1500s, looked for the same; however, pride in country, by the forces of imperialism and nationalism, stirred strong feelings about adding new territory to the motherland. Elizabethan Michael Drayton wrote, "A thousand kingdoms will we seek afar, as many nations wast in civil war."

In any event, the English became the major colonizers of the New World. The Cavaliers, who settled Virginia Colony, and the Pilgrims and Puritans, who inhabited Massachusetts Bay and Plymouth, differed on almost everything imaginable, including Christmas. The Cavaliers brought the Church of England to Jamestown. On May 14, 1607, the London Company's Robert Hunt celebrated Holy Communion on the north bank of the James River. In subsequent months, John Smith wrote: "Wee did hang an awning (which is an old saile) to three or fur trees to shadow us from the Sunne, or walles were rales of wood, our seats unhewed trees till we cut plankes, our Pulpit a bar of wood nailed to neighboring trees."[2]

It is also this same man who should be credited with bringing the spirit of Christmas to Virginia on a permanent basis. In his *General Historie*, Smith writes that he and his companies ate oysters, fish, flesh, wild fowl, and bread on December 25, 1608. "Wherever an Englishman may be," he added, "and whatever part of the world, he must keep Christmas with feasting and merriment."[3] Most of the later Virginia inhabitants, as well as settlers of the other southern colonies, followed his lead.

Except for the dissenters and nonconformists, Virginians celebrated Christmas throughout the entire colonial period. It was first and foremost a "holy day," complete with services and sacrament. But it was also a festival. Legislators in the House of Burgesses and students at the nearby College of William and Mary, for example, took a break from their duties to reside with families and to engage in feasting, dancing, carol singing, and shooting rounds. Slaves were often provided with a vacation as well, and occasionally the Christmas spirit would move the master to increase the rations and provide a cash bonus. A discourse in the *Virginia Gazette* published in December 1739 indicates Christmas was important to the sense of community, and the editor pleads for tolerance of a pleasurable Christmas:

> The Season of the Year will, I hope, excuse the Trouble which I give, in observing, that the Celebration of the Feast of *December*, and the *Freedoms* of Life which are taken therein, were in Use among the *Romans*, many Years before the Birth of our Savior *Christ*.
>
> It may not be amiss to inform the Reader, that the Primitive Christians Solemnized this Feast with the same Sacred Magnificence and Festivity, wherein they performed their *Agape* or *Love Feast*; theat Original! of the more pure and modern Manner, wherein we receive the *Eucharist* now. But then, in Process of Time, [?], Luxury, and even Vice, crept into both those innocent and holy Obs'rvances.
>
> The above mentioned *Licentiousness* of the ancient Christians is banished, no doubt, from our *Altars*; but then we cannot say, that we are altogether free from their Luxury in other Places at this Time of the Year; or that we do not imitate that pompous and profuse Manner where in the old *Roman Flamens* and *Pontiffs* celebrated their Feast of *December*, in Honour of *Saturn*.
>
> But to be clear in what I intend to say on this Subject at this Time, I observe,
> 1. That some Christians celebrate this Season in a Mixture of *Piety* and *Licentiousness*.
> 2. Others perform their Offices in a *pious Way* only.
> 3. Many behave themselves *profusely* and *extravagantly alone*. And,
> 4. Too many, who call themselves *Christians*, pass over this *Holy Time*, without paying any Regard to it at all.
>
> From all which we conclude,
> 1. That those Persons must stand self-condemn'd, who throw these *Holy Days* into the common Portion of Time; because, both Heathenish and Christian Ancients witness loudly against them.

2. Little need be said to those who celebrate this Festival in Extremes. 'Tis as ridiculous to do nothing but fast and mortify all *Christmas*, and to keep a Monkish Holiday, as it is to banquet and carouse alone, and make a *Bacchanalian* Time of it.

What past at *Bethlehem*, calls not for the same Behaviour with what happened at Mount *Calvary*; and tho' we are to offer Wine and Frankincense, and are taught to sing *Gloria in Exelsis*; yet we are forbid Excess in such like Sacrifices, and every Degree of Rant and Riot in expressing our Exultation and Joy.

3. The Persons chiefly to be addressed to, are those who stand first in my Division, and who celebrate the Nativity in a Method composed out of both these Extremes, and behave themselves both piously and [impiously] on the Occasion. There are People who prepare themselves most religiously for the approaching Rituals, and who, upon the Day, perform their Offertory and [Sacraments], the most Solemn Forms of Religion; but their [?] end with that Night; and *The other World*, [when] they had to [?] bid for on *Christmas Day*, is quite [?] in the *good things* of the [*present world* a few days after].

On the whole, they who will be over-religious at this Time, must be pardoned and pitied; they who are falsely religious, censured; they who are downright criminal, condemned; and the Little Liberties of the old *Roman December*, which are taken by the Multitude, ought to be overlooked and excused, for an Hundred Reasons, which hardly any Understanding can be ignorant of.[4]

our own familiar and festive concepts of Christmas, we can
tify more readily with Philip Vickers Fithian, a young tutor,
wrote in his diary on Christmas 1773, at Nomini Hall,
oreland County, Virginia.

rday 25. [Christmas Day] I was waked this morning
uns fired all round the House. The morning is stormy
·lson the Boy who makes my Fire, blacks my shoes,
·ands &c. was early in my Room, drest only in his

shirt and Breeches! He made me a vast fire, blacked my Shoes, set my Room in order, and wish'd me a joyful Christmas, for which I gave him half a Bit.—Soon after he left the Room, and before I was Drest, the Fellow who makes the Fire in our School Rooms, drest very neatly in green, but almost drunk, entered my chamber with three or four profound Bows, & made me the same salutation; I gave him a *Bit*, and dismissed him as soon as possible.— Soon after my Cloths and Linen were sent in with a message for a Christmas *Box*, as they call it; I sent the poor Slave a Bit, & many thanks. I was obliged for want of small change, to put off for some days the Barber who shaves & dresses me.—I gave *Tom* the Coachman . . . two Bits . . . I gave to *Dennis* the Boy who waits at Table half a *Bit*—So that the sum of my Donations to the Servants, for this Christmas appears to be five Bits, a Bit is a pisterene bisected; or an English sixpence, & passes here for seven pence Halfpenny. The whole is 3S 1–1/2D.[5]

Fithian was not from Virginia. He graduated from college in New England, a section of the English colonies that had markedly different ideas on the celebration of Christmas.

Because New England considers itself to be the cradle of American civilization, it seems logical to assume that the "present is the past writ small": that is, the first inhabitants of Massachusetts Bay (and later Plymouth) observed the holiday as we do, only less extensively and elaborately. However, it must be remembered that the word *Puritan* came from a desire of some to "purify" the Church of England. The men and women, therefore, of Massachusetts Bay had come to the New World to continue the Protestant Reformation. Or—as Governor John Winthrop put it—to build the City on the Hill. What rankled the Puritans most was the Roman Catholic traditions that had been retained by Anglicans. The Pilgrims believed much the same, except that they wanted to separate and to build a *new* church in the New World.

In his *History of Plymouth Plantations*, Governor William Bradford chastised some newcomers in 1621 because they were "pitching the barr" and playing "stoole-ball" instead of working on Christmas Day. Thus he is often accused of being anti-Christmas. Mary Caroline Crawford, in her *Social Life in Old New England*, indicates that this is not true. Bradford, after the incident, wrote in his *Log-Book*: "If they made the keeping of it a matter of devotion, let them keep their houses, but there should be no gaming or revelling in ye streets."[6] He and others, it is assumed, were more concerned with abuse than practice.

In May 1659, some thirty-eight years later, the famous Christmas trouble occurred in nearby Boston. The General Court of Massachusetts, following the lead of Cromwellian government back in England, announced a penalty for celebrating a holiday on December 25th.

> For p'venting disorders arising in seueral places w'thin this jurisdiccon, by reason of some still observing such ffestiualls as were superstitiously kept in other countrys, to the great dishonnor of God & offence of others, it is therefore ordered by the Court and the authority thereof, that whosoever shall be found observing any such day as Christmas or the like, either by forbearing of labour, feasting, or any other way, vpon any such accounts as aforesajd, euery such person so offending shall pay for euery such offense fiue shillings, as a fine to the county.[7]

In 1681 the provision banning Christmas was repealed. Simon Bradstreet explained that a colonial law could not run counter to those of the mother country and so the paragraph was excised from the statutes. Still, the matter was not settled to the satisfaction of all. As late as 1681, Harvard rector and Boston teacher Increase Mather presented a "few arguments to the consideration of the judicious" in a London pamphlet entitled *A Testimony Against Several Profane and Superstitious Customs Now Practiced by Some in New England*. His specific words read:

> *Against profane Christmas-keeping.* In the Apostolical times, the Feast of the Nativity was not observed. The very

name of Christmas savors of superstition. It can never be proved that Christ was born on December 25. It is most probable that the Nativity was in September. The New Testament allows of no stated Holy-Day but the Lords-day. Objections answered. It was in compliance with the Pagan saturnalia that Christmas Holy-dayes were first invented. The manner of Christmas-keeping, as generally observed, is highly dishonourable to the Name of Christ.[8]

Cotton Mather, his son, followed in his father's shadow, at least on this subject. In 1712 he said, "Can you in your *Conscience* think, that our *Holy Savior* is honored by *Mad Mirth*, by long *Eating*, by rude *Revelling*: by a Mass fit for not but a *Saturn* or a *Baccus*, or the Night of the Mahometan Ramadan?"[9]

In contrast to the Mathers, who largely spoke to the literati in the colonies, the preachers in the local pulpit came to accept Christmas by the end of the nineteenth century. Pastor Henry Scougal proved to be something of a transitional figure when he spoke in 1670 on the text "Rejoice with Trembling":

'Tis high time now to apply these generals to the present occasion. We are assembled this day to commemorate the greatest blessing that ever was bestowed on the children of men; a blessing wherein all the nations of the world are concern'd, and yet whose fruits do as entirely rebound to every good man, as if it had been design'd for him alone: a mercy that doth at once astonish and rejoice the angels, who in comparison of us are unconcern'd in it. These mountains do leap for joy, because the valleys were filled with a fruitful shower, for when those glorious spirits did behold God stooping to the condition of a man, & man raised above the lowliness of his state, and the happiness of all the angels, they were transported with the admiration of the mystery and joy, for the felicity of their fellow-creatures; and did with the greatest chearfulness perform the embastes they were sent upon in this great affair. For having before advertised the blessed virgin of her miraculous conception, lest her modesty should have been offended at so strange an accident, and having removed the suspicion of her betrothed husband, they rejoiced to bring the first news of that infinite mercy which we remember this day: *for as certain shepherds were feeding their flocks by night, an angel of the Lord appeared unto them, and the glory of the Lord shone round about them;* and when this glorious appearance had confounded their senses, & almost scattered their understanding, the angel said unto them, *fear not for behold I bring unto you tidings of great joy, which shall be unto all people: for unto you is born this day in the city of David, a Saviour, which is Christ the Lord; and suddenly there was with the angel a multitude of the heavenly host,* the whole choir of glorious spirits, who all join'd in this heavenly anthem, *Glory to God on high, on earth peace, and good-will towards men.* And may not that help to heighten & advance our joy & our thankfulness? Can we be insensible of our happiness, when angels do so heartily congratulate it? 'Tis a nativity which we celebrate, & any birth doth much rejoice persons interested; a woman forgets her pangs when a man-child is born into the world.[10]

In the 1700s the battle to celebrate Christmas in New England was largely won by Episcopalian churchmen. At Marblehead, Massachusetts, on January 4, 1729, George Pigot answered Thomas de Laune, John Barnard, and a certain Mr. Whifton, who had asked on the previous Christmas Day, "Will you never be done with your Popish ceremonies . . . ?" His twenty-five-page sermon, entitled "A Vindication of the Practice of the Ancient Christian, As well as the Church of England, And other Reformed Churches, in the Observation of Christmas Day,"[11] is a ringing defense of the holiday. (Later, when the sermon was published, he added an additional forty pages on Old Testament holidays.) In 1798 Thomas Thatcher, of the Congregational Church, was invited to deliver a guest sermon on Christmas in the Dedham, Massachusetts, Episcopal Church. Toward the end of his remarks, he told his listeners: "Something will be expected concerning the religious festival itself. A question of this kind will naturally arise in your mind, why, if the birth of Christ be attended with so many advantages to mankind, should not this day be honored with religious solemnity."[12]

Thereafter, Thatcher listed the reasons given by members of his own denomination in not celebrating the holiday. For himself, he explained:

> I have the highest veneration for the founders of the New England churches, yet I conceive it may be possible that, with hearts filled with piety, they might vibrate to an extreme in lesser matters. As a mere *human* and compulsive injunction, I should protest against the observation of the day. But as a free-will offering to the Lord Jesus Christ, as a voluntary honor to the season of his birth, I could heartily wish, that every temple consecrated to the most high God throughout the land were opened to commemorate, with proper sensibility and fervent gratitude, the benevolence of the Deity in sending a Savior.[13]

No doubt these particular parishioners were pleased to hear these words.

The end of the American Revolution set back the December festival because the Episcopal Church was identified with English troops and American Tories. For instance, William Smith of Norwalk, Connecticut, wrote to Baptist Elder Elias Lee of Ballston, New York, on November 16, 1799, in support Christmas. Moreover, he added, "Hereafter, I shall do myself the pleasure of addressing you on the other observances and doctrines sacred to Episcopalians, with which you have taken, in my judgment, very unwarrantable freedoms."[14] In Virginia, Thomas Jefferson had already advocated separation of church and state in the New World. This move forecast an increasingly secular festival. Later, the Baptists, Methodists, and Presbyterians brought the holiday back to the pulpit and pew.

Notes

1. Translated by Rebecca Staples from Consuelo Varela, *Christobol Colon: Textos y documentos completos* (Madrid: Alianza Universidad, 1984), 97–98. I am indebted

to Ms. Staples for her translation as well as for construction, suggestions, and detailed editing of the entire prologue.

2. Clifton E. Olmstead, *History of Religion in the United States* (Englewood Cliffs, N.J.: Prentice-Hall, 1960), 41–41.
3. John Smith, *General Historie of Virginia* (London: Sparks, 1626).
4. *The Virginia Gazette*, December 1739, 14–21.
5. Hunter P. Farish, ed., *Journals and Letters of Philip Vickers, Fithian*, vol. 22, 1773–1774 (Williamsburg, Va.: Colonial Williamsburg, Inc., 1743)
6. Mary Caroline Crawford, *Social Life in Old New England* (Boston: Little, Brown, 1914), 495.
7. Nathaniel B. Shurtleff, ed., *Records of the Governor and Company of the Massachusetts Bay in New England 1650–1660*, vol. 4, part 1 (Boston: William White, 1854, 366–67.
8. Increase Mather, *A Testimony Against Several Profane and Superstitious Customs Now Practiced by Some in New England* (London, 1687), 18.
9. Abram English Brown, "The Ups & Downs of Old New England," *New England Magazine*, December 1903, 483.
10. Henry Scougal, "A Sermon Preached on the 25th of December, Being the Nativity of our Saviour" (Boston: N. E. 1637), 2–3, 15.
11. George Pigot, "A Vindication of the Practice of the Ancient Christian, As well as the Church of England, And other Reformed Churches, in the Observance of Christmas Day" (Boston: T. Fleet, 1730, 1–25).
12. Thomas Hatcher, "A Sermon Preached in the Episcopal Church in Dedham, December 25, 1979: Being the Festival of Christians" (Dedham, Mass.: Mann & Adams, 1798), 20.
13. Ibid., 23.
14. William Smith, "The Christmas Dispute Revived" (Ballston, Mass.: W. Child, 1800), 2.

I

The New Nation

Introduction

The American Revolution may have brought home rule to the colonies, but it did not settle the question of who was to rule at home. In replacing the Articles of Confederation, the Constitution provided for a stronger central government; however, not all of the people accepted the compromise document. Alexander Hamilton and Thomas Jefferson quarreled over whether the United States was to be an urban or agrarian country. Aaron Burr attempted to create another nation. Farmers in Pennsylvania revolted against federal taxation. The Kentucky Resolves argued for nullification of laws that were deemed not in the interests of the South. And finally, many individuals, such as Daniel Boone, left the problems of the East and headed west, first to the heartland, then across the wide Missouri, up over the Rocky Mountains, and finally to Mexican California.

During the period from 1790 to 1860, Christmas may have provided some respite each year to a nation that had seemingly endless challenges to face. George Washington set the tone. His first Christmas as president was spent at St. Paul's in New York, and thereafter he often returned to Mount Vernon for feasting, dancing, and gift giving. The Methodist and Baptist churches in the North and South took the lead in celebrations at local levels, offering formal services for adults, while the schools of America, both public and parochial, pioneered special programs for young people. Christmas in the West may not have been as formal as on the seacoast, but the season was celebrated with gusto just the same. In addition to enjoying food and music, Americans took stock and shared visions for the future with family and friends who were seen far too seldom.

Meanwhile, immigrants from Europe were teaching old

customs to eager subjects. Perhaps the most popular and colorful addition to the celebration came from Germany—the Christmas tree. In 1842 Charles Frederic Ernest Minnigerode, a
professor of Latin and Greek at William and Mary College,
who had come from Hesse-Darmstadt, is thought to have decorated the first tree in Virginia at the home of Judge Nathaniel
Beverly Tucker in Williamsburg. In Ohio a certain Pastor
Schwann justified placing a tree in his church as a part of the
holiday celebration. His neighbors in the Middle West—the
Pennsylvania Dutch of Lancaster and Carlisle counties; the
Swiss-Germans; the Moravians; and the new arrivals from
Sweden, Norway, and Denmark—added precious and unique
decorations such as kügels and Dresden miniatures.

As Christmas embedded itself into the marrow of the people,
the writers and artists of the nation took up their pens, to
institutionalize and create a lasting American Christmas. The
Dutch in New York contributed the first patron saint in St.
Nicholas, who drove a reindeer-drawn sleigh packed with toys
for children. Later, Washington Irving verbally painted this
scene in his *Diedrich Knickerbocker's A History of New York*
(1809). Clement Moore, in his " 'Twas the Night Before Christmas" (1822), immortalized it. And finally, Thomas Nast, a
popular cartoonist before the Civil War, made Santa Claus (an
American-British adaptation of the Dutch St. Nicholas) an
integral part of the Christmas holiday with caricatures published
in *Harper's Magazine* for almost fifty years, beginning in 1863.

Boston, the city that had once banned Christmas, passed
legislation in 1856 making the observance a state holiday. In
fact, one can make a strong argument that the capital of
Massachusetts was the home of the festival in America on the
eve of the Civil War. This was so, in part, because many of the
nation's artists and writers lived there; and, in part, because so
many of the leaders of the various church denominations often
practiced their craft on or near the Commons. The writings,
sketches, and sermons of these literati popularized the Victorian
image of Christmas here.

Santa Claus, or The Merry King of Christmas:

A Tale for the Holidays

J. H. INGRAHAM

This long and curious tale full of old-time imagery and Victorian embellishment delights the reader who has patience to pursue the deliberate and tortuous path of nineteenth-century prose. Probably written in the very same year as Dickens's A Christmas Carol, Ingraham's story shares many sentiments and symbols familiar from the great British morality tale. If not a borrowing, this is a striking case of resemblance, as evidenced in Ingraham's making the reader by magic fly through the night and peer into the countless strange windows of human behavior generated by the Christmas spirit or the lack of it. Moreover, the device of spirits as the reader's guides either foretells or echoes Dickens's treatment of Scrooge's journey.

But Dickens is only the half of it. Into this melee, Ingraham has injected also the figure of Santa Claus and his helpers—the fairies (elves) of various sizes and mien—toys for children,

---

J. H. Ingraham, "Santa Claus, or the Merry King of Christmas: A Tale for the Holidays" (Boston: H. L. Williams, 1844). I am indebted to the Athenaeum in Boston for assistance in securing this text.

mistletoe, and countless other Yuletide trimmings from long before and after Dickens.

J. H. Ingraham was a mid-nineteenth-century Boston clergyman who achieved literary recognition for establishing the "true adventure" story as an American genre. A Maine schoolteacher before he mounted the pulpit, he was an ardent opponent of slavery. In this tinsel-clad fable, we find much that was taken for granted in the sermons of the New England preacher. More important, we find Ingraham's gift to American readers— a serious perspective on the reality of rich and poor on the Boston Common.

It was the Eve of Christmas! The night was without a cloud— clear and cold. The skies were as blue as the Indian seas, and the stars sparkled like diamonds. The moon shone like a shield of silver and poured a flood of light upon the snowy roofs and towers of the city. The Common, covered with new fallen snow, lay like a floor of the purest alabaster beneath its radiant beams. The noble trees which encompassed it in majestic avenues bore, instead of the gay autumn leaves, fringes of glittering icicles pending from every branch and tendril, and as rich to the eye as drapery of gems. The snow that covered the ground had descended in the shape of minute crystals and each one reflecting the moonlight gave to the surface an appearance of being strewn with the dust of diamonds; while beneath the feet of the occasional passenger it crinkled and rustled with a pleasant tinkling sound.

It was yet two hours to midnight. The intensely piercing air had housed all whom stern necessity did not drive abroad. But, for the solitude of the shining white streets, merrier were the comfortable hearths within doors. A hundred thousand hearts, within a bell's sound, were beating with more buoyant pulsations than on other evenings, and the hoary old man, and the just tottling infant, alike felt the thrill of joy that vibrates through every bosom on the Eve of Christmas—the Echo still of that celestial strain which sang, "Peace on Earth—good will to men!" The lowly tenement of the poor man, and the marble mansion of the rich, alike shared in the blessing of the event which that night recalled; and from the crimson-hung Venetian windows of the one, and the dimly glazed panes of the other shone forth cheerful lights which told that mirth and merry-making reigned within.

Yet, doubtless, there was, here and there, many a sad heart in that vast city, and, perchance, more than one light that glimmered through the casement was the watch-light of the sick bed, or it shone only upon misery and crime, or upon Avarice counting his gains, or upon the powerful oppressing the weak! Go with us through the city, and let us see if this be so. Enter with us such abodes as we may select for our observations

Here is a stately mansion! None but the rich can dwell within marble walls and beneath sculptured architraves. Let us mount its columned portico, whose graceful shafts shine in the moonlight with wonderful beauty.—Listen! Music greets our ears, and mingled with it comes forth the merry tramp of the dancers feet and the cheerful tones of joyous laughter. We need no porter to usher us into this scene. On Christmas Eve all doors swing wide at our approach, and every dwelling is un-roofed beneath our eye. Behold in the hall these idle, costly statues, and those paintings in gold-heavy frames, the price of which would build a poor man's house. Now we enter the drawing-rooms. Mark what a scene of splendor of adornment meets the eye—and *only* the eye! For all this gear of wealth is but for the pleasure of one sense. Were the lord of the mansion blind his walls might be cold white plaster like his wood-sawyer's, and he would not be ashamed. Oh, if the rich would become self-blind, or rather could be made to realize how much more beautiful their wealth would look hung on the poor man's back and making comfortable the poor man's home, if they could be content to let the poor be the walls they love to adorn, how few young ravens would cry out to God for their bread!

See upon the lofty mantels, what a wealth of luxurious nothing's! China, India, Mexico, Paris and the ends of the earth have been brought under contribution to heap these costly showpieces upon this scarcely less costly shelf of marble! They contain in themselves the lives—which is the daily bread—of a hundred poor children, till another Christmas comes! Yet here they will stand another Christmas eve, while these children will have struggled on in hunger and want, and some, perhaps, have starved! Is cunningly cut ivory, or richly embossed silver, or chased filagrettes of gold or graceful figures in alabaster of more value than the life of a poor man's child? Yet those statues—these paintings which, exquisite as they are, are but paltry images of what God has made and given life to—these inanimate things have stood here year after year unmoved, while in the lowly dwellings of the destitute, living men, living women, living children with immortal souls have perished with hunger! Is marble fashioned by a man, of more worth than a man, that it shall not be given up to save the life of a man? Yet at this moment, as you shall see if you go with me this night, there are God's noble creatures perishing for food and warmth—which one of these dead effigies might bestow—and, lifeless itself, arrest life! It is a poor man's life I think of! but is not a poor man's life of more worth than a rich man's statue?'

You see that all here is rich and expensively arranged! There is no lack of gold where the eye of selfish man is to be gratified! Now turn and observe the inmates of these sumptuous rooms. Mark the richness of their apparel! See the jewels sparkle upon brow and bosom, one of which would make happy a whole family for life; yet it is placed there over a selfish heart only to glitter a few hours on an occasion like this! See how the bosom upon which it reposes heaves unconscious of the costly gem that it bears! Alas! how many a sighing mother's bosom heaves with a burden of woe this cold night that she beholds her little one perishing for lack of food! I see in the sparkling light of that gem a thousand bright smiles glancing! One motion of her hand guided by sweet charity could dispense them over a thousand pale, thin faces of the children of the poor! and did she know how much more beautiful the jewel would appear to her eyes, its light radiating from a troop of grateful, happy faces, she would tear it from her bosom and scatter its light in beams of blessing's. But the rich forget they are almoner's for the poor. They forget that God has blessed them that they may bless others! Like the planets, they are ordained to reflect upon the earth the light they receive. But alas, too often they revolve in their orbits, with the dark side presented to the globe which they were appointed to shine upon.

Is there no charity here?' you ask me. 'Is charity of necessity ever eclipsed in the heart of the rich?'

There is charity here, I answer!—I mean what the world calls charity The lord of the mansion gives on public occasions when men may see his good works, and he sometimes has given a small piece of silver to a beggar but he grinds the laborer in the wages due for his toil, forgetting that his wages are his all! Charity giveth *more* than is required! Rich men rarely know such charity.

Lo! the music ceases and the dancers throng that table overladen with delicacies, and decked with garlands of misletoe and flowers. Those wines are of great price and the host tells their age to his guests as a merit. Yet while those wines have been growing old many a poor man has perished for the blessings of food and shelter their luxurious cost would confer!'

'But is it a crime to be rich?'

'Yes; while a poor man dwells at thy door or hath no other home than the cold shelter of thy marble porticoes! God is not unjust. He has poured riches upon the earth, filling it with plenty for man and beast. Therefore, were true charity an inmate of the hearts of those who have gathered most, Heaven's bounties would be equally distributed and the poor would cease. In the world there is wealth enough to make the face of every man shine with joy.

'Shall the rich man then impoverish himself?'

'No. But he cannot go without judgment if he heaps his halls with idle luxuries whilst the destitute cry for bread. But let us go hence, and visit another abode!

It is in a narrow street, though near the rich man's mansion, and the tenement is a low one; for poverty hides itself in by-places and seeks humble lodgings; not that it is ashamed of itself, for Jesus Christ hath dignified poverty. Men banish it hither! Enter with me this dark abode. The step is sunken and so are the hearts of its inmates. Listen! It is not music but sounds of sorrow that greet our ears! The entry is narrow and dark, step carefully! Now look with me into this room. It is badly lighted by a dim lamp standing upon a coarse board table. Look around! There are no marble statues here, but there are naked children in drapery of rags grouped around a few coals, spectres with fleshless limbs and hollow cheeks, and large consumptive eyes! They look very wretched and are shivering with cold. They huddle together to imbibe warmth from each others' sluggish blood. Poor creatures—little enough for each one is the warmth of his own life!

You see here are no pictures other than their wan faces. There is no damask drapery. Two news-papers pinned together serve for a curtain to shield their poverty from the rude gaze of the passer-by. You look for a marble mantel-piece laden with costly baubles, in vain! There is none here! There was one of wood in the morning of this very 'merry Christmas Eve,' but stern Want took it from its fastenings and aided by the poor man's axe cast it into the chimney-place to warm the cold, cold feet, cold, cold hands of his babes!

Now turn and view the dwellers in this room. Sounds of sighing and the accents of woe fall upon the ear. They are heard above the chattering of the children's teeth who are shivering round the ashes of the old mantle-piece. They come from a wretched bed in one corner of the dingy abode. Upon it is stretched a man. Behold his features how they are stamped with suffering! He is a laborer. Six weeks ago he fell with a heavy burden and broke his thigh. Since then he has lain here, and for want of proper attendance, nourishment and care he has gained nothing in strength, and his limb being badly set now tortures him. But this suffering is the least he has to endure. He sees his children daily starving for food and perishing for warmth; while his wife silently pines away before his eyes.

Sparkling upon her bosom, you see not a glittering gem

from earth's dark mines, but an infant of but a few weeks old, a gem from the shining skies! By the bedside, holding his feverish hands she sits, sad-hearted and weary with weeping. With one hand she clasps his pulse, and with the other presses the babe to her breast which that day for the first time refused to give forth nourishment. Yet closer she holds it that her heart's weak throbbings may, peradventure, convey life to it, and round its soft limbs she wraps and doubly wraps her only shawl; for the house is very cold—scarce less cold than the street!

'Why does not the poor woman go out to beg, if she cannot work?'

She has been out, and but now returned, unsuccessful. She went to the rich man's door and rung, while we were there. The footman sternly bade her begone; and trembling and disheartened, and scarce able to move farther she hastened back to her babes to die!'

But let us leave this place—leaving them to God! Here is a house that seems neither the abode of a rich, nor of a poor man! A single ray of light streams through the massive shutters of this lower room in the rear. Let us enter the house. You see all the rooms are well furnished, and that an air of wealth pervades the whole. The occupant is rich, though the outside of his house is old and plain. He is the owner and landlord of numerous tenements. Both the rich merchant and the poor mechanic are his tenants. He has only himself and wife, and both have one mind, and one heart in getting together gold and never spending pennies.

Let us enter the closely shut room, from which the light streams forth! It is small and narrow in dimensions, and heavily guarded with bars on the windows and across the doors. You see, as its occupant, an old gray-headed man, with a hard, cold eye, and an unfeeling aspect. He is seated before an open iron-chest, with the lamp by which he sees, standing upon the corner of it. He is, you perceive, busy counting his gains; for the day before Christmas is his 'settling day.' There are piles of gold and piles of silver before him; and numerous parcels of bank notes, labelled with the names and occupations of the tenants who have paid them in, are, you see arranged upon a table by his side. There are poor men's names there, and some of those little piles he is gloating over, were gathered together by sweat and tears! But what heeds he, so that his rents are paid, how hardly the money came! He speaks! Hear him.

'John Fale is the only delinquent! He pays to-night, or to-morrow I distrain, and he goes into the street. It is after ten o'clock. There is the door bell! It may be he, for he knows how strict I am, and I give no man any favor!'

Here, you see, now comes a poor man into the room. It is the delinquent. He has a good face, but looks as if he worked hard, as he does. Hear his landlord.

'Well, John, I was about giving you up!'

'Yes, sir, I know I am late. But I have had very great difficulty to get along. It has been too cold to lay brick for some days, and the workmen are dismissed. I saved up most of the money for the rent, but none coming in, I had to take a little at one time, and a little at another, out of it, for there was the fire to warm the children, and the food to put into their little mouths, and clothes to put on their backs, and shoes and stockings to their feet—for the cold this winter has been perishing—.'

'That is enough. Have you my rent?'

'Not but half of it, sir.'

'Then the other half which you confess you had laid up for me, and then pilfered from, was as bad as stolen from my own money chest.'

'I could'nt let them perish, sir.'

'Your first thought should be your landlord! How have you dared to come to me with only half?'

'It is all I could bring you, sir, and it leaves me not a cent for the morrow's bread.'

'Your quarter's rent is eighteen dollars. You have brought me nine! Go back and get the whole by to-morrow at ten o'clock, or I distrain! This which you have brought, I will keep till then.'

The poor man sighs bitterly and sadly leaves the heartless

roof of the man who has the power to cast him and his little ones forth to perish.

'Shall he not take rent from the poor?'

'Yes; but where he finds misfortune where he looks for money, he should forgive the debt and he will for his reward himself dwell in mansions made without hands!

But let us hence for we have other abodes to visit ere midnight.

We are now in front of a mansion where dwells a fashionable woman. Let us enter:—but first, we will suffer this poor, thinly clad, young girl who is waiting for the door to open to go in with the bundle and band-box she carries beneath her arm. Now we will follow her. The lady, you see, is seated before her toilet glass, arranging diamonds in her hair. She expects to attend a distinguished dinner party and ball the next day and evening and is now trying the effects of costumes and jewels. The dressing maid ushers in the young girl and the lady turns towards her with a stern look. She addresses her—

'So, you have come at last with my dress! It is well you did not disappoint me. I must try it on by the lights so that I may see its effects at the ball. I have been waiting for you this two hours!'

'My mother and sisters with myself have been working steadily at it up to the moment I left the house, madam!'

'You should have worked more industriously. Take it out, Anny, and let me see it. Well, it is divine! Your mother and sisters deserve the reputation they have. You may go and call next week for your bill!'

'My mother desired a part of it now.'

'I have no money to-night. You must come next week!'

'The young girl turns away with a sad look of disappointment, and, as you see, silently leaves the house. Let us follow her.

It is a humble but neat abode into which she enters. Poor girl, her fingers are so benumbed with the cold she can scarcely turn the knob of the door.—Let us go in and see for ourselves why she saddened that the payment for her labor was refused.

You find here a comfortable room plainly furnished. A pale, genteel woman and two young women are seated by a small table on which is a frugal repast. They do not touch it yet, though they have not eaten since dinner, so diligently had they worked to finish the fashionable lady's dress. They wait for the return of the young girl, and now as they hear her, they start and look eagerly up. See! they are anxious to learn the result, but seeing their sister cold they give her a place by the fire, which they brighten with a few chips.

'Well, Mary!' the mother now says to her.

'She did not pay me, mother! She said I must call next week!'

'Next week! alas, next week is not to-morrow!'

The poor mother speaks very sadly, and well she may. Her daughters weep at this and well they may! Late and early they have worked the last four weeks for the rich and fashionable and on some pretence or other payment had been delayed. They worked thus hard, the mother and three daughters, to redeem a brother and son from prison. He had been imprudent and now lies in prison for a debt due an inexorable man. He had never been absent from his mother's roof at Christmas, and they had struggled to pay the debt that night, late as it was, that he might be with them on the morrow! They have with all their disappointments enough to pay it, if the fashionable woman had settled her bill. But now there is no hope, for the creditor is a hard man, and will demand the uttermost farthing. Therefore they weep, and well may they weep over the cold indifference of the rich and fashionable and their own bitter disappointment. It will be a sad Christmas to-morrow with this sorrowing family.

But you weary visiting with me the abodes of the miserable and oppressed, and think I give you but a sad entertainment for a merry Christmas Eve. Come then to other scenes, and let us see the sunny side of the clouds under whose shadows we have been so long lingering. We shall, perhaps, find smiles where we have met with tears, and out of all this evil educe good.

End of Part I.

Part Second

The scene of our Christmas Tale now changes to the Common. The moon still shines cold and clear in the deep blue skies; and the stars sparkle like gems. Fewer lights are seen in the windows and fewer passengers in the streets. The well-wrapped-up watchman walks slowly up and down his beat warming his fingers with his breath. The Common is silent and still. Not an object moves on its white floor of alabaster. In its midst the "OLD OAK" stood in stern majesty like the monarch of the wintry scene. Far and wide he flung abroad his massive limbs beneath whose leafy shelter in a summer's day, a thousand men might stand in shade. His huge, dark trunk of vast circumference, firmly rooted in the earth, stood like some mighty column of an ancient ruin, out of which a forest had up-grown, and flung wide their branching antlers to the storms.

All was dazzling moonlight! No sound was heard save the occasional dropping of an icicle from a limb, striking with a sharp noise into the crystal snows beneath the trees.

Suddenly comes from one of the far off streets that, like arteries, diverge from the Common, the deep, mellow cry of a watchman—

'Twelve o'clock, and a merry Christmas morning!'

At the same time, mingling with his sonorous voice came the deep-mouthed clock-tongues tolling the midnight hour from steeple and tower far and near.

As the first stroke rung clearly out upon the moonlit air and was borne towards the OLD OAK, all at once a strange movement was visible throughout the whole tree! Its branches began to wave and bend, and the icicles which were hung upon them in glittering fringes, striking together, tinkled with soft wild music, like a myriad of little silver bells. As the last stroke of twelve floated through the air, the tree was as full of music as an organ. The huge limbs as they swayed against each other, gave out deep bass notes, and from the lighter branches and more slender tendrils, came the sweet notes of a glauichord.

Never was heard such unearthly harmony. It seemed as if a choir from fairy-land had lit upon the tree, and filling its branches, like birds, were playing for joy that 'merry Christmas' had come!

Suddenly this strange, harmonious music, died away, and a silence followed as if some great event was about to happen. All at once from the vast trunk came forth a deep sound like that of a bassoon, and the tree on the side towards the city, slowly opened, leaving an arched way like the entrance to some Lilliputian gothic temple. As soon as this door in the trunk was wide open there came out of the body of the tree as if from a great distance, the notes of a trumpet. It came nearer and nearer, and as it approached other instruments of music was mingled with it, till at length a whole band of musicians seemed rapidly advancing from the deep recesses of the Oak towards the entrance!

Still nothing was yet visible to the eye, save the dark cavernous opening into the bowels of the tree, that resembled the vista of a long cathedral aisle dimly lighted.

Louder and nearer sounded the instruments of music, and although I could distinctly hear clarions and horns, bugles and drums, serpents and cymbals, yet they appeared to me to be Lilliputian players, and from the noise they made, I felt satisfied that the instruments could not be much larger than children's toys. All at once I heard the rattling of wheels and the shouting of tiny voices, and amid the shadows that enveloped the opening in the oak I beheld lights flashing, and then came galloping out a chariot and six horses, accompanied by out-riders and followed by a dense multitude, some on horseback, others on foot, and others riding astride upon humming birds and flying over the heads of the others. The out-riders bore flambeaux and before the horses rode at full speed, playing a merry peal, at least three-score musicians clad in green with silver helmets upon their heads.

A more beautiful and rare a sight than this brilliant and dashing cavalcade never was seen! The greatest wonder of it was that not one of the persons composing it was bigger than my thumb, except him who sat in the chariot and seemed the chief personage, who might have been half an inch taller than the rest. This personage was dressed magnificently in furs softer than the richest velvet. A white fur cap covered his head with a silver star glittering in the front; and about his person was wrapped a purple robe lined with ermine. In his hand he held a wooden cross and upon it was suspended an empty purse. His countenance (for I saw it distinctly by the light of the flambeaux carried by the out-riders) was very pleasing and inclined to mirthfulness; for joy sparkled in his black eyes and mirth played around his mouth. His countenance, nevertheless, was majestic and commanding, and as he wore a long, white beard, with snowy locks floating upon his shoulders, his appearance was at the same time pleasing and venerable. It at once irresistably prepossessed me in his favor.

The mounted band of musicians, after galloping on their miniature but spirited horses about a yard or a little more from the tree, drew rein and formed in line with military accuracy, while they still continued to play the most delightful strains of martial music. The chariot wheeling, dashed on past the line, and thrice drove round the oak upon the sparkling surface of the snow, the whole train, which must have numbered full ten thousand, following at full speed; some on foot running like the wind; others mounted on fleet coursers no larger than a mouse; other borne through the air on the backs of gorgeous humming-birds! The noise of their progress was like that of the wind stirring the autumn leaves, as it circles among the trees of the forest. It was a brilliant sight, with their waving plumes, their flaunting mantles, their gold, silver and steel ornaments and armor glancing in the moonlight, and reflecting back, with increased splendor, the flashing rays of the hundred tiny flambeaux!

After the third circle around the oak from which he had so strangely issued with his train, the person in the chariot waved his furred hand, and the whole cavalcade halted in front of the door in the tree, between it and the musicians. The out-riders ranged themselves on either side of the chariot, and those who were so fortunate as to be mounted on their green and gold winged coursers flew up into the branches of the tree; and as there was more than a thousand of this troop, the tree seemed to be covered with gold and emeralds, for these were the prominent colors that met the eye.

At a wave of the hand of the personage in the chariot, the music ceased and a deep silence reigned. Santa Claus, for this distinguished individual was none other than the merry King of Christmas, then rose up in his seat and thus spoke:

'Friends and followers! Once more we have come forth from our year-long retirement within the heart of this mighty Oak, to hail the dawning of merry Christmas! Without me—without you and our gifts, what would Christmas be? *Sad* instead of *merry* I wot. We administer to the happiness of millions, and this night of all nights in the year, myriads of children bless good king Claus!'

'Long live good King Claus! Long live the merry king of Christmas!' Shouted ten thousand tiny voices; while loud and right merrily sounded horn, trumpet and clarion, till the very welkin rung again!'

'Thanks, good friends and true hearts,' answered the merry monarch of the Holidays. 'Now are you ready all to do my hovel and hall to gladden the hearts of my little friends, with presents from Santa Claus?'

'We are ready, we're ready, one and all,
To fly at thy bidding to hovel and hall!'

'Right glad am I to have such faithful and loyal subjects. Now prepare your sacks!'

When he had spoken thus, I saw now for the first time, that nearly every little imp, for I know not what else to call the miniature creatures, had, slung across his shoulder, an empty stocking. Some of them were so long and large that the burden was quite as much as they could stagger under, while others were smaller and more portable. All, except the musicians and the guard about the chariot, had these socks dangling over their backs.

'Now, my children,' said Santa Claus looking around him very gravely, 'I see you expect to have your stockings filled as heretofore, from my great stocking; for I know every one of you to have a favorite child whom you design this Christmas morning to make happy by a stocking full of presents. But you see my stocking. It is empty!'

As Santa Claus thus spoke he took from the cushion of his chariot a large gray stocking, so large that it would hold hundreds of such stockings as his attendants carried, and held it up to the view of all.

At seeing it in this condition, for he turned it upside down and held it by the toe and shook it that they might be convinced it contained nothing whatever, there was a general murmur of surprise which sounded like the rustling of the leaves of the Oak when agitated by an autumnal wind. Hitherto they had always been accustomed to see the merry king's huge gray stocking crammed and sticking out and over-running with Christmas 'gifts,' from which one and all filled his own sack and flew with the gifts, each to the chamber of his own favorite; for, we are told, each of these little servants of good King Claus, chooses a child as soon as it is born, and continues to be its Christmas 'Fay' year by year, deserting it only when it commits its first sin: and then weeping, it ceases to visit it more!

'You are grieved, my merry children, to see that I have assembled you here before me beneath our Christmas tree, with no annual gifts to pour into your sacks. But cease your lamentations; for not one of you shall want that to give! nor shall one of your favorites fail to be made happy tomorrow morning as on former Christmas days! I will now tell you how this shall be accomplished. Last night as I was counting out, in my palace beneath the oak, the gold which was to fill my stocking with gifts as on other Christmas Eves, I saw, all at once, standing before me a beautiful and youthful female in silvery robes and a crown of light encircling her brow. I knew that she was an inhabitant of one of the stars, and bowing before her in awe I awaited her message. 'Oh king,' said she to me, in a voice sweetly toned with the accents of benevolence and universal

37

love, 'Thou art busy preparing thy generous donations for Christmas morn. I am come to thee to tell thee that for this time thou needest not trouble thyself to gather together gifts either for the old or young, for the rich or the poor!'

At hearing these words, I looked very sad, thinking how many tears would be shed if I had no gifts for my little ones.

'How then can there be a merry Christmas,' I said 'without Santa Claus and his presents?'

'Listen, good king Christmas!' she replied, smiling. My name is CHARITY. I am sent from Heaven, with power to rule, for this Christmas day among men. Thou art also to obey me, not because I command thy obedience, but because thy great heart will prompt thee to submission; for I see, with pleasure, my own image reflected in thy breast. Wilt thou obey me this day? Shall my will be thine?'

'I and my subjects, sweet Charity, are at thy disposal,' I said, laying my hand upon my heart; and kneeling I kissed the hem of her robe, in token of my free submission.

'Thou shalt now hear my plan of ruling for this Christmas festival, merry King Claus. Put up thy gold for this time for I want it not. The gold I shall make use of I shall seek for in men's *hearts*. Hitherto thou hast expended vast sums for this occasion and thousands of hearths have been gladdened by thy bounties. Thou hast done enough for thy part; men must, this Christmas, do their part. When the midnight hour shall toll, which ushers in Christmas morn, ride boldly and gaily forth from thy OAK, as heretofore, with all thy train, and when thy people throng around thee for gifts to scatter through every habitation, say to them that for this merry Christmas time they must make mankind the givers! 'I am,' said Charity to me with a celestial smile, 'I am this day the almoner of the rich man's wealth and the reliever of the poor man's woe. Go forth with thy people, good king, and tell them they must take this night from the rich the gifts they would bestow upon the poor, and from the poor the gifts they would bestow upon the rich. Now farewell to thee, King Santa Claus,' she added, 'and see that thou showest thyself, this merry Christmas, both a faithful servant and friend of Heavenly Charity!'

'While she was thus speaking, my children, she was gradually lost to my sight, slowly ascending upon a bright cloud, towards the skies.

As all the little subjects of King Santa Claus had kind hearts, and delighted in nothing so much as doing good, the words of their king gave them the greatest pleasure; for they at once perceived (being as intelligent as they were benevolent) how noble and beautiful was the design which Charity had originated for—not only enabling them to pursue as before their delightful employment of distributing gifts upon every threshold, but of making the rich instead of the purse of King Santa Claus the involuntary dispensers of these bounties.

Therefore, King Santa Claus had no sooner done speaking,

'Now dispense ye, messengers of sweet Christmas charity, all! Enter every abode in this vast city the halls of the rich and the hovels of the poor Mark well each beholds! Report where thou seest the rich man have more than his need—where thou seest the miser hoarding his gold while the poor man perishes for want of it; where thou seest the powerful oppress the weak, and the wicked plot the ruin of the innocent! For Charity careth for all these things! Now fly each on his message and be ye all faithful and speedy. In ten minutes report to me what ye discover! For this night Charity holdeth judgment upon earth, and I am her prime minister! Do well thy work and ye shall not lack gifts to fill thy sacks, nor want occasions of scattering abroad those blessings which, like me, it is your delight to bear to the good and innocent.'

No sooner had Santa Claus ended than there was a murmur of applause and a clapping of tiny hands that sounded like the laughing ripple of a mountain rivulet, gurgling over a bed of pebbles. Then the instruments of the band struck up a merry peal amid which rose the humming of a thousand green and gold wings, and the clattering of the feet of ten thousand coursers. Away through the air and over the snow, flying and riding and running, the messengers of Santa Claus spread themselves in all directions over the moonlit city. As they crossed the crystal snows that covered the Common they looked to the eye like a shower of diamonds and emeralds, so glittered their garments of green and their silver helms in the beams of the moon. Their passage through the air and over the snow was attended with a melodious noise like that of a hundred Aeolian harps sounding at once in the evening wind! Their speed was like the lightning! and in a few seconds they had dispersed themselves in every street, avenue, and lane, and alley in the wide, slumbering city. Those that were astride the backs of humming birds, I saw course high in the air, and then dart like shooting stars down the chimney flues. Those that were mounted on steeds entered, at top speed, through the key holes of the doors; while those less lucky ones who were on foot (and who constituted the foot-guard of good Santa Claus) got in under-neath the doors; and in poor men's houses made their entrance through broken panes and yawning chinks. And I saw, that by reason of the more numerous openings that were in the poor man's house, and therefore, the more easy access to the interior, which these little messengers of love and charity obtained, that the poor man's roof had a great many more of these blessed guests than that of the rich man!

After they had all disappeared and silence and moonlight only reigned over the city, I turned to observe king Claus, and to admire in his countenance, the benign expression of that benevolence which was planning happiness of so many beings that night; when, to my surprise a flourish of trumpets filled my ears, and amid the martial melody I beheld him with his few attendants that remained, coursing in his chariot with his six winged horses harnessed to it in silken traces, swiftly over the crystal snow in the direction of the state-house! I followed his glittering progress with my eyes and saw him gallop over intervening snow bank and hollow with the speed of an arrow; and when I looked to see the iron fence arrest him (forgetting what a miniature affair his equipage was the whole being so perfectly proportioned), I saw him pass right through between the bars without a whit lessening his speed. Following his glittering course, still, I beheld him next mount the glacis in front of the State House, and then, dashing across the portico, disappear—chariot, winged-horses, musicians, attendants and all—through one of the ponderous key holes of the great door. In a moment afterwards I beheld him re-appear in the lofty cupola above the dome; and there surrounded by his train of attendants, he sat, like a monarch upon his throne, awaiting the report of his messengers, with the snow-clad city, which for that night, he governed as the vice-regent of Charity, spread out in the bright moonlight beneath his feet!

End of Part II.

Part Third

The ten minutes which King Claus had given his numerous troop of benevolent little messengers to be absent in their mission of charity and love had hardly expired, when the whole region above the city was filled with music like a thousand harps wildly swept with the fingers. I looked up and around to discover whence it proceeded, and saw at once that it was made by the motion of the returning couriers of Santa Claus. They came, some flying in glittered bands, like trains of minute stars shooting along the air, others coursing over the silvery surface of the virgin snow, both horse and foot. They had come forth from chimney-flue, key-hole, and crevice, and were pressing towards their master and King, each more eager than his fellow. They knew, by instinct, where to find him enthroned; for, wherever he was, a chord of love was still uniting their little hearts to his great heart; and, wandered they never so far, by following this golden thread, they could always find the way back to him!

In a few seconds the vast dome and roof of the State House and even the chimney tops were covered with these little beings in gold and green; for I saw that, to the foot and horse no more than to the humming-bird dragoons the perpendicular walls of the edifice presented no obstacle; the whole troop ascending from the base of the columns to the top as easily as a fly runs up a wall. They were so great in number that they covered every spot upon the dome and roof, not leaving a place unoccupied large enough to set a lady's thimble down upon!

When all had taken their places and good King Claus had looked kindly round upon his brilliant Court he rose up in his chariot and thus spoke:

'Welcome, my children! Your prompt return shows me that you have been diligent and faithful in your tasks. Le,' he continued, addressing himself to a splendidly accoutered horseman at the head of his shining squadrons of cavalry, who wore an opal suit of armour, and upon his head a silver helmet graced by a golden plume from the crest of a humming-bird. 'Le, you are the captain of my horse, and report to me what you beheld. From each of my great captains I will hear a report, and their experience will show me what all of you have seen and observed, and my judgment shall be given accordingly!'

'Merry and good King Claus,' said Le, curbing his mettlesome courser with a master's hand and keeping his seat with grace and dignity, 'I will relate what I have seen! After leaving the Common, guided by brilliantly-lighted windows, I approached a magnificent mansion and entered it. I found myself in a gorgeous suite of rooms and in the presence of music and dancers. All was happiness, gaiety and splendor. Wines and luxuries were there and joyous laughter came from many a beautiful lip. In one room a table was loaded with game, pies, cake, fruit and every delicacy in abundance. From this abode, for I saw they all were happy without my aid, I sought one of poverty close by. It was a wretched abode, dark and cold. I saw a wife seated by a sick husband, a babe at her breast and four children huddled about her feet crying with cold, for they were too cold to sleep! I wept over the sight and wished that part of the joy I had left in the halls I had just left was bestowed upon them!'

'And where hast thou been and what hast thou seen, noble Li!' demanded Santa Claus looking very grave at the report made by his chief equestrian.

The personage addressed was no less distinguished than Le. He was the chief of the Flying Dragoons. He was mounted in a bold manner upon the back of a humming-bird of the largest size and of the most beautiful plumage. His armour was of emerald hue from casque to spur! His breastplate was a single pearl and in his hand he held drawn a glittering sword nearly as long as a cambric needle. His countenance was very handsome, as were those of all these generous hearted dispensers of Christmas Charity, and wore an expression of benignity and love. His long hair, softer than any floss, waved upon his shoulders and his lip was graced by an elegant moustache. The scabbard of his sword was studded with diamonds and the housings of his saddle blazed with jewels. The wealth and splendor of all these little beings had struck me with surprise from the first! I saw that though no two were alike in their costume yet all were equally costly and beautiful. I looked, in vain, for a humble suit—for a poor implet among them! They were all dressed equally rich though with infinite variety. Curious to know why there were none poor and humble among the subjects of good Santa Claus, I inquired of a youth in turquoise armour who was about three quarter of an inch high, and who stood upon the edge of a cornise near me, the reason of it. His reply perfectly satisfied me that Santa Claus had a just right to bring mankind to judgment. He said to me, in a voice that was scarce less sweet than the sweetest note the Norwegian Magician has ever drawn from his charmed viol,

'In the Kingdom of merry, and good King Claus, there are no poor nor rich. All are alike opulent. If any gains more than a certain sum, he casts it into the royal treasury. If any lose what he possesses, an equal contribution from each, makes him as rich as they. All are alike rich, industrious, and happy. There is no infamy so dishonorable, in our estimation, as to lay by gold, or jewels! Among men it is base to be poor. Among us it is base to be rich!'

But we must return to listen, to the report about to be made by Li.

'Most mighty King of Christmas! My first visit, was to an

abode, to which I was directed by a glimmer of light shining through a crevice in the shutters. The place was so securely shut and guarded, that I had some difficulty in finding an entrance. The light came from a small room, in which, sat a hard visaged man, adding up his yearly gains in a huge ledger. On one side of him, stood open an iron chest, nearly filled with money he had received that day for rents; for I saw by his books he was a very rich landlord. On the other side of him, was a table covered with little piles of bank notes, labelled with the names of those tenants he had received them from. Near him lay a little parcel of nine dollars, which was unlabelled, upon which, from time, he looked with an expression of ill-humor, and muttering,

'Nine dollars more wanted to balance my books! I must have it if it comes out of his blood!'

So I left him there, and next entered a poor man's abode, in an adjoining alley. I found no difficulty in finding my way in, for there were here broken panes, and fallen boards, and open panels. In an humble room, a woman young, and interesting, was trying to soothe the angry grief of her husband, who, sleepless walked the night to and fro his creaking floor.

'To-morrow, we are turned into the street! To-morrow, for the hardheartedness of man, and the want of nine dollars, we are beggars!' he cried in despair; and burying his face in his hands, the man wept like a child. Still she smiled upon him with gentle love and sympathy, and told him to hope in God, for all would yet be well. But he listened, as if he heard not, and still repeated his former words. The ten minutes had by this time expired, and I left this abode, and hastened to make my report!'

Santa Claus, when he had ended, made no remark, but only looked very grave, and shook his head.

'Now, noble Ol,' he said, addressing his Captain of Foot, 'Where hast thou been, and what hast thou seen?'

The Captain of Foot being thus addressed, advanced a little in front of his battalion, which numbered full four thousand implets, and covered half the area of the roof below the dome. He was clad in scarlet armour, which sparkled with rubies, and being tall of stature (for he was within an eight of an inch of being four inches, plumes and all) his appearance was imposing. His voice sounded like the finest not of a guitar.

'Great King! In obedience to your commands, I dispersed my people over the city, and entering myself, a house of splendid exterior, in the most fashionable quarter, I beheld a lady at her toilet trying the effect of a new dress, which, as I learned from her conversation with her maid, she intends to wear to a ball the coming evening. A diamond necklace glittered upon a black velvet cushion near her, and rings and bracelets, and various jewelry, were strewn around her in profusion. As I was admiring the beauty of the dress, I saw something sparkle upon the rich lace, with which the bosom was decorated. I drew nearer to examine it (for it shone brighter than the diamonds upon her bosom) when I saw that it was a tear! I knew then, from its brightness, that it was the tear of the poor!—a tear from the eyes of the poor working girl, who had left this costly dress! and I knew that fashionable woman was an oppressor!

I left her abode, and entered one of a more humble exterior. It was neat, yet comfortable. All that it contained was useful. Nothing was there merely to please the eye. The inmates (a mother and three daughters) had nothing, over the daily work of their hands. Life, *life* demanded all their weary earnings for itself! They were weeping; and as I listened at what they said, I knew that they wept, because their hire had been withheld by the woman of fashion, with which they hoped to free a brother—a son, from prison, and have him at their board, this merry Christmas. It was a sad scene, and I turned from it away, for my eyes were blinded with tears. The time set for my return had now expired, and I hastened hither, to make my report!'

Neither did Santa Claus make any reply, when his Captain of Foot had ceased speaking. But I saw the serious aspect of his countenance deepened, and he shook his head with a sadder air than he had yet done.

'Now, my favorite, he said to a beautiful youth, with blue eyes, and auburn-colored hair, that waved upon his shoulders like a cape of golden floss, 'what have you to tell, that you come forward thus unbidden? I have learned enough from these, my three Captains, to know how to enter upon this judgment Charity hath put into my hands! But speak, EL! Where hast thou been, and what hast thou seen?'

'Though I am but a young Page, and make but little figure among great captains,' answered El, advancing, and standing near King Claus the better to be heard, (we forgot to say that he was arrayed in a suit of gold, and carried in his girdle a stiletto no bigger tha a rose thorn!) 'What I have seen I beg you will listen to and do justice therein, oh King! I went as others did, at thy bidding, to hovel and hall. The first abode I entered was that of a poor woman, if the cellar in which I found her lying may be called an abode. She was dying of starvation, and breathed her last the moment after I entered.—Upon her dead bosom lay an infant asleep—asleep for hunger! It was a pale, wan thing! and as I saw it lay nestling there upon the cold breast of his mother, who had died of hunger and exposure in a Christian land, at a time when 'Merry Christmas' was in the hearts, and on the lips of thousands of happy ones, I sighed for human charity! I left the living babe upon its dead mother's still bosom, and entered the dwelling where lived one of the Judges of the land. His habitation was sumptuous, and luxury and taste contributed to his enjoyment. His cellar was filled with provisions, and his coal-vault held tons of the best Anthracita; yet that day he had condemned a poor man to prison for stealing a bushel of coal from a coal-yard, and had passed sentence upon a wretched woman who had pilfered a loaf of bread and a chicken, from a provision-stall. They were seated, this Judge and his wife, before a glowing grate with a table covered with Christmas eve delicacies near them; for they had entertained a party of friends who had but a short time left.—They had no children and I heard them regretting that they had none to enjoy their wealth, and render happy their declining years.

'From this mansion, where wealth did not make happiness, I went into a house opposite. A miser was up late, engaged in weighing gold, and clipping from each coin enough out of every hundred, to make one full coin. I saw upon his table, a paper by which I knew he was the harsh creditor who held in prison the widow's son! By this time the ten minutes had expired, and I hastened to tell you what I had seen!'

'You have seen much my favorite, and I thank you for telling me what you observed. Now all of you who have witnessed similar inequalities of things, will do after the same manner in all your cases as I shall command those who have just spoken to do! Hear, my three captains, how this night King Claus, directed by Heavenly Charity, shall correct the evils you have witnessed, and pass judgment upon that false social condition among mankind whereby misery exists instead of universal peace, prosperity and love!'

All of them prepared to hear with attention what Santa Claus had to say, half divining with their quick wits what it would be.

'Le,' he said addressing the Captain of Cavalry, 'haste thee with thy company to hovel and hall as before. Employ in thy service as many of thy people as thou mayest require, for thou hast much to do and will need many hands to do it. Those that you need not let them imitate thy example in other abodes. Go first to the mansion of the rich man and let thy troop fill their sacks with every delicacy from his table, with coal from his vault, with garments from his wardrobe and that of his wife and children, with sheets and blankets from his beds, with meat from his barrel and meal from his bin! Leave behind enough for all his comforts and wants, and in so doing thou dost not rob him. He, in withholding, for so long, more than his wants demanded, has been the robber of the poor! When thy sacks are filled, convey them on the shining rail-ways which Charity will lay for thee from the tall flues of the rich man's chimney down into the humble chimney of the poor sick man's habitation, where thou sawest the mother watching by his bed-side, and her cold children huddling around her feet for warmth! There busy thyself and them in making fires, preparing food, clothing the naked little ones and administering to the comfort of the sick man! These are the 'Christmas gifts' I design for them! Go on this lovely duty, and delay not; for the servants of Charity never linger!'

The words of Santa Claus were received by the whole troop which Le commanded with such demonstrations of joy as always fills the bosom of the good where good actions are to be done. Wheeling his charger and waving his hand to his battalions, the chief placed himself at their head and away they galloped down the dome with the speed of the wind, and were soon seen coursing over the sparkling ground, casque and armour glittering in the moonlight so that their passage seemed like a rivulet of parti-coloured gems moving along upon the surface of the snow.

They had no sooner disappeared than good Santa Claus whose face was now less clouded with the severe gravity which had grown darker and darker upon it as he listened to each report of his captains, turned to Li, his bold Captain of Flying Dragoons and thus addressed him also:

'Noble Li, it is my command that you take with you a suitable party and hasten to the abode of the hard hearted landlord whom you beheld casting up his accounts. Take from his iron-chest every dollar that he has rung from the poor and return it to each one of the victims of his cupidity. Take also a thousand dollars and carry it to the poor labourer. When this is done let thy people disperse and do in like manner in every abode where injustice reigns over misfortune!'

When good King Claus had thus spoken, the Captain of the Flying Dragoons signified his pleasure at the task given him to perform, and the next moment the air was musical with the flutter of a thousand little wings, and, flying over the town, they descended uppn it like a shivered rain-bow falling in a shower of glittering, parti-colored fragments.

When the last brilliant messenger of the train had disappeared, the visage of King Claus grew still more placid than before; and calling to OL, his Captain of Foot, he despatched him to the abode of the fashionable lady. 'Take her useless gems and with them make glad the heart of the widow and her daughter; for this night Equity hath come to judgment on the earth!'

I saw, then, the army of this Captain descend and spur

themselves through the streets of the city each on a message of equity and love, kindred with that committed to their Captain. The handsome little page was then entrusted with a similar duty to the cruel creditor and his prisoner, and the the rich Judge and the poor infant lying on the dead mother's breast.

'When thou comest into the house of the cruel creditor,' said Santa Claus, 'thou shalt take from his wealth all, to a farthing, that he has unjustly wrested from the poor or the unfortunate, leaving him only his honest gains. In like manner shall judgment come to all this night! When thou goest into the prison lead forth the mother's boy and convey him to her arms! When thou comest into the mansion of the Judge, convey thence such provision and coal as the families of the two unfortunate persons he has imprisoned may require, and I will see that from the coffers of the miser their hearts shall be made glad. I'faith! This shall be a right merry Christmas to the poor! and I thank sweet Charity for making me her minister in this loving matter!'

'But, oh, King,' said the Page, 'didst thou not say that not only the rich were to be involuntary givers to the poor of Christmas gifts, this night, but the poor were to bestow Christmas presents upon the rich! But so far these are gifts only on the one side!'

What I said I repeat,' answered Santa Claus. 'The Christmas presents of the rich shall come from the poor. I have a rare Christmas present for that Judge! Thou shalt be its bearer. You said he sighed that he had no children to inherit his riches. Seek out the living babe that lies nestling upon the cold bosom of its dead mother and taking it up gently bear it and lay it in his arms! Such are the gifts the rich shall have from the poor! Now hie thee on thine errands of mercy and love for thou hast much on hand to do!'

The Page, with a smile of delight that he had such delightful tasks given him, bounded from the presence of King Claus and was in a moment lost to view. When he had vanished on his mission I saw that the face of Santa Claus was now entirely free from the cloud, which had been gradually lessening as he despatched one after another of his servants on their errands of love and charity. His countenance was benign and peaceful and a noble serenity pervaded his whole manner.

All at once, while I was observing him I beheld, standing in the chariot by his side, the radiantly-bright form of Charity. In her right hand she held what seemed to me a ball of the finest silver threads. She cast the ball from her into the air, when I saw it descend and strike upon the chimney of the rich merchant who had given the Christmas Eve ball, and, thence rebounding, light upon the chimney of the poor woman, who had been turned begging from his door, leaving a silvery road along the intervening air between, and so connecting the abode of opulence with that of poverty! Then I beheld it rise into the air and light upon the flue of the cruel landlord's mansion and thence flying through the air descend the low chimney of the tenant. Thence I beheld it in the same manner connect, by a silvery road through the moonlit atmosphere, the cellar of the dead woman with the stately mansion of the Judge, and, every where, the abodes of the oppressor with the oppressed. The motion of the silvery ball with which Charity would bind all hearth stones together, grew each moment more and more rapid till I could no longer follow it with my eyes as it flew from chimney to chimney over the whole vast city binding with a silvery chord of universal charity the far-sundered extremes of the social world. In a few moments the whole metropolis, as I looked down upon it, presented one of the most beautiful spectacles that can be conceived. Over it just above the roofs was extended a network of silvery lines interlacing and crossing each other in every possible direction! It appeared as if a net of silver threads had fallen from the skies and lay upon the town!

I had hardly ceased wondering at this rare sight, when my astonishment was increased by a new thing that I witnessed, and which also, at the same time, afforded me an explanation of the uses of these silvery ways from chimney to chimney. Hardly was this beautiful net in which Charity had bound the city, completed, when I beheld it alive with the little beings who composed the subjects of King Claus, and which he had despatched on their several messages to 'hovel and hall.' They were moving upon it in all directions with the most busy activity. I could see hundreds issuing from the chimney of the rich merchant, carrying every luxury that he did not need, in cars along these shining rail-ways and disappearing with them down the chimney of the poor woman who had nothing for food or warmth for her cold and hungry little ones. Turning my eyes in another direction, I saw the page assisted by full one hundred and fifty of his Lilliputian fellows, pushing along in a golden car the dead woman's living babe, to make it a Christmas present to the childless judge; and with it they disappeared down the chimney! For at least ten minutes the whole scene was one of the most extraordinary life and motion. Cars heavily laden, were moving with the speed of lightning along these aerial roads and in every direction, while the noise they caused in their motion, fell melodiously upon the ear, like music stealing down towards earth from 'the gates of Heaven ajar!'

'Lo! now, oh king,' said Charity addressing Santa Claus, 'Equity ruleth over this mighty city. From the rich hath been taken that, and only that, which was surplus to their wants, and it is given to him whose need was fartherst removed from the rich man's fullness; for every rich man hath his poor man assigned him in the councils of Equity. There is now no more a poor man, nor a rich man in the city! The wail of want is hushed, and the guilt of the wealthy hoarder-up of gold (which contains *life*) exists no more! In a few moments thy messengers will return. Then, thyself, go and with me, behold in person the sweet fruit of this night's doings. Enter with me the abodes of those from whom thou hast taken, and convey them, in dreams to the presence of those whom their long idle-lying abundance has made happy.—Take the rich merchant to the glad home of the poor woman his riches have blessed: the landlord to the abode of his cheerful tenant; let the woman of fashion, see the good her jewels have done, and let the hard creditor behold the blessings that have followed the distribution of his ill-gotten gains. Let the Judge see from what a fate thou hast rescued the infant, and the miser witness the good the distribution of his hoarded gold has achieved. Let all from whom their overabundance or unjust gains have been taken, by my command, behold the effects produced! Let them see the dark abodes of wretchedness become sunny with cheerful comforts! Let them see the tears dried! the smile of peace light up the pale cheek of the widow! Let them all witness the varied scenes of happiness they have created! I will then lay my wand upon their hearts, and they will so love what they see, that the rich merchant shall take more delight in viewing his wealth thus bestowed, than in seeing it around him in statues and paintings! the woman of fashion shall love more to see the bright smiles of the faces of the poor children which her dispersed jewels have caused, than once she delighted in their glitter dispersed over her bosom; for a smile of gratitude is brighter to the eye of the giver than the brightest jewel of Ind!

'I will so touch their hearts with these scenes which thou shalt make them witness in their sleep, that, when they shall wake in the morning, the sweet influences shall remain! The work thou hast done this night shall they do over by day in love and charity, prompted by a desire to enjoy in reality, the happiness to which they have beheld themselves the involuntary contributors in their dreams!'

The End

The Christmas Banquet

NATHANIEL HAWTHORNE

It is fitting that Nathaniel Hawthorne—immortal American author of stories that are stark and somber, even macabre—was born in Salem of a long line of Puritans. In history and literature, in theater and film, the inhabitants of Massachusetts seacoast town still bear the historical and psychological scars of the zealots of the Bay Colony, the early American colonists who burned witches. In this 1843 story, seated around the dreariest of Christmas tables are characters who refuse to seek and will not find the joys of Christmas. Who are these people? John Humphrey Noyes believed that the "Banquet" portrayed some of Hawthorne's contemporaries. Hawthorne may have been ridiculing certain American socialists with whom he had recently affiliated. More importantly, for today's audience, it seems quite clear now that the so-called Ghost of New England is chiding, allegorically, divines and philosophers who believe Puritanism obsolete.

Nathaniel Hawthorne, "The Christmas Banquet," in *Tales and Sketches* (New York: Library of America, 1982), 849–67.

I have here attempted," said Roderick, unfolding a few sheets of manuscript, as he sat with Rosina and the sculptor in the summer-house—"I have attempted to seize hold of a personage who glides past me, occasionally, in my walk through life. My former sad experience, as you know, has gifted me with some degree of insight into the gloomy mysteries of the human heart, through which I have wandered like one astray in a dark cavern, with his torch fast flickering to extinction. But this man—this class of men—is a hopeless puzzle."

"Well, but propound him," said the sculptor. "Let us have an idea of him, to begin with."

"Why, indeed," replied Roderick, "he is such a being as I could conceive you to carve out of marble, and some yet unrealized perfection of human science to endow with an exquisite mockery of intellect; but still there lacks the last inestimable touch of a divine Creator. He looks like a man, and, perchance, like a better specimen of man than you ordinarily meet. You might esteem him wise—he is capable of cultivation and refinement, and has at least an external conscience—but the demands that spirit makes upon spirit, are precisely those to which he cannot respond. When, at last, you come close to him, you find chill and unsubstantial—a mere vapor."

"I believe," said Rosina, "I have a glimmering idea of what you mean."

"Then be thankful," answered her husband, smiling; "but do not anticipate any further illumination from what I am about to read. I have here imagined such a man to be—what, probably, he never is—conscious of the deficiency in his spiritual organization. Methinks the result would be a sense of cold unreality, wherewith he would go shivering through the world, longing to exchange his load of ice for any burthen of real grief that fate could fling upon a human being."

Contenting himself with this preface, Roderick began to read.

In a certain old gentleman's last will and testament there appeared a bequest, which, as his final thought and deed, was singularly in keeping with a long life of melancholy eccentricity. He devised a considerable sum for establishing a fund, the interest of which was to be expended, annually forever, in preparing a Christmas Banquet for ten of the most miserable persons that could be found. It seemed not to be the testator's purpose to make these half a score of sad hearts merry, but to provide that the storm of fierce expression of human discontent should not be drowned, even for that one holy and joyful day, amid the acclamations of festal gratitude which all Christendom sends up. And he desired, likewise, to perpetuate his own remonstrance against the earthly course of Providence, and his sad and sour dissent from those systems of religion or philosophy which either find sunshine in the world or draw it down from heaven.

The task of inviting the guests, or of selecting among such as might advance their claims to partake of this dismal hospitality, was confided to the two trustees or stewards of the fund. These gentlemen, like their deceased friend, were sombre humorists, who made it their principal occupation to number the sable threads in the web of human life, and drop all the golden ones out of the reckoning. They performed their present office with integrity and judgment. The aspect of the assembled company, on the day of the first festival, might not, it is true, have satisfied every beholder that these were especially the individuals, chosen forth from all the world, whose griefs were worthy to stand as indicators of the mass of human suffering. Yet, after due consideration, it could not be disputed that here was a variety of hopeless discomfort, which, if it arose from causes apparently inadequate, was thereby only the shrewder imputation against the nature and mechanism of life.

The arrangements and decorations of the banquet were probably intended to signify that death-in-life which had been the testator's definition of existence. The hall, illuminated by torches, was hung round with curtains of deep and dusky purple, and adorned with branches of cypress and wreaths of artificial flowers, imitative of such as used to be strown over the dead. A sprig of parsley was laid by every plate. The main reservoir of wine was a sepulchral urn of silver, whence the liquor was distributed around the table in small vases, accurately copied from those that held the tears of ancient mourners. Neither had the stewards—if it were their taste that arranged these details—forgotten the fantasy of the old Egyptians, who seated a skeleton at every festive board, and mocked their own merriment with the imperturbable grin of a death's-head. Such a fearful guest, shrouded in a black mantle, sat now at the head of the table. It was whispered, I know not with what truth, that the testator himself had once walked the visible world with the machinery of that same skeleton, and that it was one of the stipulations of his will, that he should thus be permitted to sit, from year to year, at the banquet which he had instituted. If so, it was perhaps covertly implied that he had cherished no hopes of bliss beyond the grave to compensate for the evils which he felt or imagined here. And if, in their bewildered conjectures as to the purpose of earthly existence, the banqueters should throw aside the veil, and cast an inquiring glance at this figure of death, as seeking thence the solution otherwise unattainable, the only reply would be a stare of the vacant eye caverns and a grin of the skeleton jaws. Such was the response that the dead man had fancied himself to receive when he asked of Death to solve the riddle of life; and it was his desire to repeat it when the guests of his dismal hospitality should find themselves perplexed with the same question.

"What means that wreath?" asked several of the company, while viewing the decorations of the table.

They alluded to a wreath of cypress, which was held on high by a skeleton arm, protruding from within the black mantle.

"It is a crown," said one of the stewards, "not for the worthiest, but for the wofulest, when he shall prove his claim to it."

The guest earliest bidden to the festival was a man of soft and gentle character, who had not energy to struggle against the heavy despondency to which his temperament rendered him liable; and therefore with nothing outwardly to excuse him from happiness, he had spent a life of quiet misery that made his blood torpid, and weighed upon his breath, and sat like a ponderous night fiend upon every throb of his unresisting heart. His wretchedness seemed as deep as his original nature, if not identical with it. It was the misfortune of a second guest to cherish within his bosom a diseased heart, which had become so wretchedly sore that the continual and unavoidable rubs of the world, the blow of an enemy, the careless jostle of a stranger, and even the faithful and loving touch of a friend, alike made ulcers in it. As is the habit of people thus afflicted, he found his chief employment in exhibiting these miserable sores to any one who would give themselves the pain of viewing them. A third guest was a hypochondriac, whose imagination wrought necromancy in his outward and inward world, and caused him to see monstrous faces in the household fire, and dragons in the clouds of sunset, and fiends in the guise of beautiful women, and something ugly or wicked beneath all the pleasant surfaces of nature. His neighbor at table was one who, in his early youth, had trusted mankind too much, and hoped too highly in their behalf, and, in meeting with disappointments, had become desperately soured. For several years back, this misanthrope had employed himself in accumulating motives for hating and despising his race—such as murder, lust, treachery, ingratitude, faithlessness of trusted friends, instinctive vices of children, impurity of women, hidden guilt in men of saint-like aspect— and, in short, all manner of black realities that sought to decorate themselves with outward grace or glory. But, at every atrocious fact that was added to his catalogue—at every increase of the sad knowledge which he spent his life to collect—the native impulses of the poor man's loving and confiding heart made him groan with anguish. Next, with his heavy brow bent downward, there stole into the hall a man naturally earnest and impassioned, who, from his immemorial infancy, had felt the consciousness of a high message to the world, but, essaying to deliver it, had found either no voice or form of speech, or else no ears to listen. Therefore his whole life was a bitter questioning of himself—"Why have not men acknowledged my mission?

Am I not a self-deluding fool? What business have I on earth? Where is my grave?" Throughout the festival, he quaffed frequent draughts from the sepulchral urn of wine, hoping thus to quench the celestial fire that tortured his own breast, and could not benefit his race.

Then there entered—having flung away a ticket for a ball—a gay gallant of yesterday, who had found four or five wrinkles in his brow, and more grey hairs than he could well number, on his head. Endowed with sense and feeling, he had nevertheless spent his youth in folly, but had reached at last that dreary point in life, where Folly quits us of her own accord, leaving us to make friends with Wisdom if we can. Thus, cold and desolate, he had come to seek Wisdom at the banquet, and wondered if the skeleton were she. To eke out the company, the stewards had invited a distressed poet from his home in the alms-house, and a melancholy idiot from the street corner. The latter had just the glimmering of sense that was sufficient to make him conscious of a vacancy, which the poor fellow, all his life long, had mistily sought to fill up with intelligence, wandering up and down the streets, and groaning miserably, because his attempts were ineffectual. The only lady in the hall was one who had fallen short of absolute and perfect beauty, merely by the trifling defect of a slight cast in her left eye. But this blemish, minute as it was, so shocked the pure ideal of her soul, rather than her vanity, that she passed her life in solitude, and veiled her countenance even from her own gaze. So the skeleton sat shrouded at one end of the table, and this poor lady at the other.

One other guest remains to be described. He was a young man of smooth brow, fair cheek, and fashionable mien. So far as his exterior developed him, he might much more suitably have found a place at some merry Christmas table, than have been numbered among the blighted, fate-stricken, fancy-tortured set of ill-starred banqueters. Murmurs arose among the guests as they noted the glance of general scrutiny which the intruder threw over his companions. What had he to do among them? Why did not the skeleton of the death founder of the feast unbend its rattling joints, arise, and motion the unwelcome stranger from the board?

"Shameful!" said the morbid man, while a new ulcer broke out in his heart. "He comes to mock us!—we shall be the jest of his tavern friends!—he will make a farce of our miseries, and bring it out upon the stage!"

"O, never mind him!" said the hypochondriac, smiling sourly. "He shall feast from yonder tureen of viper soup; and if there is a fricassee of scorpions on the table, pray let him have his share of it. For the dessert, he shall taste the apples of Sodom. Then, if he like our Christmas fare, let him return again next year!"

"Trouble him not," murmured the melancholy man, with gentleness. "What matters it whether the consciousness of misery come a few years sooner or later? If this youth deem himself happy now, yet let him sit with us for the sake of the wretchedness to come."

The poor idiot approached the young man with that mournful aspect of vacant inquiry which his face continually wore and which caused people to say that he was always in search of his missing wits. After no little examination he touched the stranger's hand, but immediately drew back his own, shaking his head and shivering.

"Cold, cold, cold!" muttered the idiot.

The young man shivered too, and smiled.

"Gentlemen—and you, madam," said one of the stewards of the festival, "do not conceive so ill either of our caution or judgment, as to imagine that we have admitted this young stranger—Gervayse Hastings by name—without a full investigation and thoughtful balance of his claims. Trust me, not a guest at the table is better entitled to his seat."

The steward's guarantee was perforce satisfactory. The company, therefore, took their places, and addressed themselves to the serious business of the feast, but were soon disturbed by the hypochondriac, who thrust back his chair, complaining that a dish of steward toads and vipers was set before him, and that there was green ditch water in his cup of wine. This mistake being amended, he quietly resumed his seat. The wine, as it flowed freely from the sepulchral urn, seemed to come imbued with all gloomy inspirations; so that its influence was not to cheer, but either to sink the revellers into a deeper melancholy, or elevate their spirits to an enthusiasm of wretchedness. The conversation was various. They told sad stories about people who might have been worthy guests at such a festival as the present. They talked of grisly incidents in human history; of strange crimes, which, if truly considered, were but convulsions of agony; of some lives that had been altogether wretched, and of others, which, wearing a general semblance of happiness, had yet been deformed, sooner or later, by misfortune, as by the intrusion of a grim face at a banquet; of death-bed scenes, and what dark intimations might be gathered from the words of dying men; of suicide, and whether the more eligible mode were by halter, knife, poison, drowning, gradual starvation, or the fumes of charcoal. The majority of the guests, as is the custom with people thoroughly and profoundly sick at heart, were anxious to make their own woes the theme of discussion, and prove themselves most excellent in anguish. The misanthropist went deep into the philosophy of evil, and wandered about in the darkness, with now and then a gleam of discolored light hovering on ghastly shapes and horrid scenery. Many a miserable thought, such as men have stumbled upon from age to age, did he now rake up again, and gloat over it as an inestimable gem, a diamond, a treasure far preferable to those bright, spiritual revelations of a better world, which are like precious stones from heaven's pavement. And then, amid his lore of wretchedness, he hid his face and wept.

It was a festival at which the woeful man of Uz might suitably have been a guest, together with all, in each succeeding age, who have tasted deepest of the bitterness of life. And be it said, too, that every son or daughter of woman, however favored with happy fortune, might, at one sad moment or another, have claimed the privilege of a stricken heart, to sit down at this table. But, throughout the feast, it was remarked that the young stranger, Gervayse Hastings, was unsuccessful in his attempts to catch its pervading spirit. At any deep, strong thought that found utterance, and which was torn out, as it were, from the saddest recesses of human consciousness, he looked mystified and bewildered; even more than the poor idiot, who seemed to grasp at such things with his earnest heart, and thus occasionally to comprehend them. The young man's conversation was of a colder and lighter kind, often brilliant, but lacking the powerful characteristics of a nature that had been developed by suffering.

"Sir," said the misanthropist, bluntly, in reply to some observation by Gervayse Hastings, "pray do not address me again. We have no right to talk together. Our minds have nothing in common. By what claim you appear at this banquet, I cannot guess; but methinks, to a man who could say what you have just now said, my companions and myself must seem no more than shadows, flickering on the wall. And precisely such a shadow are you to us!"

The young man smiled and bowed, but drawing himself back in his chair, he buttoned his coat over his breast, as if the banqueting-hall were growing chill. Again the idiot fixed his melancholy stare upon the youth, and murmured—"Cold! cold! cold!"

The banquet drew to its conclusion, and the guests departed. Scarcely had they stepped across the threshold of the hall, when the scene that had there passed seemed like a vision of a sick fancy, or an exhalation from a stagnant heart. Now and then, however, during the year that ensued, these melancholy people caught glimpses of one another, transient, indeed, but enough to prove that they walked the earth with the ordinary allotment of reality. Sometimes a pair of them came face to face, while stealing through the evening twilight, enveloped in their sable cloaks. Sometimes they casually met in churchyards. Once, also, it happened that two of the dismal banqueters mutually started at recognizing each other in the noonday sunshine of a crowded street, stalking there like ghosts astray. Doubtless they wondered why the skeleton did not come abroad at noonday too.

But whenever the necessity of their affairs compelled these

Christmas guests into the bustling world, they were sure to encounter the young man who had so unaccountably been admitted to the festival. They saw him among the gay and fortunate; they caught the sunny sparkle of his eye; they heard the light and careless tones of his voice, and muttered to themselves with such indignation as only the aristocracy of wretchedness could kindle—"The traitor! The vile imposter! Providence, in its own good time, may give him a right to feast among us!" But the young man's unabashed eye dwelt upon their gloomy figures as they passed him, seeming to say, perchance with somewhat of a sneer, "First, know my secret!—then, measure your claims with mine!"

The step of Time stole onward, and soon brought merry Christmas round again, with glad and solemn worship in the churches, and sports, games, festivals, and everywhere the bright face of joy beside the household fire. Again likewise the hall, with its curtains of dusky purple, was illuminated by the death torches gleaming on the sepulchral decorations of the banquet. The veiled skeleton sat in state, lifting the cypress wreath above its head, as the guerdon of some guest illustrious in the qualifications which there claimed precedence. As the stewards deemed the world inexhaustible in misery, and were desirous of recognizing it in all its forms, they had not seen fit to reassemble the company of the former year. New faces now threw their gloom across the table.

There was a man of nice conscience, who bore a blood stain in his heart—the death of a fellow-creature—which, for his more exquisite torture, had chanced with such a peculiarity of circumstances, that he could not absolutely determine whether his will had entered into the deed or not. Therefore, his whole life was spent in the agony of an inward trial for murder, with a continual sifting of the details of his terrible calamity, until his mind had no longer any thought, nor his soul any emotion, disconnected with it. There was a mother, too—but a desolation now—who, many years before, had gone out on a pleasure party, and, returning, found her infant smothered in its little bed. And ever since she has been tortured with the fantasy that her buried baby lay smothering in its coffin. Then there was an aged lady, who had lived from time immemorial with a constant tremor quivering through her frame. It was terrible to discern her dark shadow tremulous upon the wall; her lips, likewise, were tremulous; and the expression of her eye seemed to indicate that her soul was trembling too. Owing to the bewilderment and confusion which made almost a chaos of her intellect, it was impossible to discover what dire misfortune had thus shaken her nature to its depths; so that the stewards had admitted her to the table, not from any acquaintance with her history, but on the safe testimony of her miserable aspect. Some surprise was expressed at the presence of a bluff, red-faced gentleman, a certain Mr. Smith, who had evidently the fat of many a rich feast within him, and the habitual twinkle of whose eye betrayed a disposition to break forth into uproarious laughter for little cause or none. It turned out, however, that with the best possible flow of spirits, our poor friend was afflicted with a physical disease of the heart, which threatened instant death on the slightest cachinnatory indulgence, or even that titillation of the bodily frame produced by merry thoughts. In this dilemma he had sought admittance to the banquet, on the ostensible plea of his irksome and miserable state, but, in reality, with the hope of imbibing a life-preserving melancholy.

A married couple had been invited, from a motive of bitter humor; it being well understood, that they rendered each other unutterably miserable whenever they chanced to meet, and therefore must necessarily be fit associates at the festival. In contrast with these, was another couple, still unmarried, who had interchanged their hearts in early life, but had been divided by circumstances as impalpable as morning mist, and kept apart so long, that their spirits now found it impossible to meet. Therefore, yearning for communion, yet shrinking from one another, and choosing none beside, they felt themselves companionless in life, and looked upon eternity as a boundless desert. Next to the skeleton sat a mere son of earth—a haunter of the Exchange—a gatherer of shining dust—a man whose life's record was in his leger, and whose soul's prison-house, the vaults of the bank where he kept his deposits. This person had been greatly perplexed at his invitation, deeming himself one of the most fortunate men in the city; but the stewards persisted in demanding his presence, assuring him that he had no conception of how miserable he was.

And now appeared a figure which we must acknowledge as our acquaintance of the former festival. It was Gervayse Hastings, whose presence had then caused so much question and criticism, and who now took his place with the composure of one whose claims were satisfactory to himself and must needs be allowed by others. Yet his easy and unruffled face betrayed no sorrow. The well-skilled beholders gazed a moment into his eyes and shook their heads, to miss the unuttered sympathy—the countersign, never to be falsified—of those whose hearts are cavern mouths, through which they descend into a region of illimitable woe and recognize other wanderers there.

"Who is this youth?" asked the man with a blood stain on his conscience. "Surely he has never gone down into the depths! I know all the aspects of those who have passed through the dark valley. By what right is he among us?"

"Ah, it is a sinful thing to come hither without a sorrow," murmured the aged lady, in accents that partook of the eternal tremor which pervaded her whole being. "Depart, young man! Your soul has never been shaken. I tremble so much the more to look at you."

"His soul shaken! No; I'll answer for it," said bluff Mr. Smith, pressing his hand upon his heart and making himself as melancholy as he could, for fear of a fatal explosion of laughter. "I know the lad well; he has as fair prospects as any young man about town, and has no more right among us miserable creatures than the child unborn. He never was miserable and probably never will be!"

"Our honored guests," interposed the stewards, "pray have patience with us, and believe, at least, that our deep veneration for the sacredness of this solemnity would preclude any willful violation of it. Receive this young man to your table. It may not be too much to say, that no guest here would exchange his own heart for the one that beats within that youthful bosom!"

"I'd call it a bargain, and gladly, too," muttered Mr. Smith, with a perplexing mixture of sadness and mirthful conceit. "A plague upon their nonsense! My own heart is the only really miserable one in the company; it will certainly be the death of me at last."

Nevertheless, as on the former occasion, the judgment of the stewards being without appeal, the company sat down. The obnoxious guest made no more attempt to obtrude his conversation on those about him, but appeared to listen to the table talk with peculiar assiduity, as if some inestimable secret, otherwise beyond his reach, might be conveyed in a casual word. And in truth, to those who could understand and value it, there was rich matter in the upgushings and outpourings of these initiated souls to whom sorrow had been a talisman, admitting them into spiritual depths which no other spell can open. Sometimes out of the midst of densest gloom there flashed a momentary radiance, pure as crystal, bright as the flame of stars, and shedding such a glow upon the mysteries of life that the guests were ready to exclaim, "Surely the riddle is on the point of being solved!" At such illuminated intervals the saddest mourners felt it to be revealed that mortal griefs are but shadowy and external; no more than the sable robes voluminously shrouding a certain divine reality and thus indicating what might otherwise be altogether invisible to mortal eye.

"Just now," remarked the trembling old woman, "I seemed to see beyond the outside. And then my everlasting tremor passed away!"

"Would that I could dwell always in these momentary gleams of light!" said the man of stricken conscience. "Then the blood stain in my heart would be washed clean away."

This strain of conversation appeared so unintelligibly absurd to good Mr. Smith, that he burst into precisely the fit of laughter which his physicians had warned him against, as likely to prove instantaneously fatal. In effect, he fell back in his chair a corpse, with a broad grin upon his face, while his ghost, perchance, remained beside it bewildered at its unpremeditated exit. This catastrophe of course broke up the festival.

"How is this? You do not tremble?" observed the tremulous old woman to Gervayse Hastings, who was gazing at the dead man with singular intentness. "Is it not awful to see him so suddenly vanish out of the midst of life—this man of flesh and blood, whose earthly nature was so warm and strong? There is a never-ending tremor in my soul, but it trembles afresh at this! And you are calm!"

"Would that he could teach me somewhat!" said Gervayse Hastings, drawing a long breath. "Men pass before me like shadows on the wall; their actions, passions, feelings are flickerings of the light, and then they vanish! Neither the corpse, nor yonder skeleton, nor this old woman's everlasting tremor, can give me what I seek."

And then the company departed.

We cannot linger to narrate, in such detail, more circumstances of these singular festivals, which in accordance with the founder's will, continued to be kept with the regularity of an established institution. In process of time the stewards adopted the custom of inviting, from far and near, those individuals whose misfortunes were prominent above other men's, and whose mental and moral development might, therefore, be supposed to possess a corresponding interest. The exiled noble of the French Revolution, and the broken soldier of the Empire, were alike represented at the table. Fallen monarchs, wandering about the earth, have found places at that forlorn and miserable feast. The statesman, when his party flung him off, might, if he chose it, be once more a great man for the space of a single banquet. Aaron Burr's name appears on the record at a period when his ruin—the profoundest and most striking, with more of moral circumstances in it than that of almost any other man—was complete in his lonely age. Stephen Girard, when his wealth weighed upon him like a mountain, once sought admittance of his own accord. It is not probable, however, that these men had any lesson to teach in the lore of discontent and misery which might not equally well have been studied in the common walks of life. Illustrious unfortunates attract a wider sympathy, not because their griefs are more intense, but because, being set on lofty pedestals, they the better serve mankind as instances and bywords of calamity.

It concerns our present purpose to say that, at each successive festival, Gervayse Hastings showed his face gradually changing from the smooth beauty of his youth to the thoughtful comeliness of manhood, and thence to the bald, impressive dignity of age. He was the only individual invariably present. Yet on every occasion there were murmurs, both from those who knew his character and position, and from them whose hearts shrank back as denying his companionship in their mystic fraternity.

"Who is this impassive man?" had been asked a hundred times. "Has he suffered? Has he sinned? There are no traces of either. Then wherefore is he here?"

"You must inquire of the stewards or of himself," was the constant reply. "We seem to know him well here in our city and know nothing of him but what is creditable and fortunate. Yet hither he comes, year after year, to this gloomy banquet, and sits among the guests like a marble statue. Ask yonder skeleton; perhaps that may solve the riddle!"

It was in truth a wonder. The life of Gervayse Hastings was not merely a prosperous, but a brilliant one. Everything had gone well with him. He was wealthy, far beyond the expenditure that was required by habits of magnificence, a taste of rare purity and cultivation, a love of travel, a scholar's instinct to collect a splendid library, and, moreover, what seemed a magnificent liberality to the distressed. He had sought happiness, and not vainly, if a lovely and tender wife, and children of fair promise, could insure it. He had, besides, ascended above the limit which separates the obscure from the distinguished, and had won a stainless reputation in affairs of the widest public importance. Not that he was a popular character, or had within him the mysterious attributes which are essential to that species of success. To the public he was a cold abstraction, wholly destitute of those rich hues of personality, that living warmth, and the peculiar faculty of stamping his own heart's impression on a multitude of hearts by which the people recognize their favorites. And it must be owned that, after his most intimate associates had done their best to know him thoroughly, and love him warmly, they were startled to find how little hold he had upon their affections. They approved, they admired, but still in those moments when the human spirit most craves reality, they shrank back from Gervayse Hastings, as powerless to give them what they sought. It was the feeling of distrustful regret with which we should draw back the hand after extending it, in an illusive twilight, to grasp the hand of a shadow upon the wall.

As the superficial fervency of youth decayed, this peculiar effect of Gervayse Hasting's character grew more perceptible. His children, when he extended his arms, came coldly to his knees, but never climbed them of their own accord. His wife wept secretly, and almost adjudged herself a criminal because she shivered in the chill of his bosom. He, too, occasionally appeared not unconscious of the chillness of his moral atmosphere, and willing, if it might be so, to warm himself at a kindly fire. But age stole onward and benumbed him more and more. As the hoar-frost began to gather on him his wife went to her grave, and was doubtless warmer there; his children either died or were scattered to different homes of their own; and old Gervayse Hastings, unscathed by grief,—alone, but needing no companionship,—continued his steady walk through life, and still on every Christmas day attended at the dismal banquet. His privilege as a guest had become prescriptive now. Had he claimed the head of the table, even the skeleton would have been ejected from its seat.

Finally, at the merry Christmas-tide, when he had numbered fourscore years complete, this pale, high-browed, marble-featured old man once more entered the long-frequented hall, with the same impassive aspect that had called forth so much dissatisfied remark at his first attendance. Time, except in matters merely external, had done nothing for him, either of good or evil. As he took his place he threw a calm, inquiring glance around the table, as if to ascertain whether any guest had yet appeared, after so many unsuccessful banquets, who might impart to him the mystery—the deep, warm, secret—the life within the life—which, whether manifested in joy or sorrow, is what gives substance to a world of shadows.

"My friends," said Gervayse Hastings, assuming a position which his long conversance with the festival caused to appear natural, "you are welcome! I drink to you all in this cup of sepulchral wine."

The guests replied courteously, but still in a manner that proved them unable to receive the old man as a member of their sad fraternity. It may be well to give the reader an idea of the present company at the banquet.

One was formerly a clergyman, enthusiastic in his profession, and apparently of the genuine dynasty of those old puritan divines whose faith in their calling, and stern exercise of it, had placed them among the mighty of the earth. But yielding to the speculative tendency of the age, he had gone astray from the firm foundation of an ancient faith, and wandered into a cloud region, where everything was misty and deceptive, ever mocking him with a semblance of reality, but still dissolving when he flung himself upon it for support and rest. His instinct and early training demanded something steadfast; but, looking forward, he beheld vapors piled on vapors, and behind him an impassable gulf between the man of yesterday and to-day, on the borders of which he paced to and fro, sometimes wringing his hands in agony, and often making his own woe a theme of scornful merriment. This surely was a miserable man. Next, there was a theorist—one of a numerous tribe, although he deemed himself unique since the creation—a theorist, who had conceived a plan by which all the wretchedness of earth, moral and physical, might be done away, and the bliss of the millennium at once accomplished. But, the incredulity of mankind debarring him from action, he was smitten with as much grief as if the whole mass of woe which he was denied the opportunity to remedy, were crowded into his own bosom. A plain old man in black attracted much of the company's notice, on the supposition that he was no other than Father Miller, who, it seemed, had given

himself up to despair at the tedious delay of the final conflagra-
tion. Then there was a man distinguished for native pride and
obstinacy, who, a little while before, had possessed immense
wealth, and held the control of a vast moneyed interest, which
he had wielded in the same spirit as a despotic monarch would
wield the power of his empire, carrying on a tremendous moral
warfare, the roar and tremor of which was felt at every fireside
in the land. At length came a crushing ruin—a total overthrow
of fortune, power, and character—the effect of which on his
imperious, and, in many respects, noble and lofty nature, might
have entitled him to a place, not merely at our festival, but
among the peers of Pandemonium.

There was a modern philanthropist, who had become so
deeply sensible of the calamities of thousands and millions of
his fellow-creatures, and of the impracticableness of any general
measures for their relief, that he had no heart to do what little
good lay immediately within his power, but contented himself
with being miserable for sympathy. Near him sat a gentleman
in a predicament hitherto unprecedented, but of which the
present epoch probably affords numerous examples. Ever since
he was of capacity to read a newspaper this person had prided
himself on his consistent adherence to one political party, but,
in the confusion of these latter days, had got bewildered and
knew not whereabouts his party was. This wretched condition,
so morally desolate and disheartening to a man who has long
accustomed himself to merge his individuality in the mass of a
great body, can only be conceived by such as have experienced
it. His next companion was a popular orator who had lost his
voice, and—as it was pretty much all that he had to lose—had
fallen into a state of hopeless melancholy. The table was likewise
graced by two of the gentler sex—one, a half-starved, consumptive seamstress, the representative of thousands just as wretched;
the other, a woman of unemployed energy, who found herself in
the world with nothing to achieve, nothing to enjoy, and nothing
even to suffer. She had, therefore, driven herself to the verge of
madness by dark broodings over the wrongs of her sex, and its
exclusion from a proper field of action. The roll of guests being

thus complete, a side-table had been set for three or four disappointed office-seekers, with hearts as sick as death, whom the stewards had admitted, partly because their calamities really entitled them to entrance here, and partly that they were in especial need of a good dinner. There was likewise a homeless dog, with his tail between his legs, licking up the crumbs and gnawing the fragments of the feast—such a melancholy cur as one sometimes sees about the streets, without a master, and willing to follow the first that will accept his service.

In their own way, these were as wretched a set of people as ever had assembled at the festival. There they sat, with the veiled skeleton of the founder holding aloft the cypress wreath, at one end of the table, and at the other, wrapped in furs, the withered figure of Gervayse Hastings, stately, calm, and cold, impressing the company with awe, yet so little interesting their sympathy that he might have vanished into thin air without their once exclaiming, "Whither is he gone?"

"Sir," said the philanthropist, addressing the old man, "you have been so long a guest at this annual festival, and have thus been conversant with so many varieties of human affliction, that, not improbably, you have thence derived some great and important lessons. How blessed were your lot could you reveal a secret by which all this mass of woe might be removed!"

"I know of but one misfortune," answered Gervayse Hastings, quietly, "and that is my own."

"Your own!" rejoined he philanthropist. "And, looking back on your serene and prosperous life, how can you claim to be the sole unfortunate of the human race?"

"You will not understand it," replied Gervayse Hastings, feebly, and with a singular inefficiency of pronunciation, and sometimes putting one word for another. "None have understood it—not even those who experience the like. It is a chillness—a want of earnestness—a feeling as if what should be my heart were a thing of vapor—a haunting perception of unreality! Thus seeming to possess all that other men have—all that other men aim at—I have really possessed nothing, neither joy nor griefs. All things, all persons—as was truly said to me at this table long and long ago—have been like shadows flickering on the wall. It was so with my wife and children—with those who seemed my friends: it is so with yourselves, whom I see now before me. Neither have I myself any real existence, but am a shadow like the rest!"

And how is it with your views of a future life?" inquired the speculative clergyman.

"Worse than with you," said the old man, in a hollow and feeble tone; "for I cannot conceive it earnestly enough to feel either hope or fear. Mine—mine is the wretchedness! This cold heart—this unreal life! Ah! it grows colder still."

It so chanced that at this juncture the decayed ligaments of the skeleton gave way, and the dry bones fell together in a heap, thus causing the dusty wreath of cypress to drop upon the table. The attention of the company being thus diverted for a single instant from Gervayse Hastings, they perceived, on turning again towards him, that the old man had undergone a change. His shadow had ceased to flicker on the wall.

"Well, Rosina, what is your criticism?" asked Roderick, as he rolled up the manuscript.

"Frankly, your success is by no means complete," replied she. "It is true, I have an idea of the character you endeavor to describe; but it is rather by dint of my own thought than your expression."

"That is unavoidable," observed the sculptor, "because the characteristics are all negative. If Gervayse Hastings could have imbibed one human grief at the gloomy banquet, the task of describing him would have been infinitely easier. Of such persons—and we do meet with these moral monsters now and then—it is difficult to conceive how they came to exist here, or what there is in them capable of existence hereafter. They seem to be on the outside of everything; and nothing wearies the soul more than an attempt to comprehend them within its grasp."

Christmas, or The Good Fairy

HARRIET BEECHER STOWE

In 1853, when the author of Uncle Tom's Cabin *wrote this story, Dickens's* A Christmas Carol *had already for a decade been a seasonal morality play for Americans, who seemed to desire its message of humanity even more ardently than the author's own British countrymen. Harriet Beecher Stowe, spokeswoman for causes (abolition, temperance, and women's suffrage), probably gained stature as an American author owing more to the strength and passion of her beliefs than to the artistry of her prose. As in the case of Uncle Tom, she created a typology of characters (stereotypes if you will) that she used to personify her convictions. Although in quaint and "ladylike" terms, the self-centered, white-fingered, and bejewelled Ellen Stuart was, every bit as much as Ebenezer Scrooge, transformed at Christmas into a human being aware of poverty and her own power to reduce it.*

Harriet Beecher Stowe, "Christmas, or the Good Fairy," in *Earthly Care: A Heavenly Discipline* (Philadelphia, Penn.: Willis P. Hazard, 1853), 109–24. The text for this excerpt is on file at the Athenaeum in Boston.

Oh, dear! Christmas is coming in a fortnight, and I have got to think up presents for everybody!" said young Ellen Stuart, as she leaned languidly back in her chair. "Dear me! it's so tedious! Everybody has got everything that can be thought of."

"Oh, no!" said her confidential adviser, Miss Lester, in a soothing tone. "You have means of buying everything you can fancy, and when every shop and store is glittering with all manner of splendors, you cannot surely be at a loss."

"Well, now, just listen. To begin with, there's mamma! what can I get for her? I have thought of ever so many things. She has three card-cases, four gold thimbles, two or three gold chains, two writing desks of different patterns; and then, as to rings, brooches, boxes, and all other things, I should think she might be sick of the sight of them. I am sure I am," said she, languidly gazing on her white and jewelled fingers.

This view of the case seemed rather puzzling to the adviser, and there was silence for a few moments, when Eleanor, yawning, resumed—

"And then there's cousins Ellen and Mary—I suppose they will be coming down on me with a whole load of presents; and Mrs. B. will send me something—she did last year; and then there's cousins William and Tom—I must get them something, and I would like to do it well enough, if I only knew what to get!"

"Well," said Eleanor's aunt, who had been sitting quietly rattling her knitting needles during this speech, "it's a pity that you had not such a subject to practice on as I was when I was a girl—presents did not fly about in those days as they do now. I remember when I was ten years old, my father gave sister Mary and me a most marvellously ugly sugar dog for a Christmas gift, and we were perfectly delighted with it—the very idea of a present was so new to us."

"Dear aunt, how delighted I should be if I had any such fresh unsophisticated body to get presents for! but to get and get for people that have more than they know what to do with now—to add pictures, books, and gilding, when the centre-

74

tables are loaded with them now—and rings and jewels, when they are a perfect drug! I wish myself that I were not sick, and sated, and tired with having everything in the world given me!"

"Well, Eleanor," said her aunt, "if you really do want unsophisticated subjects to practice on, I can put you in the way of it. I can show you more than one family to whom you might seem to be a very good fairy, and where such gifts as you could give with all ease would seem like a magic dream."

"Why, that would really be worth while, aunt."

"Look right across the way," said her aunt. "You see that building."

"That miserable combination of shanties? Yes!"

"Well, I have several acquaintances there who have never been tired of Christmas gifts, or gifts of any other kind. I assure you, you could make quite a sensation over there."

"Well, who is there? Let us know!"

"Do you remember Owen, that used to make your shoes?"

"Yes, I remember something about him."

"Well, he has fallen into a consumption, and cannot work any more, and he and his wife and three little children live in one of the rooms over there."

"How do they get along?"

"His wife takes in sewing sometimes, and sometimes goes out washing. Poor Owen! I was over there yesterday; he looks thin and wistful, and his wife was saying that he was parched with constant fever, and had very little appetite. She had, with great self-denial, and by restricting herself almost of necessary food, got him two or three oranges, and the poor fellow seemed so eager after them."

"Poor fellow!" said Eleanor, involuntarily.

"Now," said her aunt, "suppose Owen's wife should get up on a Christmas morning, and find at the door a couple of dozen of oranges, and some of those nice white grapes, such as you had at your party last week, don't you think it would make a sensation?"

"Why, yes, I think very likely it might; but who else, aunt? You spoke of a great many."

"Well, on the lower floor there is a neat little room, that is always kept perfectly trim and tidy; it belongs to a young couple who have nothing beyond the husband's day wages to live on. They are, nevertheless, as cheerful and chipper as a couple of wrens, and she is up an down half a dozen times a day, to help poor Mrs. Owen. She has a baby of her own about five months old, and of course does all the cooking, washing, and ironing for herself and husband; and yet, when Mrs. Owen goes out to wash, she takes her baby and keeps it whole days for her."

"I'm sure she deserves that the good fairies should smile on her," said Eleanor; "one baby exhausts my stock of virtue very rapidly."

"But you ought to see her baby," said aunt E., "so plump, so rosy, and good-natured, and always clean as a lily. This baby is a sort of household shrine; nothing is too sacred and too good for it; and I believe the little, thrifty woman feels only one temptation to be extravagant, and that is to get some ornaments to adorn this little divinity."

"Why, did she ever tell you so?"

"No; but one day when I was coming down stairs, the door of their room was partly open, and I saw a pedlar there with open box. John, the husband, was standing with a little purple cap on his hand, which he was regarding with mystified, admiring air, as if he didn't quite comprehend it, and trim little Mary gazing at it with longing eyes."

"I think we might get it," said John.

"Oh, no," said she, regretfully; "yet I wish we could, it's so pretty!"

"Say no more, aunt. I see the good fairy must pop a cap into a window on Christmas morning. Indeed, it shall be done. How they will wonder where it came from, and talk about it for months to come!"

"Well, then," continued her aunt, "in the next street to ours there is a miserable building, that looks as if it were just going to topple over; and away up in the third story, in a little room just under the eaves, live two poor, lonely old women. They are both nearly on to ninety. I was in there day before yesterday.

One of them is constantly confined to her bed with rheumatism, the other, weak and feeble, with failing sight and trembling hands, totters about her only helper; and they are entirely dependent on charity."

"Can't they do anything? Can't they knit?" said Eleanor.

"You are young and strong, Eleanor, and have quick eyes and nimble fingers; how long would it take you to knit a pair of stockings?"

"I!" said Eleanor. "What an idea! I never tried, but I think I could get a pair done in a week, perhaps!"

"And if somebody gave you twenty-five cents for them, and out of this you had to get food, and pay room rent, and buy coal for your fire, and oil for your lamp"—

"Stop, aunt, for pity's sake!"

"Well, I will stop, but they can't; they must pay so much every month for that miserable shell they live in, or be turned into the street. The meal and flour that some kind person sends goes off for them just as it does for others, and they must get more or starve, and coal is now scarce and high priced."

"Oh, aunt, I'm quite convinced, I'm sure; don't run me down and annihilate me with all these terrible realities. What shall I do to play a good fairy to these poor old women?"

"If you will give me full power, Eleanor, I will put up a basket to be sent to them, that will give them something to remember all winter."

"Oh, certainly I will. Let me see if I can't think of something myself."

"Well, Eleanor, suppose, then, some fifty, or sixty years hence, if you were old, and your father, and mother, and aunts, and uncles, now so thick around you, laid cold and silent in so many graves—you have somehow got away off to a strange city, where you were never known—you live in a miserable garret, where snow blows at night through the cracks, and the fire is very apt to go out in the old cracked stove; you sit crouching over the dying embers the evening before Christmas—nobody to speak to you, nobody to care for you, except another poor old soul who lies moaning in the bed—now, what would you like to have sent you?"

"Oh, aunt, what a dismal picture!"

"And yet, Ella, all poor, forsaken old women are made of young girls, who expected it in their youth as little as you do, perhaps!"

"Say no more, aunt. I'll buy—let me see—a comfortable warm shawl for each of these poor women; and I'll send them—let me see—oh! some tea—nothing goes down with old women like tea; and I'll make John wheel some coal over to them; and, aunt, it would not be a very bad thought to send them a new stove. I remember the other day, when mamma was pricing stoves, I saw some, such nice ones, for two or three dollars."

"For a new hand, Ella, you work up the idea very well," said her aunt.

"But how much ought I to give, for any one case, to these women, say?"

"How much did you give last year for any single Christmas present?"

"Why, six or seven dollars, for some; those elegant souvenirs were seven dollars; that ring I gave Mrs. B—— was ten."

"And do you suppose Mrs. B—— was any happier for it?"

"No, really, I don't think she cared much about it; but I had to give her something, because she had sent me something the year before, and I did not want to send a paltry present to any one in her circumstances."

"Then, Ella, give ten to any poor, distressed, suffering creature who really needs it, and see in how many forms of good such a sum will appear. That one hard, cold, glittering diamond ring, that now cheers nobody, and means nothing, that you give because you must, and she takes because she must, might, if broken up into smaller sums, send real warm and heart-felt gladness through many a cold and cheerless dwelling, and through many an aching heart."

"You are getting to be an orator, aunt; but don't you approve of Christmas presents among friends and equals?"

"Yes, indeed," said her aunt, fondly stroking her head. "I

have had some Christmas presents that did me a world of good—a little book mark, for instance, that a certain niece of mine worked for me with wonderful secrecy, three years ago, when she was not a young lady with a purse full of money—that book mark was a true Christmas present; and my young couple across the way are plotting a profound surprise to each other on Christmas morning. John has contrived, by an hour of extra work every night, to lay by enough to get Mary a new calico dress; and she, poor soul, has bargained away the only thing in the jewelry line she ever possessed, to be laid out on a new hat for him."

"I know, too, a washerwoman who has a poor lame boy—a patient, gentle little fellow—who has lain quietly for weeks and months in his little crib, and his mother is going to give him a splendid Christmas present."

"What is it, pray?"

"A whole orange! Don't laugh. She will pay ten whole cents for it; for it shall be none of your common oranges, but a picked one of the very best going! She has put by the money, a cent at a time, for a whole month; and nobody knows which will be happiest in it, Willie or his mother. These are such Christmas presents as I like to think of—gifts coming from love, and tending to produce love; these are the appropriate gifts of the day.

"But don't you think that it's right for those who have money, to give expensive presents, supposing always as you say, they are given from real affection?"

"Sometimes, undoubtedly. The Saviour did not condemn her who broke an alabaster-box of ointment—very precious—simply as a proof of love, even although the suggestion was made, 'this might have been sold for three hundred pence, and given to the poor.' I have thought he would regard with sympathy the fond efforts which human love sometimes makes to express itself by gifts, the rarest and most costly. How I rejoiced with all my heart, when Charles Elton gave his poor mother that splendid Chinese shawl and gold watch—because I knew they came from the very fullness of his heart to a mother that he could not do too much for—a mother that has done and suffered everything for him. In some such cases, when resources are ample, a costly gift seems to have a graceful appropriateness; but I cannot approve of it, if it exhausts all the means of doing for the poor; it is better, then, to give a simple offering, and to do something for those who really need it."

Eleanor looked thoughtful; her aunt laid down her knitting, and said, in a tone of gentle seriousness:

"Whose birth does Christmas commemorate, Ella?"

"Our Saviour's, certainly, aunt."

"Yes," said her aunt. "And when and how was he born? in a stable! laid in a manger; thus born, that in all ages he might be known as the brother and friend of the poor. And surely it seems but appropriate to commemorate His birthday by an especial remembrance of the lowly, the poor, the outcast, and distressed; and if Christ should come back to our city on a Christmas day, where should we think it most appropriate to his character to find him? Would he be carrying splendid gifts to splendid dwellings, or would he be gliding about in the cheerless haunts of the desolate, the poor, the forsaken, and the sorrowful?"

And here the conversation ended.

"What sort of Christmas presents is Ella buying?" said cousin Tom, as the waiter handed in a portentous-looking package, which had been just rung in at the door.

"Let's open it," said saucy Will. "Upon my word, two great gray blanket shawls! These must be for you and me, Tom! And what's this? A great bolt of cotton flannel and gray yarn stockings!"

The door bell rang again, and the waiter brought in another bulky parcel, and deposited it on the marble-topped centre table.

"What's here?" said Will, cutting the cord! "Whew! a perfect nest of packages! oolong tea! oranges! grapes! white sugar! Bless me, Ella must be going to housekeeping!"

"Or going crazy!" said Tom: "and on my word," said he,

looking out of the window, "there's a drayman ringing at our door, with a stove, with a tea-kettle set in the top of it!"

"Ella's cook stove, of course," said Will; and just at this moment the young lady entered, with her purse hanging gracefully over her hand.

"Now, boys, you are too bad!" she exclaimed, as each of the mischievous youngsters were gravely marching up and down, attired in a gray shawl.

"Didn't you get them for us? We thought you did," said both.

"Ella, I want some of that cotton flannel, to make me a pair of pantaloons," said Tom.

"I say, Ella," said Will, "when are you going to housekeeping? Your cooking stove is standing down in the street; 'pon my word, John is loading some coal on the dray with it."

"Ella, isn't that going to be sent to my office?" said Tom; "do you know I do so languish for a new stove with a tea-kettle in the top, to heat a fellow's shaving water!"

Just then, another ring at the door, and the grinning waiter handed in a small brown paper parcel for Miss Ella. Tom made a dive at it, and staving off the brown paper, developed a jaunty little purple velvet cap, with silver tassels.

"My smoking cap! as I live," said he, "only I shall have to wear it on my thumb, instead of my head—too small entirely," said he, shaking his head gravely.

"Come, you saucy boys," said aunt E——, entering briskly, "what are you teasing Ella for?"

"Why, do you see this lot of things, aunt? What in the world is Ella going to do with them?"

"Oh! I know!"

"You know; then I can guess, aunt, it is some of your charitable works. You are going to make a juvenile Lady Bountiful of El, eh?"

Ella, who had colored to the roots of her hair at the expose of her very unfashionable Christmas preparations, now took heart, and bestowed a very gentle and salutary little cuff on the saucy head that still wore the purple cap, and then hastened to gather up her various purchases.

"Laugh away," said she, gaily; "and a good many others will laugh, too, over these things. I got them to make people laugh—people that are not in the habit of laughing!"

"Well, well, I see into it," said Will; "and I tell you I think right well of the idea, too. There are worlds of money wasted at this time of the year, in getting things that nobody wants, and nobody cares for after they are got; and I am glad, for my part, that you are going to get up a variety in this line; in fact, I should like to give you one of these stray leaves to help on," said he, dropping a $10 note into her paper. I like to encourage girls to think of something besides breastpins and sugar candy."

But our story spins on too long. If anybody wants to see the results of Ella's first attempts at good fairyism, they can call at the doors of two or three old buildings on Christmas morning, and they shall hear all about it.

Christmas at Sutter's Fort in 1847

JOHN BONNER

Fifty years after an 1847 Christmas, early American author John Bonner vividly described, from a turn-of-the-century perspective, a Yuletide celebration that bridged two eras. Captain Sutter, a baron on European soil, was the Swiss, German, and (now, with the Mexican-American War about to end) American master of New Helvetia, California. From miles around he welcomed to a great fiesta the settlers—Americans, British, Europeans, ladies and gentlemen, Indians, trappers, prospectors, ranchers—with the combined opulence and splendor of Old Mexico and Europe, to share in the openhanded, ranch-style hospitality of the new American West. More significant than this blend of cultures was a meeting in the quiet of the Baron's study when the revelry was at full pitch: Sutter, the also-baronial Vallejo, and one other man were remarking on a metallic object, picked up from a dry stream bed ten miles from the hacienda. Gold! the first sign of an overwhelming wave of change about to wash over California and indeed over the entire North American continent.

John Bonner, "Christmas at Sutter's Fort in 1847," in *Christmas in California* (San Francisco: California Historical Society). I am indebted to Martha Kendall Winnacker, publications director of the California Historical Society, for her assistance with this text, and for permission to reprint.

Perhaps the most remarkable Christmas in the history of California was the one kept with revel at Capt. Sutter's settlement of New Helvetia in 1847, nearly half a century ago. The great California Baron was in high spirits, as might have been expected. Things had come about as he had anticipated. The country had passed into American hands, and for a long time he has been a better American than Swiss, German or Frenchman. He was as undisputably monarch of all he surveyed as Robinson Crusoe on his island. He had an estate larger than a German principality or an English shire. It was peopled by several hundred Indians, who were as absolutely his slaves as the negro fieldhands of Alabama were the slaves of the planters. To conduct his various enterprises he had several score of white men—Americans, Germans, Englishmen, Frenchmen, Spaniards—over whom his authority was absolute. His cattle were past counting. Time had been when the natives had stolen a few head here and there, but he had a way of punishing thieves which prevented a repetition of the offense.

His fort had been completed in 1845. It was a quadrangular stockade, fifteen feet high and 500 feet long by 150 feet wide. To an assailant without artillery it was impregnable. On two of the corners rose stout blockhouses which mounted a cannon each; other pieces of artillery were placed en barbette on the top of the wall so as to command the approach from the river. Within the quadrangle adobe houses furnished shelter for 500 men. There was a storehouse full of supplies, furs and ammunition, likewise a dwellinghouse in which Sutter had lived before he built his ranchería on the Feather and where he still kept his office.

His fort was the first resting place which Eastern immigrants struck after crossing the mountains. Here they found food and shelter. Sutter turned no man away on the petty pretense that he was penniless. Careless of paying his own debts, he was indulgent to his debtors. Nor did he too closely scrutinize the reasons which immigrants gave for moving to California. His broad, generous soul forgave everything but horsestealing.

When his family joined him—he had a wife, daughter and

two sons, all of whom have passed away—he built him a ranchería on the Feather River, which he called Ranchería de Hoch, and in which he spent most of his time. The building consisted of three or four gables, whose ends fronted the river. Here he sat on his balcony, watched his men catch salmon in the sparkling waters of the Feather, and speculated on what would become of his baronial estate when he was gone. He had tasted adversity, he had courted danger; was the present halcyon era of prosperity and eminence going to last? Thoughts passed through that far-reaching mind which he told no man. In the dim vista of the future he discerned many things. The one thing which he did not clearly foresee was that he would die in poverty in Pennsylvania without an acre of land which he could call his own, or a dollar except what he derived from the grudging charity of the Legislature of California.

On the Christmas day of 1847 he resolved that he and his should be merry. His man James W. Marshall had selected a site for a sawmill in a valley which the Indians called Culuma, which meant in their tongue "pleasant valley." It was in the heart of a forest of big trees. When their trunks were sawn into boards he could substitute frame houses for the adobes in which his people lived. His orchards and his vineyards were thriving; his herds had multiplied amazingly; he had horses which could cover the distance to Sonoma in a day and the distance to the Bay in a day and a half. People were growing to understand him, and the better they knew him the more they liked him. Even Vallejo, who had once called him a pestilent intruder, had been won over by his kindness at the time the Lord of Sonoma was imprisoned by the Bear flag insurgents and was his good friend.

He resolved that his retainers should keep Christmas royally. A feast should be given within the fort, which they would remember to the end of their days. The fattest cattle in his herd were slaughtered and the flesh cleaned from the ribs to make frezadas. The Indians cared little for meat or pork; their chief delicacy was fried jackass meat, and the captain sacrificed several burros to gratify them, though a donkey was worth four times as much as a horse. There were hecatombs of frijoles and tortillas, and salmon was served in many shapes, boiled, baked and fried. From the storeroom, fruits of all kinds, the products of the New Helvetia orchards, were taken with a lavish hand and set down on the long board table. Barrels of wine were set out and their contents drawn off in pannikins and pitchers. When Sutter founded this fort he found the valleys covered with the wild grape, from which he made a wine which was agreeable to the taste of trappers, hunters and Indians. This was supplied in profusion, and in deference to the occasion the Baron pretended not to notice the ravages the fluid wrought on the wits and muscles of his guests. To his European proteges he served aguardiente in bottles. The banquet began at noon; before the Christmas sunset the interior of the fort was strewed with inert revelers, who lay where they originally fell.

The Baron entertained his personal friends at his Ranchería de Hoch. To that hospitable resort the neighbors had been invited from far and wide. Guests had come from such distant points as San Francisco and Sonoma. From the rancheros along the river whole families had ridden, the ladies in saddle, their courtiers sitting behind to hold them straight on their horses. An army of Indian hostlers took charge of their beasts when the riders dismounted. For those who arrived early and who wished to stimulate an appetite for dinner, lunches had been provided on the river; the young men fished and shot ducks and geese; while for the ladies, Sutter's new stern-wheel steamer offered a new and exciting form of promenade.

Dinner was at five. Sutter had lived in Geneva and Paris, and knew what a good dinner should be. He had one or two cooks whom he had trained on sound gastronomical principles. They made him a soup of many ingredients; it could not have been surpassed in New York. Besides the salmon which he caught at his own door, the fish we now call the Sacramento perch, the brook trout, and the barracuda from the coast, were served with suitable sauces. After these came several entrees—pozoles or pig's feet, and peppers, frijoles and the delicate parts of the beef, with chile and tomatoes, an olia podrida, containing all manner of meats and vegetables stewed together, and various fricasses of chicken and turkey. The roti was veal, though a tender sirloin occupied one corner of the board; and the dinner closed with an assortment of feathered game—quail, grouse, ducks, geese and pigeons—fit to bring the water to the mouth of a gourmand. In his own house he did not drink the wine from the native grape; he had planted the mission grape and had a cellar full of the wine; nor was champagne wanting, brought up the river from San Francisco.

The guests were all in full dress; the men in silk jackets, embroidered waist-coats, velveteen breeches with gilt lacings and open below the knee and a sash round the waist; the ladies in bare arms, without corsets, in silk or crape gowns, sashes of bright colors, satin shoes and scarlet or flesh-colored stockings. Both sexes wore jewelry; jewels flashed from the ears and necks of the pretty girls.

After the feast was over and the wines drunk, the party adjourned to the long room which Captain Sutter had built expressly for balls and assemblies. There had been some impromptu dancing on the grass in true California fashion, but at the close of December the days are short and as night falls the air is nipping; the captain's guests were not sorry to take refuge indoors.

A guitar and a violin were tuned, and the piano, which Sutter had imported from France, soon began to give voice. The fun commenced as usual with a jota, in which every lady in turn was taken out by the master of ceremonies and danced a few steps, singing at the same time a little verse which she was supposed to improvise. Then followed the bamba, the zorrita, the fandango, the jarabe, and the ball wound up with the contra danza. Dancing was kept up till the tops of the sierras began to be tipped with gold, and the senoras and senoritas and their cavaliers reluctantly retired to the rooms provided for them.

The Baron had left the ballroom when the festivities were at their height and had closeted himself with two or three friends in an inner chamber. They smoked, and over goblets of aguardiente punch they discussed the inexhaustible topic of the day— the American occupation and its consequences. With the exception of Vallejo and another, the Hispano-Mexicans were sure that the advent of the gringo meant ruin. Sutter was not so sure of that. He observed that what the Californians lacked was energy and push and get-up-and-get; those were just the qualities in which the Americanos excelled. It seemed to him just possible that these gringos who were flowing across the mountains and coming to him to feed them on their way might develop the resources which lay dormant in California and which he had not yet had time to exploit. He had demonstrated that California could grow more and better fruits and cereals than any other part of the world which he had visited. The Mexicans had never taken the pains to cultivate them industriously, might not the Americanos do better?

Vallejo, who was the most farsighted man of his race in that day, and whose tongue had been loosed by generous bumpers of mission wine, said that in his opinion they might and probably would.

"There is another matter to be considered," observed the host. And drawing from his pocket an object which appeared to be metallic, and which shone in the lamplight, he asked if they knew what that was. They turned it over in their fingers, examined it, and returned it in silence.

"That," said Sutter, "is gold. It is not from San Fernando, the place where our good friend, Governor Alvarado, got the gold to make the ring he wears. It is from a spot which has never been suspected of containing gold. It was picked up not ten miles from here, in the gravel of a stream which had run dry in the heats of summer. Now, in the country where I was brought up, in Switzerland, gold is found in the sands of Alpine streams, but in such small quantities that it does not pay to hunt for it. Suppose it should be more abundant in the streams of California. I have read that in Northern Africa, 2000 years ago, the natives used to gather gold out of their streams and exchange the dust with the Carthaginians for goods. Suppose such rich streams should be found here. Would not the find be followed by a rush of people who would neglect the profits of horticulture and agriculture?"

Vallejo laughed heartily at the idea of California becoming a land of gold, and offered to wager with his host that he would carry off in his serape all the gold that would ever be found in the province.

Sutter did not join in the laugh nor take the wager.

"I am puzzled," said he. "I do not pretend to be a prophet, nor do I know enough of geology to form an opinion whether or no nuggets of gold will be more abundant here than they are in the East of Europe. But this I am sure of: If gold is found here in large quantities the real resources of the country, which I am spending my life trying to develop, will be passed over by the goldseekers, my object in founding New Helvetia will be defeated and I may die in the poorhouse."

One month from that day Marshall came riding in the rain through brush and brier from Coloma to the fort with a bag of gold nuggets under his arm, and Captain Sutter knew that the destiny he had feared had come.

II

The Gilded Age

Introduction

From 1877 to 1917, the nation's history moved so fast that it is hard to dwell on just the Civil War and Reconstruction. The peopling of the West proceeded with such dispatch that, as the superintendent of the census reported in 1890, this country no longer had a western frontier. In the name of greatness, the star-spangled banner was taken to Alaska, Hawaii, Samoa, and the Philippines in the Pacific; and the Virgin Islands, Puerto Rico, and Cuba in the Atlantic, with Teddy Roosevelt securing the Isthmus of Panama so that east and west could finally meet. John D. and William Rockefeller and Andrew Carnegie were some of the men who took America through the Industrial Revolution in half the time that it had taken Great Britain. And the Industrial Revolution spawned cities (complete with immigrant ghettos), pools, trusts, holding companies, labor unions, reform movements, and an emphasis on science as opposed to old-time religion.

In this atmosphere, American Christmas changed, too. More than anything else, it became, as writes Daniel J. Boorstin in his book *The Americans: The Democratic Experience*, "a spectacular nationwide Festival of Consumption."[1] His arguments to prove the case are most convincing. Beginning on December 24, 1867, R. H. Macy's store had a record one-day receipt of $6,000 by staying open until midnight for the first time. By 1899, the department stores named after F. W. Woolworth were selling more than $800,000 worth of Christmas ornaments annually, and holiday bonuses had to be given to employees who sometimes doubled their normal work week in November and December. Hawking wares at these stores were men in red and white suits, some of whom had attended a school in Albion,

New York, where the curriculum included "indoctrination in the history of Santa Claus, dressing for the role, wearing beards, handling children, and other special techniques."[2]

New visuals added to the color of the Christmas scene. A German immigrant, Louis Prange, pioneered in the making of holiday cards that individuals could send to keep in touch with families that had been separated as loved ones played out their various parts in the Industrial Revolution. More famous was a lithograph firm in New York named Currier and Ives. Nathaniel Currier and James Marriott Ives joined forces to depict life in America, portraying such heroes as George Washington and Andrew Jackson, whom all citizens could hold in common. Images of America abounded: the Brooklyn Bridge, steam locomotives, and the transcontinental railroads; the clipper and the steamship; America at play—baseball, hunting and fishing, rural festivities, sleigh rides. A single reproduction entitled "The Road—Winter" (actually Currier in a sled with his wife on a wintry night) was a favorite on countless parlor walls long before Christmas cards became popular. Christmas touched Americans at every level, from the tenements to the White House. President Benjamin Harrison decided that he should be a model for all when he said: "I am an ardent believer in the duty we owe to ourselves as Christians to make merry for children at Christmas time, and we shall have an old-fashioned Christmas tree for the grandchildren upstairs; and I shall be their Santa Claus myself. If my influence does for aught in this busy world let me hope that my example may be followed in every family in the land."[3]

Notes

1. Daniel J. Boorstin, *The Americans: The Democratic Experience* (New York: Random House, 1973), 158.
2. Ibid., 160.
3. Quoted from W. F. Dawson, *Christmas: Its Origin and Associations* (London: Elliot Stock, 1902), 313.

Civil War Album

As civil war threatened the Union, Americans north and south relied on holiday feelings to bind families and friends together. General Robert E. Lee, who holds a more lasting place in the hearts of most Americans than the Confederacy he fought for, wrote from the battlefield on December 25, 1861, to his wife and daughter. He enclosed violets gathered early that morning in the frost and referred to Christmas, war notwithstanding, as "this day of grateful rejoicing." In 1864, on December 25, war still raging, another Confederate soldier, a captain in Lee's cavalry division, wrote to his mother from Georgia: "Our affairs just now are as blue as indigo. In Virginia alone Confederate arms maintain their own ground position." But, "This is Christmas day, dear Mother, and doubtless as you sat around your dinner table at home, you have thought and talked of your absent son." On the Union side, there was sometimes outright revelry. Oliver Willcox Norton, Yankee soldier at Camp William Penn, wrote home in 1863 that "Christmas in camp went merry as a marriage bell, big dinner, sham battle, etc. etc." A

The texts for these excerpts are:

Robert E. Lee, in The Civil War Christmas Album, ed. *Philip Van Doren Stern (New York: Hawthorn Books, 1961), 18–19; Francis G. Dawson, in* Reminiscences of Confederate Services, ed. Bell I. Wiley *(Baton Rouge: Louisiana State University Press, 1980), 208–10; Oliver Willcox Norton, ed.,* Army Letters 1861–1865 *(Chicago: O. L. Deming, 1903); John L. Ransom, ed.,* Andersonville Diary *(New York: Haskell House Pub., 1974), 227–30. The letters of Robert E. Lee are in the Virginia Historical Society, Mss/L51 C330.*

year later, still at the front, from a Virginia home where he and other soldiers were guests, Norton described a lavish Christmas dinner with the band of the regiment playing in front of the house. Although victorious, not all Yankees celebrated. In the wretched prison at Andersonville, Georgia, some Union captives spent more than one Christmas. As the conflict neared its end, the growing despondency reflected in entries from prison diaries reminds us that in war, no one really wins.

Coosawhatchie, South Carolina
December 25, 1861

I cannot let this day of grateful rejoicing pass, dear Mary, without some communication with you. I am grateful for the many among the past that I have passed with you, and the remembrance of them fills me with pleasure. For those on which we have been separated we must not repine. If it will make us more resigned and better prepared for what is in store for us, we should rejoice. Now we must be content with the many blessings we receive. If we can only become sensible of our transgressions, so as to be fully penitent and forgiven, that this heavy punishment under which we labor may with justice be removed from us and the whole nation, what a gracious consummation of all that we have endured it will be!

I am here but little myself. The days I am not here I visit some point exposed to the enemy, and after our dinner at early candle light, am engaged in writing till eleven or twelve o'clock at night.

As to our old home, if not destroyed, it will be difficult ever to be recognized. Even if the enemy had wished to preserve it, it would almost have been impossible. With the number of troops encamped around it, the change of officers, etc., the want of fuel, shelter, etc., and all the dire necessities of war, it is vain to think of its being in a habitable condition. I fear, too, books, furniture, and the relics of Mount Vernon will be gone. It is better to make up our minds to a general loss. They cannot take away the remembrance of the spot, and the memories of those that to us rendered it sacred. That will remain to us as long as life will last, and that we can preserve.

In the absence of a home, I wish I could purchase Stratford. That is the only other place that I could go to, now accessible to us, that would inspire me with feelings of pleasure and local love. You and the girls could remain there in quiet. It is a poor place, but we could make enough corn bread and bacon for our support, and the girls could weave us clothes. I wonder if it is for sale and at how much. Ask Fitzhugh to try to find out, when he gets to Fredericksburg.

You must not build your hopes on peace on account of the United States going into a war with England. She will be very loath to do that, notwithstanding the bluster of the Northern papers. Her rulers are not entirely mad, and if they find England is in earnest, and that war or a restitution of their captives must be the consequence, they will adopt the latter. We must make up our minds to fight our battles and win our independence alone. No one will help us. We require no extraneous aid, if true to ourselves. But we must be patient. It is not a light achievement and cannot be accomplished at once.

I wrote a few days since, giving you all the news, and have now therefore nothing to relate. The enemy is still quiet and increasing in strength. We grow in size slowly but are working hard.

Affectionately and truly,
R. E. Lee

Coosawhatchie, South Carolina
December 25, 1861

My Dear Daughter:

Having distributed such poor Christmas gifts as I had to those around me, I have been looking for something for you. Trifles even are hard to get these war times, and you must not therefore expect more. I have sent you what I thought most useful in your separation from me and hope it will be of some service. Though stigmatized as "vile dross," it has never been a drug with me. That you may never want for it, restrict your wants to your necessities. Yet how little will it purchase! But see how God provides for our pleasure in every way. To compensate for such "trash," I send you some sweet violets that I gathered for you this morning while covered with dense white frost, whose crystals glittered in the bright sun like diamonds, and formed a brooch of rare beauty and sweetness which could not be fabricated by the expenditure of a world of money.

May God guard and preserve you for me, my dear daughter! Among the calamities of war, the hardest to bear, perhaps, is the separation of families and friends. Yet all must be endured to accomplish our independence and maintain our self-government. In my absence from you I have thought of you very often and regretted I could do nothing for your comfort. Your old home, if not destroyed by our enemies, has been so desecrated that I cannot bear to think of it. I should have preferred it to have been wiped from the earth, its beautiful hill sunk, and its sacred trees buried rather than to have been degraded by the presence of those who revel in the ill they do for their own selfish purposes.

I pray for a better spirit and that the hearts of our enemies may be changed. In your homeless condition I hope you make yourself contented and useful. Occupy yourself in aiding those more helpless than yourself. Think always of your father.

R. E. Lee

Camp Wm. Penn, Philadelphia
Thursday, Dec. 10, 1863.

Dear Sister L.:—

I have just time to write you a line. I had just two days to
spend at home. Trains not connecting and being behind time
delayed me. I got here to the camp last Monday and was
immediately assigned the command of a full company.

Next day I was put on as "officer of the guard" and my
letter writing and everything of the kind are coming out slim.

My regiment is full. The field officers are Colonel Chas. W.
Fribley, Lieutenant Colonel N. B. Bartram, formerly Lieutenant
Colonel Seventeenth New York, and Major Loren Burritt. The
second lieutenant of my company is Jas. S. Thompson.

The regiment is in barracks, just moved in on Tuesday. We
are eight miles from Philadelphia, but the cars pass frequently
and it is not too far for camps, twenty minutes trip.

I was officer of the guard the day we moved and not allowed
to leave my guard, and when the officers' baggage was unloaded
some one took my valise and I cannot find it. It was worth sixty
dollars to me at least, and all my papers were in it. It may come
to light and the end of the world may come in 1867. One is as
probable as the other.

The weather is clear and very cold. I must close. Will tell
you more next time. Write soon. Address "Lieutenant O. W.
N., Company K, Eighth United States Colored Troops, Camp
W. Penn, Philadelphia, Pennsylvania."

Oliver W. Norton

Camp Wm. Penn, Philadelphia
Dec. 26, 1863.

Dear Sister L.:—

A Happy New Year to you if it isn't too late. Christmas in
camp went "merry as a marriage bell," big dinner, sham battle,
etc., etc.

At night I went to the theater in town. Saw Edwin Forrest in
"Metamora." I send you a "phiz." Will send you a full length

when they come. I have just time to say I have been appointed Acting Quartermaster on the staff of Major Burritt, commanding three companies Eighth United States Colored Troops, to be sent to Delaware on recruiting service. I shall have a horse to ride, of course. Write soon and direct as before till I send my new address.

Oliver W. Norton

Chapin's Farm, Va.,
December 26,
1864.

My Dear Sister L.:—

This will not reach you in time to present my respects in a "Merry Christmas," so I will wish you a "Happy New Year" and many returns of the season, and tell you how I spent my Christmas. There are so few Sundays in the army that the occurrence of the holiday on that day was no drawback. The military part of the festivity was a Division Dress Parade and the social, or our social part was a dinner at "Ye Quartermaster's." Lieutenant Burrows is a capital hand at carrying out anything of that kind and he determined to do the thing up right.

We had two guests, Colonel Samuel C. Armstrong, of the Eighth, and Lieutenant Colonel Mayer of the Forty-fifth, two men who would be considered acquisitions in almost any social circle. Colonel A. was born in the Sandwich Islands and Colonel M. in Buenos Ayres, South America, and both are full of stories of adventure, travel and society. Mayer is the hero of half a dozen duels, which is not much of a recommendation, I know, but the custom of his country makes it a very different thing from dueling here.

I will not undertake to describe our dinner in detail, but we had oyster soup, fish boiled, roast fowl (chicken) and mutton, potatoes, peas and tomatoes, oysters, fried and raw, and for dessert mince pie, fruit cake, apples, peaches, grapes, figs, raisins, nuts, etc., and coffee, and for wassail a rousing bowl of punch. The band of the regiment played in front of the house during dinner, and the leader says he played three hours. The long and short of it is we had as elegant and *recherche* an affair as often comes off in the army, enjoyed ourselves thoroughly and nobody went home drunk.

Do you know that since my last letter to you I have passed my twenty-fifth birthday? And now I am beginning my twenty-sixth year. My years would indicate that I ought to be a man, but I must confess to much of the boy in my nature yet. To be sure I have grown some in strength of character since I was twenty-one, but I seem to be a long way off from the condition of a man in society. Do you think I will be married before I am thirty? I don't see much prospect of it. I am twenty-five and not in love yet, and sometimes I think it is the best thing that could have happened to me that I have been beyond the reach of temptation in that line, until I had strength of character enough to look at this matter as a man should. God willing, I mean to have a wife and a home, but when, is beyond my knowledge.

Oliver W. Norton

Andersonville Diary—J.L. Ransom:

Dec. 24.—Must hang up my stocking to-night for habit's sake, if nothing else. I am enjoying splendid health, and prison life agrees with me. Wrote home to-day.

Dec. 25—and Christmas.—One year ago to-day first went into camp at Coldwater, little dreaming what changes a year would bring around, but there are exchange rumors afloat, and hope to see white folks again before many months. All ordered out to be spuadded over again, which was quite a disappointment to our mess, as we are making preparations for a grand dinner, gotten up by outside hands, Mustard, Myers, Hendryx and myself. However, we had our good things for supper, instead of dinner, and it was a big thing, consisting of corn bread and butter, oysters, coffee, beef, crackers, cheese, &c.; all we could possibly eat or do away with, and costing the snug little sum of $200 Confederate money, or $20 in greenbacks. Lay awake long before daylight, listening to the bells. As they rang out Christmas good morning, I imagined they were in Jackson, Michigan, my old home, and from the spires of the old Presbyterian and Episcopal churches. Little do they think as they are saying their Merry Christmas and enjoying themselves so much, of the hunger and starving here. But there are better days coming.

Dec. 26—News of exchange and no officers over from Libby to issue clothing. Extra quantity of wood. Rebels all drunk and very domineering. Punish for the smallest kind of excuse. Some men tunneled out of the pen, but were retaken, and were made to crawl back through the same hole they went out of, and the Lieutenant kept hitting them with a board as they went down, and then ran back and forward from one hole to the other and as they stuck up their heads, would hit them with a club, keeping them at it for nearly an hour. A large crowd of both Rebels and Yankees collected around to see the fun.

Dec. 27—Colonel Sanderson and Colonel Boyd came over this morning in a great hurry and began to issue clothing very fast, saying an exchange had been agreed upon, and they wanted to get rid of it before we all went away. Pretty soon the news got inside, and the greatest cheering, yelling, shaking of hands and congratulating one another took place. Just before dinner five hundred were taken out, counted and sent away. Everybody anxious to go away first, which of course they cannot do. Sergeants Hight and Marks stand at the gate with big clubs, keeping order, letting them out two at a time, occasionally knocking a man down, and it is seldom he gets up again very soon. Some of the outside went and the rest go to-morrow. It is a sure thing—a general exchange, and all will be sent away immediately. Everybody in good spirits. Guess Northern folks will be surprised to see such looking objects come among them. They are the worst looking crowd I ever saw. Extra ration of food and wood to-night, and am anxiously waiting for the morrow.

Head Quarters Lee's Cav Division
Dec. 25, 1864

My dearest Mother,

A few days ago I recd your letter of Oct 26 and immediately sent a reply to Wilmington, but my friend Capt Cavendish tells me that he will start for England in a day or two and I cannot lose the opportunity of writing to you again. This is Christmas day, dear Mother, and doubtless as you sat around your dinner table at home in quiet Isleworth you have thought and talked of your absent son. You are always present in my mind and more particularly on such a day as this when we have been accustomed to meet at our home. For the past ten days we have been riding nearly night and day to check the movements of the Yankee cavalry who were making a raid on Gordonsville and I have been pretty nearly worn out. On Tuesday we marched all night, we had already gone 30 miles since morning, the snow was falling in small flakes mixed with hail which froze as it touched your clothes, my hat was as stiff as a board, icicles hanging all around the brim, my coat shining with ice, my horse slipping and sliding at every step, we started at 1 o'clock in the morning and rode fourteen miles before we struck the Yankee camp, we had but 500 men and there were 3000 Yanks, we got within 200 yds of their fires about break of day, formed our troops and with a yell and shout charged right down on them, it was a perfect surprise, and after a short fight drove them off in headlong confusion. Our loss was very slight and we captured a number of horses and prisoners. A bullet struck me on the leg, cutting my trousers and drawers and just breaking the skin, so much for luck. Yesterday Gen Lee gave me permission to come down to Richmond to spend Christmas, and I have thus the opportunity of quietly writing this. My friends in Richmond are particularly kind to me. I have always a home here at Mr. Tyler's whenever I come to town. I know not how to appreciate sufficiently the uniform courtesy and consideration which has been extended to me. Your last letter gave me great satisfaction, and I was delighted to find that affairs were no worse with you. I had been very anxious, but I now hope that with the blessing of Providence father will be able to surmount all his difficulties and see his way clear to a comparatively prosperous career. I feel very deeply all father's troubles and trials. I know how much he has still struggled on, tell him from me that I am with him heart and soul in all his labors, and beg him always and often to write to me and tell me all that he is doing, all his plans and all his intentions, don't let me think that I am estranged from you because I am not in England, don't let me think that distance or time makes me any the less your affectionate Son. Thanks for your news from Bartley, I have not yet received his letter, tell him I shall not forgive him until I receive a letter with all the news. Henceforth direct my letters as follows, Capt Francis W. Dawson, Maj. Gen. Fitz:Lee's Staff, care of Messrs. Mitchell & Tyler, Richmond, Virginia. C.S.A. You can send through Major Walker, or Messrs Fraser, Trenholm & Co of Liverpool, or Messr A. Collie & Co. of Leadenhall St will I am sure send on your letters. Perhaps William will call on Messrs Collie and ask them, their ships are coming over constantly and it would be a safe and expeditious channel for you.

Our affairs here just now are as blue as indigo, in Georgia everything seems to go wrong, in Virginia alone Confederate arms maintain their own ground position, but a brighter day will soon come and we shall be able soon to recover our lost ground and show Europe that the South is still able to conquer and maintain her independence. Tis sad, sad, indeed to see the ruin and desolation which now reign in some of the most beautiful portions of this once happy land, no man, whatever his fortune, is safe, a Yankee raid may in an hour make beggars of the richest: not a family but has lost some near and dear one, how then can the North or England think, that we shall be willing to allow all these fearful sacrifices to be made in vain; how could we affiliate with those who have murdered brothers, fathers, sons, who have reduced thousands of affluent families to beggary; shall we brand ourselfs as recreant cowards by relinquishing the contest: shall we disgrace the memory of the thousands who have fallen, by allowing now that we have been persecuting an unholy and unjustifiable war: No! whatever our disaster the South can never give up, we must struggle, still struggle to the last.

Your letters can never be uninteresting to me so long as they contain news from home, do not fear then that the details of your quiet domestic life have no attraction for me. I like to know all that is going on at home. I don't expect you to write of wars and rumours of wars, of political debates and party struggles. I have enough of those here, all that I want is news, news of home. William is I am sure treading unswervingly his path in life, may he always be as prosperous as he deserves, his kindness to you and the children has placed me under a debt towards him beyond any repayment that I hope to make a wish he would write to me. Tell Joe to work on and work hard during the golden hours of youth, and he will hereafter reap a rich harvest from his labors, whatever his future career in life, his success will and must depend on the use he makes of the time and opportunity he can now command. Kiss sister for me, tell her that if by God's blessing I live till the war is over, I will certainly go home again, if only for a month or two. Give my kindest regards to the Plaisirs, tell them I could write to them separately, but I am moving about all the time and, as many of my letters, may miscarry I wish as frequently as possible, to write to you. Send me the address of my cousin Mr. White in Baltimore, and the No of Mr. White's firm in London, if I should accidentally be taken prisoner Mr. W. of Baltimore might be of great assistance to me. Do not forget in each of your letters to mention the dates of the last 3 or 4 letters you have had from me, so that I may know which have been lost and what news to repeat.

Thank Mother Teresa and the good nuns and Granny for

their kindness and prayers, beg of them still to pray for me, to your prayers and theirs, under God, do I alone attribute the safety which has hitherto attended me.

With reiterated assurances of affection and sympathy

Believe me to remain, My dear father & mother,

Your affectionate Son

FRANCIS W. DAWSON

Cap & c

P.S. Ask Mr. Steel to write, give him my kindest regards

Christmas Is For Children

As America took Christmas celebration more and more to heart, the schools became strong supporters of this cultural trend. In 1863 Edith Parker, daughter of Chief Justice Joel Parker of the Massachusetts Supreme Court, prepared an oration for her high school graduation. Intending to argue that English Christmas was not the model for American festivities, she named a half dozen jolly practices we inherited, if not from the British Isles, from Charles Dickens's beloved A Christmas Carol: the Yule log, the mistletoe, Christmas caroling from house to house, and the wassail bowl, among others. In praise of the Yankee emphasis on Santa Claus and gift giving, however, she made her point that Christmas in America is a children's holiday (as if this had been overlooked by Dickens when he gave us the unforgettable character of Tiny Tim). The holiday was similarly defined by the Children's Aid Society on the Eastern seaboard, whose annual broadsides, pleading with more fortunate families to help poor children, contained facts and figures about homeless children in nineteenth-century New York, and what was being

Edith Parker's "Christmas in Different Lands and Places" is in the J. Parker Manuscript Collection in the Massachusetts Historical Society, Boston, Massachusetts. The broadside entitled *Christmas Appeal for Poor Children*, (New York: Children's Aid Society, 1864) is in the manuscript files of the same institution. I am indebted to Louis L. Tucker, Director, for permission to reprint. The letter of William Lloyd Garrison to Wendell Garrison, December 23, 1873, is in the manuscript papers of William Lloyd Garrison, Rare Book Room, Boston Public Library in Boston, Massachusetts. This document is reproduced here by courtesy of the Trustees of the Boston Public Library.

done to make their Christmas merry. William Lloyd Garrison, aging abolitionist, in 1873 gave a more personal and poignant twist to the point of view that Christmas is for children, in a letter to his son.

Christmas in Different Lands and Places

EDITH PARKER

O ur Christmas, the American Christmas, and the American way of celebrating it are not, as is generally supposed, of English origin. Our good forefathers never heard of such a thing as hanging up their stockings. Though in the days of long stockings and small clothes it would certainly have been a good idea, for Santa Klaus never leaves a stocking half filled. And as to the good old Saint himself, our English ancestors would have thought you insane, had you talked of his reindeer, his sleigh and the budget of toys slung over his back. No, the unfortunate lords of Merry England knew nothing of such mummeries, as they would probably have termed them. Santa Klaus is from Holland, though I think hanging up stockings is an American invention. If so, we certainly deserve the palm for making Christmas merry, notwithstanding the claims England lays to it. The Merry Christmas of Old England was the Christmas of the ancient baronial half of the masquerade and wassail bowl. For thus did our ancestors make up for the want of Santa Klaus. An Old English Christmas was celebrated in the hall by attending church in the morning, enjoying a sumptuous dinner of roast beef and plum pudding after which came the renowned wassail bowl, a mixture of the choicest wines and spices and esteemed by an Englishman the most delectable of beverages. This was accompanied by the singing of Christmas carols; and a masquerade and dance in the evening finished the day. The masquerade was generally performed by poor persons, with the object of making a little money. They went about from house to house on Christmas Eve, performing their little play and received such rewards as the people chose to give. Every year on Christmas Eve an immense log, either the trunk or root of a tree, was brought into the hall by the servants and amid great rejoicing laid in the fireplace and lighted with a brand carefully saved from the log of the last year. This was called the Yule Log, and there were many superstitions connected with it. It was thought a sign of great ill luck if it went out before morning.

Nor was Christmas less merry in kitchen than in hall. The mistletoe boughs were hung from the low rafters, and by the laws of ancient customs each had the privilege of kissing a maid every time he plucked a berry off the branch, and much merriment was occasioned by the sport. Other games and romping country dances occupied the time when the berries were gone, and the good cheer, if less choice, was quite as plentiful as at their master's table. This was the Christmas of Merry England.

But let us look across the water, let us glance a moment at Germany. The church service there is at midnight. Its grand dinner no Christmas carols are there, no wassail bowl or mistletoe bough, but these to a German mind are amply made up for by the tasteful supper, the brilliant Evergreen Tree, with its tapers and bonbons, and the profuse and elegant presents, with which they endeavor to make their Christmas merry. But what merriment under the mistletoe bough or around the evergreen tree can compare with that which echoed through the house when the stockings are pulled from the chimney corner and the bounties of Santa Klaus are eagerly drawn from their depths? What jokes at an English dinner or compliments in the shape of German bonbons are half so pleasant as the noisy shouts of delight at the contents of the stockings. How much to be pitied is the unfortunate individual who is never waked on Christmas morning by the pattering of little feet on the stairs, and the Christmas greeting, called from one to another through the house; who has never known the pleasure of personating the Jolly Old Elf in his office of filling the stockings, or watched the bright faces as the parcels were undone, the happy smile or joyous exclamation as some long wished for treasure reveals itself, or a merry laugh as some funny little image of the good saint is drawn forth, or a momentary expression of disappointment when the last little bundle is reached.

Oh let the children believe in Santa Klaus! What harm can it do? They enjoy their gifts so much more for this little mystery connected with them. Child life should be ever joyous and happy, let not worldly wisdom come too soon, let them people the air and earth with elves and fairies, if they find pleasure in such fancies. Let children be childlike; do not disturb them with doubts and puzzling questions; they grow wise all too fast in this fast age. And they are so happy in their simple faith, it is so pleasant to see their happiness, and they remember it with so much pleasure in after years! It is Santa Klaus that makes Christmas merry, and would you take the merriment from Christmas?

Christmas Appeal for Poor Children
CHILDREN'S AID SOCIETY

The day is approaching which, as the happiest in the history of the world, ought to be made the happiest of the year to the poor and unfortunate. ON CHRISTMAS DAY, all those who are enjoying the re-union of friends and dear ones at the family festival, who sit at well-filled tables and by cheerful hearths, and who call up all the sacred and social associations of the holiday, should remember the thousands and thousands of our City-poor who have not even a home; who are weak with hunger and shiver with cold, while others have abundance; whom no man calls friend, and who live neglected and unhappy. Especially should the children of the more highly favored and well-off think on that happy day of the children of the poor and the unfortunate. Let them remember, then, how many a little boy has, through all the great city, not a place he can call *home*, but must sleep in boxes and cellar-ways; how many a little girl has no shoes, or hood, or outside garment for the winter's cold; how many a child runs barefooted to the Industrial School through the December snow, and many a little mouth gets its first meal at the school dinner.

Will not the children do their part to make Christmas Day joyful to the poor children of New York, by their kind gifts?

It is well known that the Children's Aid Society has under its charge now several thousands of these poor children. We propose, if the public second this appeal, to give a joyful Festival to these unfortunate little ones.

Some who are homeless, and who are willing to go, we shall provide with a Christmas Home, by sending them, under charge of our experienced agent, Mr. Friedgen, to good families in the West.

To others, we shall give gratuitous lodgings in the News Boys' Lodging House, and the Girls' Lodging House; hundreds of others will be provided with shoes and stockings and warm garments, and at least one good meal.

Who will give a home to the homeless boys and girls? The expenses for this have increased, and will amount now to at least $20. Who will send money for a pair of shoes, or a hood, or a warm garment, or a bed-comforter for these destitute little ones? Who will give them a dinner?

C. L. Brace, Secretary

CHILDREN'S AID SOCIETY

A winter of business depression is a hard one for the children of the poor. The father is out of work, and the children find "hunger watching at the door." Families are broken up by want of employment, and the little ones sent out on the street to beg or steal.

This winter hundreds of poor children come through the cold and the winter's storm to our schools without shoes. Hundreds more creep from their boxes and cellars to our Lodging-Houses, ragged, barefooted, and hungry. Our citizens will see them shivering and wet in the storm, or crouching under shelter, or silently and piteously asking aid by their misery and homelessness.

THE CHRISTMAS season should bring a brief happiness even to the most outcast and miserable; and in memory of what ONE has given to the world, those who have, should give to those who have not. We earnestly call upon the well-off and fortunate to do something this year, which shall make the Christmas time the happiest of their lives to the poor and houseless children.

The CHILDREN'S AID SOCIETY gives for its best gifts a HOME to the street-children. Its own treasury is empty; but FIFTY DOLLARS will send three homeless children to homes in the country.

A HUNDRED DOLLARS will give dinners to a hundred and fifty children in the Industrial Schools for a month. FIFTY DOLLARS will put shoes on thirty bare-footed children.

This SOCIETY desires, if the means be given, to send out a Christmas party of homeless children to the West; to distribute clothing and shoes and food among thousands of destitute little ones in their schools; and to give good Christmas dinners and pleasant festivals to the homeless little ones in their Lodging-

Houses. Who will help to make a happy Christmas to the children of the poor?

It is earnestly asked that the children of Sunday-Schools and Day-Schools would remember these little ones who have no home or friends.

Roxbury, Dec. 23, 1873

Dear Wendell:

Last evening I dropped into the P.O. box a letter for Mr. Bleby addressed to your care; intending it for the night mail. But our footman anticipated the time some four or five minutes of emptying the box before I got to it, and taking its contents to the general P.O.; so it will not reach you any sooner than this. As Mr. Bleby sails for Nassau to-morrow, it is hardly probable that he will be able to call at your office, and if it so happen, I do not wish you to take any trouble to convey the letter to him, as it was merely a hasty farewell. If, therefore, he fail to get it, then destroy it, and I will write another to him to his address in the Bahama Islands. Frank wishes a dollar to be handed to Mr. Bleby should he call, as due him; he having left with Frank, last spring, on leaving us, six dollars to pay for two visits of a physician (regular charge)—but Dr. Jackson asked only five dollars for his services. This was a slip of memory when Mr. B. was here last week, which Frank wishes to have rectified, if opportunity offer. In case you pay the dollar, it will, of course, be refunded by Frank.

Christmas is at hand, and the little folks every where are expecting to be remembered in some way or other. At such a distance from your darlings, it is difficult to decide what toys would please them best; and therefore I enclose a little spending money to be used in their behalf as you or Lucy may think judicious. Or half of it may be given to Lucy for "fun money." I am sorry it is so small an amount; but what with the other grandchildren, and various relatives and friends to be remembered, and a diminished and diminishing income, and some large medical bills, etc., etc., my pockets are well "cleaned out." And yet, my dear boy, I want to send *you* something, in season at least for a New Year's token—not in accordance with any wishes or expectations of your own, I know, but for my parental gratification. I will leave it for Lucy "unbeknownst" to you, to suggest something for my guidance in making a purchase.

I am improving in my general health, but not much in the knee.

A Merry Christmas to you all!
In great haste,
Your loving Father
William Lloyd Garrison

Christmas on the
Prairie Frontier

KATHERINE FOUGERA

As Americans advanced across the continent in search of a manifest destiny, the phrase "the only Good Indian is a dead Indian" appeared all too often in newspapers and pulp Westerns. The mindless and heartless slogan was usually associated with General George Armstrong Custer, who led 200 men from the U.S. Seventh Cavalry to their death and his own in an 1873 campaign against the Sioux on the Little Bighorn River. But this reminiscence by Katherine Fougera, a pioneer woman and widow of Seventh Cavalryman Captain Francis Gibson, illustrates that not all people in frontier outposts were without compassion toward the "vanishing American."

With the approach of roaring December my husband and I decided to give a Christmas tree party at our quarters on Christmas Eve, but where to find either tree or trimmings was the problem. The trader's store offered a meager assortment of articles, and the commissary could supply only such staples as

Katherine Gibson Fougera, "Christmas on the Prairie Frontier," in *With Custer's Calvary* (Caldwell, Idaho: Caxton Printers, 1942), 237–44. Permission to reprint has been granted by Gordon Gibson.

sugar, coffee, flour, and other simple necessities. However, soldiers were sent out to scour the neighborhood for anything that looked like a tree and finally returned with some forlorn bunches of squatty sage and cedar brush. The outlook was discouraging, but it stimulated imagination, and we started to fashion something that at least resembled a tree. We hung the plants in relays from the ceiling down to within a few feet of the floor, and beneath them was placed a wash-tub decorated with gaily painted paper and filled with sand and whatever crude presents the town of Bismark afforded. A sort of Christmas pie idea. So far so good, but now for the trimmings, and in this paper played the most conspicuous part. Paints were produced and brushes wielded, while plain paper took on startling colors, and scissors were busy cutting yards and yards into strips, which served as festoons or were converted into cornucopias to be filled with homemade candy. Some thrifty souls had garnered a few nuts, and these were dexterously covered with silver foil salvaged from cigars and then hung upon the tree along with ancient Christmas cards, resurrected from trunks, and tied with scraps of faded ribbon which had been ironed and freshened.

Jack Sturgis and some other youngsters just out of the Point displayed hidden artistic talents. They colored candles bright red, cut them in two, and perched them jauntily on the branches. They fashioned a huge paper bell, also painted red, pasting on the edges cut-out pictures of Santa Claus, and when the work was completed the ensemble stood forth as a thing of beauty.

The refreshments would be sandwiches, cake, and candy, lemonade made from the usual citric acid crystals, and, of course, ice cream evolved from condensed milk, whipped-up gelatine, and the whites of eggs. The eggs by the way, wrapped in cotton, were brought from Bismarck by the mailman, who, to keep such precious articles from freezing, always carried them inside his buckskin shirt, against his bare chest.

Christmas Eve dawned bright and clear, and the temperature had moderated. Someone brought an old banjo, another had unearthed an antique guitar, another a jew's-harp. With such dance music provided we swung into the Virginia Reel with much merriment, and then the old square dances had their turn. What a beautiful time we had! Finally, before midnight, Lieutenant Gibson, being Officer of the day, had to make his rounds of the outposts, and shortly afterwards the party broke up, everyone tired but happy.

When the last guest had departed, I thought I would take a peep into the kitchen, now dark and deserted, so, with lighted candle held high, I opened the door. As the flame stabbed through the blackness I suddenly gasped and gazed before me with startled eyes, for on the side porch appeared some strangers huddled together—strangers of juvenile stature, one barely tall enough to see above the window casement. In short, my uninvited guests were small Indian children, who were staring through the glass at the tree in mesmeric entrancement. For a moment I was held spellbound in surprise, then, cautiously, so as not to frighten them, I opened the porch door and motioned them to enter. At first they cowered and shrank away, then a straight-backed youngster in buckskin, dragging by the hand a diminutive squaw about four years old, stepped into the room, the others following warily, single file. How had they gained entrance to the garrison, I wondered? Then I recalled a slight breach in the stockade wall, just big enough to admit the wriggling in and out of one small body at a time.

I turned to the supposed leader of the party and, speaking slowly, asked, pointing to the tree, "Someone tell Indian boy about it?"

He nodded, as the little hostiles around the agencies picked up a smattering of English very quickly.

"Who tell Indian boy?"

"Horn Toad."

Horn Toad was a good-natured Indian scout, adored by all the children in the garrison.

"Oh," I nodded, while the little frozen band huddled about the stove in stolid silence, "and who is she?" indicating the wee squaw.

"Sister," replied the boy, while the little girl clung more

fiercely to his hand. My eyes ran over the tiny figure, and my heart contracted. The poor tot shivered and drew across the shoulders of her calico dress an impromptu shawl made of gunny sack, and a strip of the same material served as her only headgear. Her moccasins and leggings were of buckskin. The young warriors were clad in whole suits of it, but, evidently, when it came to the females of the species, the supply had given out. It was a miracle that the little band hadn't been frozen to death.

Just how, where, or why at this season of the year these people were abroad instead of being under shelter at the agencies did not matter. The fact remained that they and at least some of their tribe had set up their wickiups somewhere near by. I mentally shook myself. What an unconscionable hour for these children to be up. They must be returned to their mothers at once, and yet, as I looked into their timid, expectant faces, pity stirred within me, and my logic went woefully awry. Heaven only knew how long they had waited out there in the cold, feasting their eyes upon this glittering paradise, and that set me thinking. Quickly I drew them into the living room and towards the Christmas tree pie, which, I was confident, still held a few treasures, and, digging into the sand myself, I fished out a Jack-in-the-box which I presented to the little lady. Her black eyes leaped with surprise and joy, and her wee hands trembled as she clutched the toy. Then, making a motion for them to continue, I flew to the kitchen to heat up what cocoa still remained. The striker was just leaving for his barracks when I called to him.

"Oh, Alkorn," I instructed, "go to the nearest bastion and tell the sentinel to relay to other sentinels that, in the event of any Indians hanging around and looking for children, they are at Lieutenant Gibson's quarters and will be along soon."

During my absence my guests had certainly explored the entire contents of the tub. The appearance of the Jack-in-the-box had dissipated their last vestige of hesitation, and they plunged feverishly into the sand, and with each rag doll, toy pistol, or other treasure exhumed, they became in fact wild

Indians—wild with delight—the boys voicing their emotions in short grunts, the wee one in squeals of rapture.

It was upon this scene of oozing, scattering sand that I entered, bearing a pot of steaming cocoa, but the children refused to abandon the magic tub until the very last toy had been salvaged. Then they drank long and thirstily of the refreshing beverage, and soon color returned to their pinched cheeks and warmth crept back into their little chilled fingers. Noting all this, I communed with myself thoughtfully. I should have sent them home right away, I told myself severely, yet I continued to heap their laps with goodies, popcorn, nuts, and candy. Besides, there was some ice cream left over and cake, too, that were begging to be eaten, and what was a party without them? So, before they knew it, mounds of pink and white concoction were whisked in front of the little savages, who immediately plunged small eager fingers into the pretty, fluffy stuff, only to recoil from the sudden chill. The tiny squaw was the first to experiment with it, by cautiously licking some off her palm, and her cherubic smile would have inspired a masterpiece from Raphael. They needed no further urging and attacked the ice cream, stuffing themselves with all the abandon of healthy, hungry children.

While they were thus engaged, I ran upstairs looking for old blankets, woolen stockings, and socks. I found a short coat of my own, some mittens and galoshes and warm mufflers. Suddenly queer sounds coming from below sent me scurrying halfway downstairs, where I paused. The noise started with the clapping of hands, accompanied by a weird chant. This was followed by the sound of softly muffled feet and short, sharp whoops, at first faint but growing louder and louder. I sank upon the stairs and peered through the bannisters into the living room, and what I beheld kept me rooted to the spot. My eyes dilated before a picturesque phase of barbaric expression.

The straight-backed boy, evidently wishing to do his part and that of his tribe toward the entertainment, was staging a performance of his own and was directing the others in some kind of dance. One boy and the diminutive squaw stood at the side clapping their hands and chanting monotonously, the latter moving her hips and body in imitation of the older squaws while, circling the stove in single file, the young braves stamped upon the carpet with the firmness of buffaloes combined with the whirlwind lightness of the wildcat, their lithe frames swaying like the prairie grasses and with a rhythm as perfect as a set measure. Backwards and forwards they flung themselves as though made of elastic rubber, bending pliant heads and necks and emitting long-drawn-out whoops of joy. The crunching into the carpet of ruinous sand mattered not, for on the step I sat like petrified wood, lost in wonder at the wild beauty and cadence of that native dance. Why, I pondered, did white children have to spend money to attain anything like the grace of these aborigines to whom it seemed as inborn and as natural as a spring of cool, pure water. The dirge changed, and the little redskins swung into close, group formation, each executing fast, fantastic steps. Followed more insistent hand clapping and droning. The young bucks quickly flung back into single file, whereupon the dance became fiercer, the whoops louder and longer, and with a frenzy that almost shook the floor they fairly leaped about the stove until the leader held up his hand and stopped. The droning ceased, the embryo braves threw themselves, gasping, upon the carpet, and the wee one slid down beside the young chief.

I drew a deep breath, hurried back upstairs, and brought down an armful of clothing and blankets. Then I bundled up the wee squaw like a bale of cotton, tied my too-big mittens on her warm little hands, and gave the rest of the blankets, mufflers, and galoshes to the boys. After that I stripped the tree of its remaining gifts, put candy and cake in a bag, which I consigned to the care of the straight-backed boy, and very reluctantly let my guests out again into the night. I glanced up at the clock in the hall. Already it was Christmas. The snow crunched crisply beneath light retreating steps while again and again the happy children, clutching their cherished toys, turned radiant faces over their shoulders for one last look and smile.

Finally, the small, straight-backed Indian boy, bringing up

the rear with his Christmas burdens, patted his mouth with his slim hand and emitted the farewell call of his tribe, which seemed to linger on the air even after the little band had faded from view.

I smiled to myself, blew out the kerosene lamp in the hall, and trudged wearily upstairs while, drifting through the still, approaching dawn and echoing from bastion to bastion, came the comforting call of the sentinels, "One o'clock and all's well."

The Original Mister Santie Claws

HELEN WARD FIELDER

No anthology of Christmas in America would be complete without one story that is set in the classroom. In the late nineteenth and early twentieth century, prior to lawsuits and school board rules and regulations that permit only a cultural celebration, the heart of Christmas was often found in the proverbial little red schoolhouse. Occasionally the school had the only sizeable decorated tree in town and more often than not the last Friday evening prior to vacation marked a delicious potluck, a recitation of lessons, and then an evening of entertainment. In this story, a small school in rural Texas prepares for a turn-of-the-century celebration by writing letters to Santie Claws.

Days were getting troublesomely short in San Jose. That was the only visible sign of the approach of Christmas. One need not hope for frosted panes or gleaming holly in Texas. In the little schoolhouse at San Jose the signs of the season were

Helen Ward Fielder, "The Original Mister Santie Claws," *Sunset Magazine*, January 1919, 44–45, 60. This essay is included here through the good offices of William Marken, executive editor, *Sunset Magazine*.

exhibited by a troupe of shivering youngsters who hugged their pitifully thin coats about them as they scurried meekly to their places. The schoolhouse was warm. There a fire burned always. My attendance was very good. They did not even look forward to the holidays with pleasant anticipation—for ten days there would be no fire in the schoolhouse stove.

To be sure the sun still shone warmly on mountains of blue velvet, but his heart was not in the work. He merely fulfilled his contract. There were no lingering twilights. After delivering his sunset in the approved manner he rushed himself off to bed. The same mountains lost their soft baby blue and became ugly, cold and threatening. The whole world seemed to huddle itself together and wait patiently for another dawn.

As teacher, friend, confident (and janitor) of the San Jose school it became my task to revive the holiday spirit and talk of Christmas. It is easy enough to encourage that spirit among citizens whose well-filled pocketbooks form a solid foundation for indulgence, but my material was different. As well talk to them in terms of lobster suppers and tango teas as to mention our modern, lavish, cranberry Christmas. They all knew and understood the story of the Christ Child and loved to repeat it in their adorable broken English, but what knew they of turkeys and theatre tickets, of well filled stockings, or even of well filled stomachs! It was bitterly paradoxical to talk to the poor little half-starved waifs about Santa Claus and the chimney myth when some of them did not even possess a stocking to hold the gifts.

In my own heart the spirit of Christmas, only remnant of my childhood, bubbled rebelliously. I was obliged to tell a few stories just to satisfy my conscience and hush that wayward youthfulness, so unbecoming in an old maid. My eager listeners snatched up these story crumbs and begged for more. They spread my doctrines abroad and in a few days my roll of attendance had swelled. The new applicants had heard my Santa Claus fable and believed that by remaining on the scene of action until after my Christmas program was rendered, they could at least give the old gentleman an opportunity to prove himself genuine.

Felipe Duran escorted the first newcomer to my desk one morning.

"His name are Manuel Arrelanes," he stated, "and he have come from Salinas, Mexico. Never have go to school in El Paso, but have four years in the school of Salinas. He like much you for teach him."

After this informal introduction the frightened Manuel, who appeared in danger of immediate heart failure, produced two badly soiled books in Spanish, decorated with numerous indigestible looking illustrations. He was so proud of them that I allowed him to keep them. They couldn't do any harm, and he seemed to have a superstition to the effect that they would aid him in learning the English language.

Felipe immediately adopted Manuel as his protege, and initiated him in all the pleasures and mysteries of San Jose society, which swung impartially between the church and the school. At church one received holy cards and dew-drop medals or images of the Virgin Mary; one sang in the choir and received Holy Communion. At school there were weekly programs when one said one's "piece" trembling with pride and misery; there were yearly picnics, which they called "pignigs" and then this wonderful "Chrissen tree" celebration. These constituted the gay life of the younger set in San Jose. Felipe was the recognized leader on all occasions.

A few days later I overheard an interesting conversation between the two of them at the noon hour. I was eating cold sandwiches with the indifference born of habit, while I figured just what it would cost to give thirty small heathen a taste of Christmas joy. I was also frantically adding relatives and multiplying price tags. I never realized how true it is that "all the world is akin" until about Christmas time. The sound of voices interrupted my calculations:

"For why did you not come to school by the bell this day?" accused Felipe.

"Because it is my clock," Manuel defended himself. "On

my house I have two clocks, big and little—so. The big one she
have feet alright but cannot go, and the little one she runs
without the feet. How is it that I can tell where she go?" he
demanded with dramatic emphasis.

Felipe was very properly provoked to mirth by this said state
of affairs. He laughed long and loudly. Manuel became violent.
There was a torrent of Spanish, which I could only half inter-
pret, but I recognized "fool" and "imbecile" several times; then
he slowed down to grumble in English:

"I can go back to Salinas," he finished miserably, "the pretty
school of the *Americanos* is not for me. Maybe you think I is
one nigger! Maybe you think the teacher love you more or
anybody! She do not! She has much love for all the children,
and I is good as you, Felipe Duran! Maybe you think the teacher
is going for marry you when school is out! Bah!" his disgust
was audible.

Felipe seemed thoroughly subdued. He descended from his
pedestal gracefully:

"No, no, you must not think 'bout going for Salinas now!"
he soothed. "Two or three days more and we going to have that
Chrissen tree. You is good to eat candies and the orange like all
of us. In Salinas they do not eat the fruit and make speeches for
Chrissen."

"You was here the year of yesterday," suggested Manuel.
"Tell it to me 'bout the Chrissen and that man Santie Claws
what Miss Fieldern is all time talking 'bout."

"Santie Claws," began Felipe proudly. "Oh, Miss Fieldern,
she knows that man good; he are one friend of her family. She
says he come to her house when she was one little chile, and
bring much gifts. She tell me all 'bout Santie Claws! He lives in
one big Chrissen tree, and eats much of the reindeers. He have
not got any children because is not one married man. But he
loves much to them and brings things for the good ones because
he has much money to buy at the stores."

Manuel was sad. "For two years now I have want for one
thing," he mourned, "and all the time I not know about this

Santie Claws man what is so big fool to bring you things for nothing!"

"What do you care for that?" laughed Felipe. "Now you can write him one letter and give to Miss Fieldern. She will help you; she is one friend of his. When he is got the money we should be glad he is one fool!"

Here the conversation drifted to baseball and being only an ordinary woman I didn't try to follow it. But in that moment of eavesdropping I had discovered my cue.

The following day I confronted my audience with a plan that promised to divulge the secret desire of Manuel before he ever learned of "that old fool Santie Claws."

"This evening," I suggested briskly, "we are all going to write letters. You will write a letter to Santa Claus and tell him what you want him to bring you and where he can send it. Sign your name down here like this—."

I drew a minute and painstaking diagram on the blackboard. After half an hour of patient explanation and many questions they seemed almost to understand what I meant. Black heads were bowed in pensive thought, and a few well chewed pencil stubs began to travel laboriously across tablets.

Manuel was seized with happy inspiration. Here at last was his chance to put in a claim with the Santa Claus person! He wrote desperately, evidently hoping to get his letter in first and thus insure it the proper amount of attention. I mentally resolved that it should, if I had anything to do with it. Bless their little hearts! How pitifully simple were their wants and how easily gratified! How sensible, compared to the requests of the children of my own country!

I observed that one of my little girls, Juaquina, was sitting rigid and idle with an expression of disapproval.

"Do you need help?" I offered. "Can't you think of anything you want for Christmas?"

"Many things I want," replied that young lady with dignity, "but no get them from Santie Claws. I have tried that man two year now and when I want somethings, I buy from the store. He brings me things that is no good, and all the time when I ask for one thing he brings me some other. The other Christmas I ask for one piano and he send the ribbons for my hair! And when I ask for one dress of blue, what he brings me is a green handkerchief of the silk! That man!—he knows *nothing*! I will go to El Paso and buy."

With difficulty I persuaded her that this was only a daily lesson and she must do her part. With sullen reluctance she obeyed.

"Now, Felipe, you may begin."

Felipe seized what appeared to be half a tablet and read: "Dere Mr. Santie Claws, Sir:—I have not paper for write much. These little things I wish because my body needs it:—One coat, one shoes, two hats—one of brown and one of blue; one brush for my teeth—my teacher have one like it—a little soap for Sunday, and I no have got stockings. I would like one dog what is good to kill the rabbits and if you is got—"

"That will do, Felipe," I begged. "We won't have time to hear all of it. You mustn't ask for so many things. Remember, there are many children. Now Juaquina."

"Mr. Santie Claws," was Juaquina's formal heading. "My teacher says I must write one letter to you. This is because. I wish one box of pretty pencils this Christmas which I will buy from the store in El Paso. I knows you do not know anything about pencils. You will send me books, maybe. I will buy one doll for my sistern, and one hold card for my mama, with pigture of Jesus. If you got anything you don't want you can give to me, but I no ask for nothing."

The rebuke was eloquent.

"Now, Manuel, we will just have time for your letter before we go home," I suggested.

Manuel caught his breath with excitement and began to read:

Most Honorable Santa Claus of the Chrissen:—I have hear from my teacher how you is good to boys what is poor and want for things. You are man of business and have no time to buy what I want, so if you send the moneys I will get him. I know where is one two handed (second-hand) Ford, and I think I can get him cheaper than you. This have the seat for five peoples and I can learn to run him. Would like so much to take my mother for rides on the Sunday. You can always ride for nothing with me. Thank you many times for this good thing. Some times maybe I can do anything for you.

Your very good friend,
Manuel.

I fell back paralyzed. Good heavens! Where was the flitting dream of being able to grant Manuel's humble little request! Yes, these Mexican children were simple in their demands, and sensible enough! A second-hand Ford would be useful to a great many families, certainly!

I stared at Manuel dazed, until little circles of black and green began to dance like a halo about his head; then my sense of humor came to the rescue.

"Put away your books," I commanded. "Jose, pass the hats. Now—one, two, march!"

On the morning of the twenty-second of December each child, in my room was presented with a pink mosquito-netting bag of assorted candies, one shiny orange and one picture post-card. There was great rejoicing, and so hearty a demonstration on their part that with relief I put on my hat and realized that I was going to have ten days of rest.

In the cloak room I met Manuel. He was visibly troubled about something, and his unopened bag of candy dangled gingerly by the string.

"'Scuse me, teacher," he apologized, "but please, that Ford car have not come to my house yet. Would you ask your friend, Mr. Santie Claws, when you see him?"

"Why—yes," I assented gravely, "I'll do that; but you must not count on it too much. You know he is a very busy person, so many people want things."

"Yes, I know," he sighed patiently, "but I *is* one good boy, teacher. *You* know I is good *several days*! And he can ride for nothing."

"Well, I'll do my best," I assured him, trusting that by the time the holidays were over he would have forgotten it and be nursing a new ambition.

It was at Christmas dinner that I told the story of the letters and Manuel and his two-hand Ford. There was a hearty laugh of appreciation.

"Poor little cuss!" sympathized my father. "What a shame he can never get what he wants so badly! Like all the rest of us, he aims too high!"

"Oh, I don't know!" argued Mr. Mason. He was fresh from the east, and studied "the Mexican question" with a good deal of enthusiasm. "He's got the ambition and the energy all right. I dare say he could run the car, too, if he had it. The fellow ought to have a chance."

Throughout the remainder of the evening Mr. Mason appeared abstracted, and broke into fresh chuckles now and then over nothing in particular.

When I returned to San Jose after the holidays Manuel was missing from the ranks. A week passed and still no Manuel. All my questions brought no knowledge of his whereabouts. He had vanished mysteriously and his absence was accepted with true Mexican philosophy, which is indifference.

"Has he gone back to Salinas?" I asked.

They shrugged their shoulders denying all knowledge or responsibility.

"He isn't sick, is he?" I demanded.

"*Quien sabe?*" came the characteristic chorus in reply.

Finally I gave up in despair; then the following Saturday I met Manuel himself. I was hurrying home across the street, heavily burdened with packages from my shopping tour, when a happy voice called:

"It is my teacher!"

I looked up to see a Ford, with a huge, glaring sign stretched across the front reading: "Jitney Bus—El Paso To Alfalfa—15 cents." From behind that sign had come the voice, and behind it was seated Manuel at the wheel, smiling happily. He helped me in with all the airs of a gentleman and, with mingled pride and prayerfulness, I allowed him to drive me a few perilous blocks.

When I got out I offered him a dime, but he refused it vehemently:

"No, no! For you it is nothing always!"

"Aren't you coming back to school anymore?" I asked.

"I am much afraid I can not," he apologized discreetly. "I make too much money here and in a little while I can come back to San Jose and make one store of the groceries for my mother. Your friend Mr. Santie Claws was very good with me. I wish you to please give him this." He handed me a dirty dollar bill. "Because he got this job for me."

The same day I received a brief explanatory note from Mr. Mason:

> "Dear Lady:
> Surely you will pardon me for snatching one of your young hopefuls so rudely from the fountain of learning. I couldn't help it. After I saw the kid and talked with him I knew he had it in him to make good. I couldn't resist the chance to make that Ford dream come true!"

No wonder Manuel had felt so highly honored! Had not the giver of all gifts come in person to attend to his little affairs? Truly here was an example of the faith that moves mountains!

With a sigh and a twinge of regret I crossed his name from my roll-call. Then I mailed the precious dollar bill to Mr. Mason, and on the sheet of paper I wrote only the words:

"To the Original Mr. Santa Claus."

Christmas in a Country Doctor's Home

MATILDA ROSE McLAREN

Matilda Rose McLaren, an attorney in Springfield, Illinois, long before women entered the professions, and the mother of five children, writes here of Christmas in her youth. This essay faithfully recreates the holiday as it was practiced by German immigrants in the Midwest. Matilda's father, one of nine physicians in the family, controlled when the celebration would begin, because he often had to leave unexpectedly to make house calls and the family had to work around his schedule. The children carefully noted which bag Papa took when he left the house: the brown bag held maternity paraphernalia, meaning that he would be gone all night; the black bag meant that he might be home so that the celebration could be held in a timely manner.

Each December I asked "Mama, why can't we have our Christmas in the morning like other people?" and every time the answer was:

Matilda Rose McLaren, "Christmas in a Country Doctor's Home," *American Mercury*, December 1960. I am indebted to the author for her permission to reprint this essay.

"Because your papa is a doctor yet. If we wait till morning, somebody'll be sure to have a baby already. He'd miss the fun."

At our house in Millstadt, Illinois, Christmas was *always* fun; but, for some unexplainable reason, my tenth Christmas stands out most vividly.

Papa, Mama, Martha, Fred and I lived in an 11-room house which was both home and office. In the barn stood four horses; in the buggy shed, Papa's summer top buggy, his glassed-in winter storm buggy and Mama's surrey. This called for two servants, Jacob, our middle-aged hosteler who whistled *Ach du lieber Augustine* unceasingly as he groomed the horses, fired the furnace and did the yard work. Maud, the hired girl, was the daughter of one of Papa's farmer-patients. She helped Mama where-ever needed to the tune of "*Meet Me In St. Louie, Louie*," in a voice that sounded an awful lot like the nine o'clock curfew. Both had been with us so long they were considered "family."

Before Thanksgiving, Papa dug out the mail order catalog and, with a twinkle in his blue eyes announced: "Now, children, I think me Santa can't do all the planning. You better help him out once." So, on the kitchen table with its red and white checked cloth, we filled sheaves of order blanks with hints for every one from the Grandmas, through aunts, uncles and cousins, right down to Jacob and Maud.

"By golly," Papa exclaimed, "if you want that much, you'll have to be good children."

While for us children Advent called for "extra special good behavior," for our parents it meant innumerable trips to town. Papa seldom stomped through the snow to the Post Office without shopping, en-route. Had we seen the sled at Marxer's? The doll with real hair at Uncle Phillip's? Suddenly, the corn crib was locked.

We started hanging our long black stockings up on our bed posts on December sixth, St. Nicholas' birthday. Why he was described as "The old boy with sausages in his eyes," we never knew. But every "A" spelling paper induced him to drop red and white striped sticks of candy into our stockings: sometimes a shiny apple; occasionally gilded English walnuts with short messages inside. Sunday mornings, we found *oranges*. Farmers who took wagon loads of poultry and dairy products to St. Louis on Saturday, picked up Papa's medicines at Merrill Drug Company; and oranges for Mama at Union Market.

"Oranges!" Maud exclaimed. "You don't know how lucky you are. Borrow me one?"

All through December Mama was busy baking clothes-basketfuls of cookies. *Lebkuchen, feffernus, springerlies, sugar cookies* were cut into animal, flower and doll designs, then frosted with thick, white icing and decorated with lemon peel, raisins and colored sugars. Whole evenings were spent covering the long table with these objects of art. Of course, we bought sugar and flour by the barrel, butter by the tub, molasses by the keg and lard by the ten gallon can. As extra-curricular, Mama prompted our Christmas "pieces," speeches in which she was always letter-perfect first. With her legs wrapped around chair rungs, she sat creaming a huge crock of sugar and butter with her hands and coaxed, "Now, Matilda, it goes like this: *Alle Jahre wieder, kommt das Christus Kind*," for we are German-Americans whose forebears arrived in 1862 on the *Concord*, the *Mayflower* of *central* Europe.

When the last cookie was baked, Martha and I got to help fill the cookie bags. These were paper sacks large enough to hold two pounds of sugar. Into them we dropped fruits, nuts, candies and cookies. Every one who was on the regular gift list, every caller . . . in home or office . . . every stranger within our gates received such a sack; and we received them in the homes of our aunts and friends. "How else," laughed Mama, "can you compare your baking, or check the diligence of your in-laws already? Only a lazy *hausfrau* bakes less than two dozen kinds," and when my Mama laughed the checks in the gingham apron across her dumpling stomach jumped up and down with glee.

Because Papa was generous with his prescription brandy, making the Christmas mince meat was a potluck affair. While aunts Lu and Maggie ground meat, Maud washed raisins and uncle Ed chopped citron, Papa and Mama debated just how much brandy they'd put in the year before last, when it was best yet. Soon the air was tantalizing with the combination of spices, apples and lemons, beef and pork simmering on the back of the huge black cookstove. Jacob made excuses to come in with armloads of wood, and Martha and I breathed and *breathed*. She'd play she was a Physical Ed teacher:

"Inhale, *one!* Hold it! Exhale!" then we'd end on a long *aah*.

Kris Kindchen, Santa's wife, was busy, too. She ran up and down our village streets in her long nightgown and ominously snapped her switch. Often, her husband towered beside her. From a block away we'd call, "Yes, we say our prayers every night!" If that pair felt like it, they'd make us pray right then and there. Any night during December, we'd jump at unexpected knocks on our kitchen door and Santy would come stalking in. Mama filled his pockets; maybe a smoked goose breast sandwich, always cookies and candies were offered to appease him before she begged him to leave. She didn't like the idea of frightening little children.

Some evenings, only one member of the Claus family called, occasionally as many as ten, in relays. Because the refreshment racket was so worthwhile, it might have been the same one in different costume. Some Santas looked no bigger than eighth graders; in fact they often came in corduroy knickers and stocking caps that looked just like those worn by our twin cousins across the street, the Kern boys, Armin and Irving . . . Only their faces looked like Santa's.

Those twins! They were identical and proved that two heads are stronger than one. Weren't they smart enough to discover "Uncle Doc's" digitalis pills fit their B-B guns? Weren't they the lads who taught Daisy, our old gray mare, to like beer from a bottle? Never again could Papa stop at a half-way house and get by with just one bottle. Weren't they smooth enough to sneak the old gal out and gallop her all the way to the cemetery and back before Jacob even missed her?

"Just you wait till Christmas comes," he growled at the

snickering pair while wiping the foam off her and throwing a heavy warm blanket on her back. "I'll learn you to laugh so dumb the world in. You'll find out if the wind blows whitch or whatch way."

Such Christmas cleaning as went on at our house was never seen elsewhere on land or sea. Every lace curtain came down from every one of our more than 20 windows to be starched and stretched to within a stitch of its life. Carpets came up; floors were scrubbed; fresh straw spread for padding. Then, the whole family got on its knees to pull and groan until carpet edges were anchored under quarter rounds again. Dusting the winding stairway and its banister of dozens of spindles was always assigned to the daughters of the house. Martha started at the bottom and worked up; I, at the top and worked down. Mama checked the work with a dainty lace handkerchief.

"Girls," she exclaimed, "it wonders me for why you always miss that middle landing!"

For why indeed! That was where we met and went into a huddle:

"Does Papa have any X's on his desk calendar? Will it give Christmas babies?"

"Oh, if he gets called out on Christmas Eve, we'll have to wait for our presents till morning."

"Let's write the stork a letter and ask him to have mercy on us."

"Him have mercy? Don't you remember last year's calendar what hung beside President Teddy's picture? It showed the stork flying just ahead of the doctor's horse and buggy?"

"Ja! But I betcha Daisy could beat him, though." With this big worry hanging over us, how could we remember to dust that middle landing?

Maud had her cleaning troubles too. She loved to see her big black cook stove shine, "Like mine Sunday patent leather shoes." . . . and those twins loved to spit on it. They named the three biggest skittering bubbles *Shadrach*, *Meshach* and *Abed-*

nego. Then they'd bet on which bubble could endure "hell's" fire the longest . . . and Maud's stove was ruined, again.

December 23 was filled with goose-pimple-raising activity. Since our house stands cata-corner from our church, we Rose sisters scraped peep holes in Jack Frost's handiwork on our dining room windows to await the arrival of the two huge cedar trees our farmer-deacons brought in from their own woods.

"Look once," cried Martha, jumping from one foot to the other, "those trees are so big they stick out the back of the sled a half a block already. Let's go over and watch."

Wrapping red wool fascinators over our heads, we stole quietly into the church and sat shivering on the icy-cold pews while the men set up the trees, one on each side of the altar. They reached the Gothic ceiling and were always topped with twinkling stars. Once the trees were in position, Sunday School teachers took over to finish the job with long strings of pop corn and cranberries; fruits, cookies; small pictures and huge candles.

"Those trees look like twins," Martha whispered, and I could see my cold breath as I whispered back, "But they don't get into trouble like Armin and Irving."

When we got home we found the corn crib door stood, suddenly, wide open . . . but now the parlor door was locked. We could hear Santy at work, the real St. Nicholas, not the one who frightened us and begged for goodies at the kitchen door. We knew because this one laughed "Ho, ho," every once in a while as he wound music boxes that played the *Blue Danube* and put dolls through their "mama" cries. As we lay on our stomachs in the hall and tried to peep under the door we simply stopped breathing.

For Christmas Eve supper Mama served oyster stew about which Papa complained, "That's thin as greeting soup."

She explained, "I don't want you should eat so much that you can't enjoy the Christmas goose."

That *piece de resistance* had been won at a rifle raffle. Our farmers raised geese, ducks and turkeys by the hundreds and then, as the holidays approached, held rifle matches. "Doc" Rose was such a crack shot he could plink a dime off the barn lot fence from the back porch. Tavern keepers, who wanted birds to serve as free lunch, were always glad when Papa got called away from the match.

After the oyster stew, our program pieces were given their final rehearsal . . . church bells would ring in an hour. Then rag curlers were carefully removed from our tortured tresses; the fourth and fifth petticoats donned and the beautiful accordion plaited red cashmere dresses with "welwet wests" were carefully dropped over our heads. This required the combined efforts of Mama and Maud. What with hooks and eyes getting caught in curls, Mama always bit her tongue.

This was the moment we started keeping a weather eye on that brown bag. If Papa grabbed *that* and went lickety-out out the back door, there'd be no Christmas celebration at our house after church this night. The brown bag meant a baby! He carried the black one for insignificant things like broken legs and pneumonia. People were welcome to small pox, even; but, "Please God no babies tonight!" It was a sincere prayer.

Just before leaving for church I peeped into the office. Papa was on a house call. Where was Jacob? I found him in the basement contentedly reading the *Globe Democrat*, sucking his pipe while toasting his feet on the furnace door.

"Vell," he philosophised, "I got no orders to harness up yet; but you never can sometimes tell. Outside its giving snow like goose feathers. The worser the night, the surer we get called."

"Tell me once, Jacob," Maud sounded like the curfew again. "for why do you roast yourself like a goose on that furnace? Come, Matilda, it's time to go already."

While Uncle Schoppe, who gave all of us our piano lessons, played the familiar *Tannenbaum* and *Stille Nacht* on the church organ, I sat in the cedar-candle fragrance with half my mind on the program; the other half at home. The service over, would our parlor window shades be raised? *Our* candles glow? This was the signal that Papa hadn't been called out and all the aunts, uncles and cousins could come home with us. They had their own celebrations next morning.

"And there were shepherds in the same country, abiding in the fields," Rev. Wendt sonorously intoned. Then the upside-down red velvet dunce-cap-on-a-pole was passed for collection. The choir sang, *Oh, du frohliche Weihnachtszeit*. Some of us forgot our pieces. . .the altar was so high and Mama so far away and, anyhow, if Mrs. Schmachtenberg nursed her baby it wouldn't cry so loud. Wasn't it too bad Emily had to wear black hair ribbons even on holidays when the rest of us strutted red shoo-flies? Finally, everybody rose for the Lord's Prayer, accompanied by tolling bells, which gave Santy his clue to raise that shade at home. Now, Deacons passed the cardboard churches filled with goodies, first to the children down front, then to the ladies who sat on the left side of the aisle, then to the men on the right. At last, we were outside, on the church step.

I held my eyes shut, tight. Oh, if our parlor shade wasn't up! I made a trellis of my fingers. Cautiously I peeped through. *It was up!*

"Come on over!" I waved an invitation to every one in hearing distance. "Papa's home!"

Into the office across the hall from our living room we trooped. Shedding coats, kicking off smelly rubbers, dropping caps and mufflers onto the green leather couch, we were oblivious of non-relatives gathered outside our windows to watch the show. At just the right moment the parlor sliding door inched open. . .and there stood *Mr.* Santa Claus beside the candle-lighted tree; resplendent from black shiny boots to red cap.

"*Liebechen*, recite for me your piece," he kindly asked our youngest. Fred was so awed he came up with: "Blessed are the peace makers for they shall come home wagging their tails behind them."

I couldn't understand why Maud was with us for the "party" but Jacob wasn't. Or why Santy so enjoyed making the twins actually get down on their knees to say their prayers to the accompaniment of wince-producing whacks across thickly sweatered backs. "Irving," he commanded, "Say your prayers!" Then, "Now, Armin, you!"

"I've just said mine," Armin fibbed, so Santy dashed back to Irving who obliged twice. . .and bore his brother's stripes.

"Don't you laugh me out," grumbled the man with the big belly before turning to the next cousin.

When the ceiling lights came on we checked our loot with those Thanksgiving Day mail orders. For each grandma, red flannel petticoats and black wristlets; shawls for aunts; striped nightshirts and plug tobacco for uncles; beads, ribbons, dishes, leather music rolls, burnt wood boxes for handkerchiefs or gloves, pocket cloths or hand shoes for girl cousins; mouth harps and steam engines that whistled and sawed cords of toothpicks for the twins. Of course dolls, hobby horses, tool chests for the children of the house, and books for everybody, accompanied by: "By golly, we almost forgot *her*!"

When the wee ones started playing with their toys, adults and older children gathered around the piano with Uncle Schoppe at the keyboard. If you were more than eight years old and didn't know every verse of every carol (in German) without looking at the book, shame on you. Aunt Tillie's alto, Uncle Henry's base, Uncle Ed's tenor and Mama's soprano as lead voices made up a *Liederkranz* that was better than any Edison gramophone cylinder we owned.

After a while Mama and Maud circulated with trays. We drank toasts of "Happy birthday, dear Jesus," and "Merry Christmas dear Grandma, dear Papa, dear Mama, dear Children.". . .When the list was exhausted, Uncle Schoppe modulated into "God be with you till we meet again." On the way out, each guest helped himself from the mountain of cookie bags beside the door. Soon we climbed the stairs, taking the new dolls with us.

After Christmas breakfast of dunked stollen, we visited the homes of relatives, ostensibly to admire what Santy left for them; but every aunt knew we came on personal business. Purposely she postponed tipping her hand until we burst out with: "Well, we must be going once!" Then out came the hand knitted stockings and ear muffs. After the third or fourth call, before the next aunt could get her door open very wide, we sang, "Merry Christmas, well we must be going." About this time Jacob and Daisy caught up with us to cache our gifts in the buggy.

Papa hurried through morning calls to be home promptly at noon. Our menu consisted of roast goose with onion and nutmeg dressing, mashed potatoes, sauerkraut, cranberries, creamed peas, brine corn, hot mince meat pies . . . cut in quarters . . . and gallons of coffee; jellies, pickles, jams to "help fill up the cracks."

That year our dinner was interrupted by an accident. A farmer, while "shooting-in" Christmas, blew off his thumb.

"Well, just safe my piece of pie for supper once." Nothing upset Papa who, days before, had prepared for such annual emergencies. Mama, though not a registered nurse, gave the anesthetic for these impromptu operations. While our parents were out, Grandma wiped the dishes while Maud "played" them and explained:

"Shooting-in Christmas started in northern Europe years ago. There the Christmas season is so dark the sun seldom shines. It's just like night for weeks and people used to fear witches. So, they'd shoot into the air to scare them away. In Serbia, where whole roast pig is the Christmas meat, farmers raced each other to see who could get his pig barbecued on outdoor open spits first. The winner let it be known to his neighbors right away by firing his gun. Now, here in Illinois, me thinks it's just a noisy hangover from those early days to spoil your Papa's Christmas!"

But it didn't spoil Papa's Christmas. Smelling of iodoform and chloroform, he returned to the living room with a big smile on his face and a mischievous twinkle in his merry blue eyes to ask:

"Does it give cookies for a hungry man once? See if you can find me a springerlie, *Dootchen*."

And when he called me *that*, all was well with my world.

The Kid Hangs Up
His Stocking

JACOB RIIS

Jacob Riis was a nineteenth-century immigrant from Denmark whose own mastery of his new language and environment must have been an inspiration to the less fortunate new Americans he concentrated on helping. A confirmed city-dweller and a reporter for the New York Tribune *and* Evening Sun, *he wrote countless stories about slum dwellings and abuses in lower-class urban life. His own success led him to found a pioneer settlement in New York (named after him in 1901) and to aid materially in the establishment of urban parks and playgrounds. Using dialect in storytelling with more subtlety than many of his adopted countrymen, Riis here pulls at heartstrings with a story of compassion among waifs who surely must have been modeled after the homeless children in the settlement houses of Manhattan.*

Jacob Riis, "The Kid Hangs Up His Stocking," in *Children of the Tenements* (New York: Macmillan Co., 1905), 21–27. This story was published first in *Century Magazine*, December 1899. Appreciation is extended to J. Riis Owre for permission to reprint the story here.

The clock in the West Side Boys' Lodginghouse ticked out the seconds of Christmas eve as slowly and methodically as if six fat turkeys were not sizzling in the basement kitchen against the morrow's spread, and as if two-score boys were not racking their brains to guess what kind of pies would go with them. Out on the avenue the shopkeepers were barring doors and windows, and shouting "Merry Christmas!" to one another across the street as they hurried to get home. The drays ran over the pavement with muffled sounds; winter had set in with a heavy snow-storm. In the big hall the monotonous click of checkers on the board kept step with the clock. The smothered exclamations of the boys at some unexpected, bold stroke, and the scratching of a little fellow's pencil on a slate, trying to figure out how long it was yet till the big dinner, were the only sounds that broke the quiet of the room. The superintendent dozed behind his desk.

A door at the end of the hall creaked, and a head with a shock of weather-beaten hair was stuck cautiously through the opening.

"Tom!" it said in a stage-whisper. "Hi, Tom! Come up an' git on ter de lay of de Kid."

A bigger boy in a jumper, who had been lounging on two chairs by the group of checker players, sat up and looked toward the door. Something in the energetic toss of the head there aroused his instant curiosity, and he started across the room. After a brief whispered conference the door closed upon the two, and silence fell once more on the hall.

They had been gone but a little while when they came back in haste. The big boy shut the door softly behind him and set his back against it.

"Fellers," he said, "what d'ye t'ink? I'm blamed if de Kid ain't gone an' hung up his sock fer Chris'mas!"

The checkers dropped, and the pencil ceased scratching on the slate, in breathless suspense.

"Come up an' see," said Tom, briefly, and led the way.

The whole band followed on tiptoe. At the foot of the stairs their leader halted.

"Yer don't make no noise," he said, with a menacing gesture. "You, Savoy!"—to one in a patched shirt and with a mischievous twinkle,—"you don't come none o' yer monkey-shines. If you scare de Kid you'll get it in de neck, see!"

With this admonition they stole upstairs. In the last cot of the double tier of bunks a boy much smaller than the rest slept, snugly tucked in the blankets. A tangled curl of yellow hair strayed over his baby face. Hitched to the bedpost was a poor, worn little stocking, arranged with much care so that Santa Claus should have as little trouble in filling it as possible. The edge of a hole in the knee had been drawn together and tied with a string to prevent anything falling out. The boys looked on in amazed silence. Even Savoy was dumb.

Little Willie, or, as he was affectionately dubbed by the boys, "the Kid," was a waif who had drifted in among them some months before. Except that his mother was in the hospital, nothing was known about him, which was regular and according to the rule of the house. Not as much was known about most of its patrons; few of them knew more themselves, or cared to remember. Santa Claus had never been anything to them but a fake to make the colored supplements sell. The revelation of the Kid's simple faith struck them with a kind of awe. They sneaked quietly downstairs.

"Fellers," said Tom, when they were all together again in the big room,—by virtue of his length, which had given him the nickname of "Stretch," he was the speaker on all important occasions,—"ye seen it yerself. Santy Claus is a-comin' to this here joint to-night. I wouldn't 'a' believed it. I ain't never had no dealin's wid de ole guy. He kinder forgot I was around, I guess. But de Kid says he is a-comin' to-night, an' what de Kid says goes."

Then he looked round expectantly. Two of the boys, "Gimpy" and Lem, were conferring aside in an undertone. Presently Gimpy, who limped, as his name indicated, spoke up.

"Lem says, says he—"

"Gimpy, you chump! you'll address de chairman," interrupted Tom, with severe dignity, "or you'll get yer jaw broke, if yer leg *is* short, see!"

"Cut it out, Stretch," was Gimpy's irreverent answer. "This here ain't no regular meetin', an' we ain't goin' to have none o' yer rot. Lem he says, says he, let's break de bank an' fill de Kid's sock. He won't know but it wuz ole Santy done it."

A yell of approval greeted the suggestion. The chairman, bound to exercise the functions of office in season and out of season, while they lasted, thumped the table.

"It is regular motioned an' carried," he announced, "that we break de bank fer de Kid's Chris'mas. Come on, boys!"

The bank was run by the house, with the superintendent as paying teller. He had to be consulted, particularly as it was past banking hours; but the affair having been succinctly put before him by a committee, of which Lem and Gimpy and Stretch were the talking members, he readily consented to a reopening of business for a scrutiny of the various accounts which represented the boys' earnings at selling papers and blacking boots, minus the cost of their keep and of sundry surreptitious flings at "craps" in secret corners. The inquiry developed an available surplus of three dollars and fifty cents. Savoy alone had no account; the run of craps had recently gone heavily against him. But in consideration of the season, the house voted a credit of twenty-five cents to him. The announcement was received with cheers. There was an immediate rush for the store, which was delayed only a few minutes by the necessity of Gimpy and Lem stopping on the stairs to "thump" one another as the expression of their entire satisfaction.

The procession that returned to the lodging-house later on, after wearing out the patience of several belated storekeepers, might have been the very Santa's supply-train itself. It signalized its advent by a variety of discordant noises, which were smothered on the stairs by Stretch, with much personal violence, lest they wake the Kid out of season. With boots in hand and bated breath, the midnight band stole up to the dormitory and looked in. All was safe. The Kid was dreaming, and smiled in his sleep.

The report roused a passing suspicion that he was faking, and Savarese was for pinching his toe to find out. As this would inevitably result in disclosure, Savarese and his proposal were scornfully sat upon. Gimpy supplied the popular explanation.

"He's a-dreamin' that Santy Claus has come," he said, carefully working a base-ball bat past the tender spot in the stocking.

"Hully Gee!" commented Shorty, balancing a drum with care on the end of it, "I'm thinkin' he ain't far out. Looks's ef de hull shop'd come along."

It did when it was all in place. A trumpet and a gun that had made vain and perilous efforts to join the bat in the stocking leaned against the bed in expectant attitudes. A picture-book with a pink Bengal tiger and a green bear on the cover peeped over the pillow, and the bedposts and rail were festooned with candy and marbles in bags. An express-wagon with a high seat was stabled in the gangway. It carried a load of fir branches that left no doubt from whose livery it hailed. The last touch was supplied by Savoy in the shape of a monkey on a yellow stick, that was not in the official bill of lading.

"I swiped it fer de kid," he said briefly in explanation.

When it was all done the boys turned in, but not to sleep. It was long past midnight before the deep and regular breathing from the beds proclaimed that the last had succumbed.

The early dawn was tinging the frosty window panes with red when from the Kid's cot there came a shriek that roused the house with a start of very genuine surprise.

"Hello!" shouted Stretch, sitting up with a jerk and rubbing his eyes. "Yes, sir! in a minute. Hello, Kid, what to—"

The Kid was standing barefooted in the passageway, with a base-ball bat in one hand and a trumpet and a pair of drumsticks in the other, viewing with shining eyes the wagon and its cargo, the gun and all the rest. From every cot necks were stretched, and grinning faces watched the show. In the excess of his joy the Kid let out a blast on the trumpet that fairly shook the building. As if it were a signal, the boys jumped out of bed and danced a breakdown about him in their shirt-tails, even Gimpy joining in.

"Holy Moses!" said Stretch, looking down, "if Santy Claus ain't been here an' forgot his hull kit, I'm blamed!"

III

The Big
Change

Introduction

Most of the people in the United States were excited with the prospect of a new century. On the homefront, the x ray was starting to revolutionize diagnostic medicine and surgery. Walter Reed was well on the way to conquering the dreaded yellow fever. Gramaphones and pianolas were bringing the music of the day into the parlor. Houses were lit with electricity, and homemakers, who were increasingly taking jobs in the marketplace, were pleased to have new kitchen conveniences, like the toaster. More and more homes were being constructed with garages to hold the motor cars that were just beginning to be produced on the mass assembly line. Chicago and New York even had taxi cabs running on hard-surfaced streets.

Abroad, however, there were clouds on the horizon in the early 1900s. Young Winston Churchill was bogged down in the Boer War, Kaiser Wilhelm was building a powerful German navy, the Boxer Rebellion in China was aimed at reducing the number of foreigners there, and, in Russia, a revolution was being plotted by young dissidents. These shadows would eventually have their effect on the United States, and America would lose its innocence in the years ahead.

Along the Eastern seacoast, the Christmas festival of consumption remained fairly well intact until the crash and Great Depression produced a more sober atmosphere than prevailed in the so-called Aspirin Age of the twenties. On the other hand, the last West, the Rocky Mountain and Southwest region, was in the news, thanks largely to Teddy Roosevelt and a myriad of writers, such as Pearl Zane Grey, the New York dentist turned novelist who lived in California, wrote in Arizona, and fished in the waters of the Pacific from Hawaii to Australia. Elizabeth

Bacon Custer, who survived her husband George by nearly fifty-seven years, wrote, "Sometimes I think our Christmas on the frontier was a greater event to us than to anyone in the states."1 The isolation and loneliness of living in sparsely settled areas inspired a desire to make Christmas *the* season of the year. In the lower Southwest, Anglos were introduced to piñatas and luminarios—Mexican customs that had been carried across the border. In rude farm and ranch homes, trees were cut from mountain slopes and brought home so that young people could string popcorn, cranberries, and make ribbons from discarded clothing. In Navajoland, an elder would often tell the Navajo creation story in a hogan on Christmas eve while nearby trading posts held community celebrations for the Indians as well as the Anglos. These homespun Christmases often created memories that were passed down from one generation to the next.

During the 1930s and 1940s, sectional differences in the United States diminished somewhat because of the commonality of the Great Depression and World War II experiences. Individualism gave way to collective security. The same radio programs and films were heard and seen by Americans of varying ages, creeds, and cultural backgrounds. The standard fare did not have great quality, but the quantity made up for it.

News broadcasts and newsreels were the best of radio and films. News broadcasts brought instant coverage of contemporary events, like World War I, the flight of the *Spirit of St. Louis*, the explosion of the *Hindenburg*, and the Scopes trial in Dayton, Tennessee. Newsreels from Hollywood, such as those produced by Adolph Zukor, may have been slightly delayed in portraying recent developments, but they added geographical background and faces to the voices that had only been read in print or heard on the air before. At Christmas, colorful broadcasters in radio and film looked for stories of cheer and charity in order to set the tone of peace and goodwill across the land.

Notes

1. Quoted from Walter F. Pederson, ed., "Christmas on the Plains," *The American West* 1, no. 4 (Fall 1964): 54.

How the Indians Spend Christmas

FRANCIS E. LEUPP

Almost three hundred years after John Smith came to "keepe Christmas among the salvages" in the New World, American Indian customs were still being appraised in terms of their similarity to those of the white man. Pedestrian though the writing may be, this report on Indian Christmas from Francis E. Leupp, U.S. Commissioner of Indian Affairs in the early 1900s, is also revealing. Leupp's straightfaced cataloging of Indian Yuletide observation was obviously not singled out for its literary power of description, but to afford white Americans a glimpse of the kinds of ceremonies and customs the Indians considered fitting for Christmas and the extent to which these were copied from our own. The commissioner has also shown us the prevailing bias of his time: not necessarily unfavorable, but certainly stereotypical in its assessment of the Indians, "in whose primitive ideals of happiness the full stomach takes an important place," possessed of "an instinctive taste for ceremonial and the strong strain of sentiment." Elsewhere the non-nomadic tribes of Oklahoma—the Cherokee and Choctow—are

---

Francis E. Leupp, "How the Indians Spend Christmas," *LADIES' HOME JOURNAL*, 24 December 1906, 18. This essay is reprinted through the courtesy of the *LADIES' HOME JOURNAL*.

*referred to as "the five civilized tribes" (because their culture
was thought to resemble that of the white man). And it is
virtually impossible not to notice certain "primitive" aspects of
white civilization, by contrast.*

In view of their instinctive taste for ceremonial and the strong
strain of sentiment running through their nature, it seems
strange that our North American Indians have not developed
from their own sources anything corresponding very nearly to
our Christmas idea. They have memorial festivals at which they
offer gifts to their deities, partly in gratitude for having brought
their tribe through some great crisis in the past, but more
particularly by way of insuring similar favors in future crises.
They have also tribal gatherings, with sacrifices of a propitiatory
character, just before the planting season, or just before the
spring flood, or when a harvest is threatened by unfavorable
weather conditions.

New Year's Day Is Sometimes More in Favor

Among the Northern tribes long contact with the whites has
brought about some changes in the holiday dates, but stamped
the beginning of the new year with more favor, in some respects,
than Christmas. Among the Flatheads of Montana and their
allied tribes, for example, gift-making and treats of various
sorts are the rule on New Year's Day. This appears to be a relic
of the Hudson Bay Company's occupation. The Company used
to take the end of one year and the opening of a new one as the
time for balancing accounts, and usually accompanied the settlement with a present of some sort for "good will and good
measure." The Chippewas of the Mississippi learned their custom of celebrating New Year's Day from the old French voyageurs. They called it "kissing day" because of the custom of the
voyageurs to kiss each other when exchanging greetings and
gifts. At the New Year season, also, the traders used to keep an

open table for three or four days, every comer being welcome to eat all he could. These practices have now pretty well died out.

The Menominees of Wisconsin have a "New Year's kiss" which they give and receive, but they early learned the meaning of Christmas, whose celebration they extend over a considerable period, embracing both New Year's Day and "Three Kings' Day"—otherwise the sixth of January. This last holiday is always celebrated by a feast of very ancient origin, in which the chief feature is a cake with three beans cooked in it. Everybody who comes to the table must have a piece of the cake, and whoever finds a bean in his slice becomes one of the three kings of the feast and must bear his share in preparing the next year's celebration.

This notion of feasting and conviviality is the first one associated with any holiday in the minds of most of the Indians, in whose primitive ideals of happiness the full stomach takes an important place. Among the Pimas, Christmas, New Year's, Easter, and Thanksgiving are all grouped under the broad designation, "eating days." The Shoshones call Christmas the "big eating." When the celebration was first introduced at Lemhi, Idaho, then the good deaconess at one of the mission schools who had the enterprise in charge thought she would inquire among the Indians and see how many really understood what the day meant. Most of those whom she questioned professed utter ignorance; but one old blind man assured her that he knew, and explained: "Christmas all same Fourth of July—white man get heap drunk."

Here and there, of course, the inner significance appeals to the minds of the Indians, especially to tribes with a rather serious moral bent. The Northern Cheyennes call Christmas "Big Sunday," and the Arapahoes, "the birthday of the son of the stranger on high." At the Saddle Mountain Indian Mission in Oklahoma, on the old Kiowa Reservation, the day is given its full sentimental value as the birthday of Jesus Christ, and the Indians bring gifts to Him, in the form of money for spreading His message to mankind. But the conception which makes the feast the most prominent thing in sight is almost everywhere dominant. Usually the Christmas dinner is given at the local school, or by the missionaries, or by the traders, and the Indians figure as guests; but the Indians are always encouraged to do as much as possible for themselves.

A touching feature of all the Christmas dinners among the less advanced tribes is the presence of a number of old men and women who, never having been to school and learned to sit at the table and use a knife and fork, squat against the side walls of the room and are there served by kind-hearted teachers and employees, eating their food in the more primitive way to which they are used.

The Christmas Tree Catches Their Fancy

When the white people brought to the notice of the Indians the Christmas tree with its annual crop of beauties and benefits, the pretty fancy caught hold of their minds very promptly. Indeed, Chief Ring Thunder, on the Rosebud Reservation in South Dakota, who once used to hate the "white man's ways," acknowledged his conversion in the presence of a Christmas tree set up by a trader for the Indians of his camp by saying to the donor: "My friend, you have made our hearts glad. Our children are happy, and you tell us that this is good—that it is the right thing to do. If it is such a good thing we ought to have one of these trees every week!"

The Southern Cheyennes have given the Christmas tree the pretty title, "the giving tree." Trees generally are among the most conspicuous objects of worship in the pantheistic religion shared by most of our Indians; and evergreens are regarded with especial reverence as the trees that are "ever living." One of the Indian ceremonials, which, perhaps, bears a closer relation than any other to our Christmas tree celebration, may be found among the traditions of one of the groups in North Dakota. Many years ago, it runs, during the days of the "medicine clans," a cedar tree was always brought in by the leading medicine-men in the early spring, before any medicine ceremony could be performed. The cedar tree was adored on account of the length of its life, and called "Grandmother."

The tree was always planted directly in front of the medicine lodge. Before it was put into its accustomed place people were invited to make offerings to the "Grandmother." Calicoes, shawls, moccasins, robes, etc., were brought and placed on the tree, chiefly by the children and youth, much in the same manner as we place our gifts on the Christmas tree. Every one who brought anything to the "ever-living Grandmother" was absolved for any wrong he had committed, and received a benediction from one of the four leading medicine-men, who ended the ceremony by an earnest prayer that those who had honored the "Grandmother" by gifts might be blessed with health, goodness and long life—the same as she herself enjoyed. The gifts were afterward distributed.

After the season of medicine ceremonies was over, in the late autumn, the tree was hung with little children's moccasins. A prayer was then offered by one of the four leaders that the owners of the footwear might be blessed with good health and long life. The leaders then took up the tree, and, with a crowd of the people following, carried it to the Missouri River. There they put it into the water and began to sing, while the "ever-living Grandmother" floated down the river with its burden of little shoes until it was lost to sight.

Mr. and Mrs. Santa Claus Both Go Around

Among the Lower Brule Sioux a committee of young men is appointed to go about with a subscription list and make a collection for the purchase of provisions for a Christmas feast. This money is turned over to a purchasing committee, who submit lists of what they want to all the stores in the neighborhood and get bids on them, and then award the contract to the lowest bidder, just as would be done among shrewd and careful white people.

On the Cheyenne River Reservation such a committee is appointed a month before Christmas. At a later meeting certain officers for the tree ceremonies are elected, including a "Grandfather," who corresponds generally to our idea of a Santa Claus. Speakers are named also, and a "Censor of Speech." When the eventful evening arrives and the people assemble around the tree, the Censor announces the names of the speakers, and after that his duty is to confine them to the subjects assigned them— a task of some difficulty among a people so given to elocution. After the oratory, with possibly some music interspersed, "Grandfather" distributes gifts.

The Standing Rock Sioux have introduced an improvement into this dramatic feature of the celebration by having Mrs. Santa Claus accompany Mr. Santa Claus on his rounds. She is usually impersonated by a young woman, wrapped in the old-time blanket and leaning on a staff, and carrying a basket of apples for distribution among the old persons and little children. The too prevalent popular notion that the Indian lacks a sense of humor is promptly dispelled for any one who looks in upon one of these entertainments. The jokes cracked by the gift-dispensers produce great hilarity; and when some squaw rather notorious for her temper unrolls a mysterious package and discovers a neatly ornamented piece of broomstick, or a gray-haired and dignified headman finds that the tree has borne him a red and yellow jumping-jack, the quips and laughter know no bounds.

As a rule, there is very little exchanging of Christmas gifts between Indian adults, and comparatively few are made by children to the elders of their families. But the parents who are not too poor to respond take great interest in sending to the school authorities such presents as they have in mind to give to their children, and let these be placed on the trees on Christmas Eve. The Kiowas enter into the spirit of the occasion so that in some instances they have been known to slip into the room where a tree was in process of decoration, and hang upon it surreptitiously small packages addressed to themselves. This device had the double merit of contributing to the fullness of the program and of insuring its authors against being forgotten.

No Child Is Forgotten at Christmas

The kinds of gifts made to the Indian children at the schools do not vary greatly from those made to white children at Christmas. The teachers and employees write to the parents, reminding them of the approach of the festival. The parents respond according to their means, usually with small sums of money which they ask to have spent for their children. Then the traders on the reservation, and the contractors who supply the commissary, and others who depend upon the patronage of the Indians and the Government for their business, contribute more or less liberally. Finally the school authorities themselves, after figuring over the matter and discovering whether any of the children have been or are likely to be overlooked, draw upon their slender purses for a sum sufficient to preclude any such discrimination. From headquarters in Washington we commonly send a small but practical contribution in the shape of authority to add a few fancy touches to the regular school dinner.

The children everywhere are encouraged to prepare little souvenirs for each other—things made with their own hands; but our worthy effort is occasionally distorted to unseemly ends, as in the case of a school largely attended by Navajos, to whom comes down in their blood a very distinct trend toward dainty artisanship. Several of the boys at this school started the idea of melting the solder from tin cans, carving matrics in sandstone, pouring in the melted solder and thus making various ornaments for Christmas presents to their teachers. Under such a drain the supply of available cans in due course gave out; but the moulding work continued undisturbed till somebody discovered the disappearance of a large number of Government spoons from the dining-room, and an extinguisher had to be placed at once upon a most promising infant industry.

Perhaps the largest single present, in point of bulk, which

any of the Indians give away at Christmas is a horse. Sometimes the horse is a gift from one friend to another or from a parent to a child; more often, though, it is a gift from an Indian to the mission church he attends or to the school which has charge of his children.

Indians Who Have Learned What Christmas Is

Some of the customs of the Indians who have learned what Christmas is and stands for are decidedly picturesque—at Saint Joseph's Mission among the Nez Perces, for instance. For several days before Christmas the Indians come in from the surrounding country and camp around the mission, where they attend services twice a day, reciting their prayers and catechism in their own language aloud and in common, with a musical rhythm.

Throughout the last day and evening before the holiday itself their confessions are heard in the church, and about eleven o'clock in the night the bell summons to midnight mass those who are shriven. A bonfire is thereupon built in front of the church, and the Indians form a circle around it. The chief men in turn address the rest on the nature and significance of the Christmas festival, and exhort them to celebrate it in a becoming manner. At midnight the bell is rung again, and all enter the church, where the priest, with his assistants and altar boys, begins high mass, the Indians singing in Latin the parts appointed for the choir, and in the intervals singing and praying in their own tongue. Another mass follows, and then the sisters and the children sing English hymns till two A. M., when all retire quietly.

The San Felipe Indians in New Mexico evidently were indoctrinated with the Christmas idea by the Jesuit fathers who lived among them long ago; but, like most primitive people, they make an odd jumble of things Christian and pagan. For example, they go to the mission church for Christmas morning service and then a number of them file out upon the plaza and start a dance which lasts three days. The non-dancers load their tables with the best viands they know how to prepare, and keep open house for all their friends. The season is the great one of the year, also, for making calls, and the callers partake of some refreshment at each house.

The neighboring Laguna Indians still retain, though substantially only as a tradition, a practice handed down to them from their fathers, who learned it from the early Spanish missionaries. For some time before Christmas they would busy themselves making little clay images of sheep, goats, horses, cattle, cats and dogs and vegetables, which they would take into the church on Christmas Eve and lay upon the altar, where the priest would bless them during the midnight service. They would then take the blessed effigies away and distribute them—the horse in the barn, the sheep, goats and cattle on the mesas, the cat and dog in the house, the vegetables in the garden patch— where each could keep watch and see that the coming year should be a propitious one for its kind; and the amateur sculptors would join in a dance lasting four days. They still keep up the dance with vigor. The pueblo is divided between four clans, who meet on the dancing-ground; each sings its own clan song and then all join in a common one.

Our Family-Fireside Commencement:

An American Message of Christmas Good Cheer, with Some Helpful Thoughts Also for the Germans

BRAD STEPHENS

As immigration to the United States increased, so did social and economic tensions. Everyday Americans tended toward xenophobia. Eastern Europeans, the Jews in particular, were isolated in ghettos. Blacks were segregated in the cities and American Indians in the countryside on land nobody else wanted. The buildup of these pressures made it easy for the man in the street to turn against German-Americans at the outbreak of World War I. Not only pamphlets such as the following, but also Saturday matinees, Sunday sermons, and extemporaneous stump speeches fostered bans on the German language, attacks on German churches, and the trial of innocent civilians on bogus charges. Hard as it is to believe that the joy and warmth

Brad Stephens, *Our Family-Fireside Commencement: An American Message of Christmas Good Cheer, with Some Helpful Thoughts Also for the Germans* (Boston: Heintzemann Press, 1917), 3–12. This pamphlet is in the Boston Public Library.

of American Christmas could be combined with jingoism, in fact, Brad Stephens's 1917 "gift book" specifically denied all Germans any role in the folk history of Christmas, any genuine religious feeling, or any honesty, courage, and intellectual power—using this flamboyant assault to fire up American "ideals." Little is known of Brad Stephens but the document was probably written for George Creel's Committee on Public Information, a wartime group identified by its vitriolic speeches against the nationality that brought the Christmas tree to America.

One reason why Germany is going to be licked is our American Christmas. It's a good thought to carry with you this holiday season. The 25th of December is our most important educational anniversary. Our colleges have interesting exercises every year which they call commencement, but every one knows that the real commencement is in the life of the family, and that the true commencement anniversary is when we renew our loyalty to the old folks at home, and to their teachings at Christmas time.

We have endowed with many millions of dollars colleges and universities without number. The pathway to higher education is easier in our country than in any other. But the great hope for the preservation of America does not rest in these academic institutions of learning. That hope can only rest in the lessons learned around the family fireside in the average American home.

This is so because the love of truth, and justice, and human liberty that endures must be planted in the mind of the child. No educational system can keep the heart of the nation sound like the family fireside. And unless the story of democracy means something deep and consecrated to a boy or girl of twelve or fourteen years of age, it is likely never to mean anything at all.

But in Germany there has been no story of democracy to tell.

At Christmas it is appropriate and inspiring for us to think about these things. Our family-fireside traditions have made the ideals of America the hope of the world. "Peace on earth, good will to men" is still the wish sincere in every true American heart. It is not for ourselves alone that we would have the joys of the Christmas time. We none of us have any desire to light our Christmas fire with the rafters of a Belgian peasant's ruined home, or to pledge the health of our friends and kindred in wine that has been looted from a Frenchman's cellar.

But in Germany they haven't said "Merry Christmas" in more than forty years without a mental reservation, meaning, for Germans only.

And so they planned in Germany to plunder the world. Their first step in preparation was to poison their own family-fireside councils with hate and lies. They doctored their religion, they doctored their philosophy, and they doctored their history. And when the God of Abraham, and the God of Isaac, and the God of Jacob refused to stand for the teachings of Treitschke, they dethroned Him and set up a new God, a German God to sit on the right hand of their Prussian king.

"No God shall stand before me and my desire," said the Kaiser.

May our God, who was the God of Abraham and of Isaac and of Jacob, who marks still even the fall of a sparrow, preserve us this Christmas time from this sort of German efficiency!

But even in Germany the day is foretold when the people will say, as did Wolsey, "Had we but served the God of Abraham and Isaac and Jacob as we have served our Kaiser, He would not have deserted us now in our adversity."

Having deceived the world for half a century regarding their plans, they thought also to deceive us after the war was started. They wanted to establish their dream of a great middle European empire from Berlin to Bagdad, free from the interference of any power that could thwart their will. And they relied upon their spies and their propaganda to keep England, Italy, the

United States and South America out of the conflict. In this, German efficiency scored its first fall. We and our allies found out that the war, like many of the products we had been using, was made in German, too.

But, then, nothing ever made in Germany was "conceived in liberty and dedicated to the proposition that all men are created equal."

Lies were their emissaries everywhere at home and abroad. They deceived us all for a time regarding the exact date when their mobilization was ordered. They attempted to deceive us about the invasion of Belgium, and to whitewash the outrage and murder of thousands of men, women and children. Whatever the lie that was needed, everybody in Germany was ready to serve. Their Kaiser lied. Their chancellor lied. Their fifty leading college professors lied. Their ministers lied. Their newspapers lied.

But in Germany, you see, there was no story of George Washington and the cherry tree to illustrate the honor in telling the truth.

They recommended themselves and their works most highly, the Germans. That was German propaganda, too. But, ah, the fatal error! They came to believe that they were the supermen that their writers and their rulers had described. They knew that might wasn't right. It was only because they thought they had the might to terrorize the world that they started the war. As is said in sporting circles, they were the greatest "sure-thing gamblers" in the world. The survival of the fittest meant the disappearance of the unfit to them only on the basis of their hypothesis that the Germans are the fittest to survive.

But with all the cards stacked in their favor, as they have described them, the Germans welsh when they are called upon to face cold steel.

In their mass plays and in their mob strategy, the German soldier is no doubt the equal of any other soldier in the world. It is when he has to stand out alone and face an individual foe on equal terms that his inferiority becomes apparent. Then the yellow streak generally shows. Then the heart of him grows flabby. Then he blubbers, and sticks up his hand, and cries, "Kamerad."

But the German who asks for mercy gives none when mercy is his to show.

Does anyone doubt the truth of this indictment? Does anyone want to know further reasons why most Germans are cowards? Cross out everything that has been written so far!

When before in modern times and in modern warfare have white men with an open Bible done such things as the Germans have been doing for the past three years? The shooting of Captina Fryatt and of Edith Cavell; the shelling of open boats; the outraging and oftentimes the torture in the public square of little girls under ten and twelve years of age in every town they have occupied; the rape and deportation of Belgian and French women by the thousands; the bombing of cities and towns and hospitals by airships; the murder of Red Cross nurses; the sinking of hospital ships; the shooting and bayonetting of women and children; the looting and burning of homes; and the systematic devastation of all territory which they have once held and been forced to evacuate!

Will brave men do these things at the bidding of any king or kaiser?

"Cruelty springs from weakness," said Seneca. That partly explains the trail of outrage and murder that follows every German army—the weakness in the character of the German people; that claiming love and affection for the wives and children of their own family firesides, they show none for the weak and the helpless of a fallen foe; that making much of the Christmas ceremonies in the Fatherland, they have revealed nothing of the Christmas spirit in their dealings anywhere with the rest of the world. But the thing that most adequately explains their record, the blackest so far in the history of mankind, is the fact that the heart of Germany is rotten.

But we might have known beforehand, from the shabby

regard in which they hold their own women, and their virtue, what the ideals of the family fireside amounted to in Germany.

The Kaiser ejected his own mother from the home where she had passed the happiest years of her life when he became king. His jokes and salacious stories concerning the virtue of women are notorious throughout the courts of Europe. Once he was brought to book. On board of one of his battleships one day he passed a scurrilous remark about a young woman, who chanced to be the cousin of a young officer who was standing near by. The young officer felled the Kaiser with a blow. But the young man had to commit suicide to save himself from court-martial and a firing squad.

Such is the condition of servitude in Germany! No man can defend the good name or virtue of a woman against the Kaiser or any officer in the German army or navy. There is no chivalry in German militarism. An officer can pull a shop girl or a stenographer into an alley and outrage her, and neither her father, her brother, nor anybody else dare say a word in protest. And pushing women off the sidewalk into the street is every-where recognized as one of the prerogatives of Herr Lieutenant or Capitan. Where these ideas prevail concerning womanhood, can any one wonder why 33 1/3 per cent of the births in the great cities of Germany were illegitimate before the war. What will the percentage be after the war is over?

But Gott mit Uns in Germany reckons not with virtue in their women, legitimacy in their children, honor in their state-men, faith in their generals in keeping the Articles of War, or manhood in their Kaiser.

Out on the Western Front this Christmas there are soldiers who have all the ideals in their hearts that German efficiency, German militarism, and German Kultur have ignored. They have been schooled in the traditions of democracy. They haven't been fed up on lies. Their histories, their geographies, and their religion have not been doctored to fit the ambitions of a predatory ruling class, or of a paranoic and predatory kind. They fight fair even against a blackguard foe.

"What's your religion?" asked a French officer of a poilu who had just performed an act of signal bravery.

"My religion," said the poilu, "is that kind of religion that looks God in the eyes."

And so America, and England, and France, and Italy, and all our soldiers, look God in the eyes and this great struggle.

Can the might of the Hun prevail? With all of the advantages of man power and gun power against them, the soul power of the French poilu and the British Tommy held the Germans back at the Marne, before Calais, and at Verdun. And soon now, added to our soul power, we will have the man power and the gun power, too. What then will be the answer to God from Germany?

Courage to face cold steel reverts back to the ideals of the family fireside, and of the Family-Fireside Commencement which we celebrate this 25th of December. And thank God, there has always been plenty of this kind of good courage in our family ideals. It alone brought us through times darker by far than the present hour, from Magna Charta and the Bill of Rights to the Declaration of Independence and our United States Constitution. It will continue to carry us through, as long as there are a majority of us who still remember the history of our country and the ideas for which it stands—that compact in the cabin of the Mayflower; the bloody footprints of our soldiers in the snows at Valley Forge; and the pure heart and the wisdom of the railsplitter who became president.

Never more so than in a crisis like the present must we look to the homely ideals of our American firesides to hold us true. Our family commencement with the old folks at home must be an educational anniversary, to quicken the memories of child-hood, and to strengthen us anew in the lessons of truth and justice and liberty, which, God help them now, they have over-looked in Germany for many years.

Dancing Dan's Christmas

DAMON RUNYON

There is something uniquely American about Dancing Dan, as there was about most of the New York tales of Damon Runyon, whose slangy idiom and underworld characters are probably most familiar to us from the exuberant Broadway musical, Guys and Dolls. Historically speaking, the temperance movement of 1830 resurfaced in the nation a century later. This time, however, reformers substituted Prohibition for temperance, apparently no longer believing that the populace would reform itself without assistance from the law. For the first time in the American record, large numbers of citizens openly defied the law, at the same time elevating to folk-hero status the outlaws who supplied bathtub gin and ran the "speakeasies." It was the eve of the birth of the anti-hero, who for decades ahead was to dominate the American cultural scene as powerfully as did the traditional heroes and heroines of the past. Damon Runyon was a major literary voice of this era, creating street people who managed to be both lovable and lost at the same time.

Damon Runyon, "Dancing Dan's Christmas," in *The Bloodhounds of Broadway and Other Stories by Damon Runyon* (New York: William Morrow and Co., 1981), 157–70. Reprint rights have been obtained from Sheldon Abend, president, American Play Company, Inc.

Now one time it comes on Christmas, and in fact it is the evening before Christmas, and I am in Good Time Charley Bernstein's little speakeasy in West Forty-seventh Street, wishing Charley a Merry Christmas and having a few hot Tom and Jerrys with him.

This hot Tom and Jerry is an old-time drink that is once used by one and all in this country to celebrate Christmas with, and in fact it is once so popular that many people think Christmas is invented only to furnish an excuse for hot Tom and Jerry, although of course this is by no means true.

But anybody will tell you that there is nothing that brings out the true holiday spirit like hot Tom and Jerry, and I hear that since Tom and Jerry goes out of style in the United States, the holiday spirit is never quite the same.

The reason hot Tom and Jerry goes out of style is because it is necessary to use rum and one thing and another in making Tom and Jerry, and naturally when rum becomes illegal in this country Tom and Jerry is also against the law, because rum is something that is very hard to get around town these days.

For a while some people try making hot Tom and Jerry without putting rum in it, but somehow it never has the same old holiday spirit, so nearly everybody finally gives up in disgust, and this is not surprising, as making Tom and Jerry is by no means child's play. In fact, it takes quite an expert to make good Tom and Jerry, and in the days when it is not illegal a good hot Tom and Jerry maker commands good wages and many friends.

Now of course Good Time Charley and I are not using rum in the Tom and Jerry we are making, as we do not wish to do anything illegal. What we are using is rye whiskey that Good Time Charley gets on a doctor's prescription from a drug store, as we are personally drinking this hot Tom and Jerry and naturally we are not foolish enough to use any of Good Time Charley's own rye in it.

The prescription for the rye whisky comes from old Doc Moggs, who prescribes it for Good Time Charley's rheumatism in case Charley happens to get any rheumatism, as Doc Moggs says there is nothing better for rheumatism than rye whiskey, especially if it is made up in a hot Tom and Jerry. In fact, old Doc Moggs comes around and has a few seidels of hot Tom and Jerry with us for his own rheumatism.

He comes around during the afternoon, for Good Time Charley and I start making this Tom and Jerry early in the day, so as to be sure to have enough to last us over Christmas, and it is now along toward six o'clock, and our holiday spirit is practically one hundred per cent.

Well, as Good Time Charley and I are expressing our holiday sentiments to each other over our hot Tom and Jerry, and I am trying to think up the poem about the night before Christmas and all through the house, which I know will interest Charley no little, all of a sudden there is a big knock at the front door, and when Charley opens the door who comes in carrying a large package under one arm but a guy by the name of Dancing Dan.

This Dancing Dan is a good-looking young guy, who always seems well-dressed, and he is called by the name of Dancing Dan because he is a great hand for dancing around and about with dolls in night clubs, and other spots where there is any dancing. In fact, Dan never seems to be doing anything else, although I hear rumors that when he is not dancing he is carrying on in a most illegal manner at one thing and another. But of course you can always hear rumors in this town about anybody, and personally I am rather fond of Dancing Dan as he always seems to be getting a great belt out of life.

Anybody in town will tell you that Dancing Dan is a guy with no Barnaby whatever in him, and in fact he has about as much gizzard as anybody around, although I wish to say I always question his judgment in dancing so much with Miss Muriel O'Neill, who works in the Half Moon night club. And the reason I question his judgment in this respect is because everybody knows that Miss Muriel O'Neill is a doll who is very well thought of by Heine Schmitz, and Heine Schmitz is not such a guy as will take kindly to anybody dancing more than once and a half with a doll that he thinks well of.

This Heine Schmitz is a very influential citizen of Harlem,

where he has large interests in beer, and other business enterprises, and it is by no means violating any confidence to tell you
that Heine Schmitz will just as soon blow your brains out as
look at you. In fact, I hear sooner. Anyway, he is not a guy to
monkey with and many citizens take the trouble to advise
Dancing Dan that he is not only away out of line in dancing
with Miss Muriel O'Neill, but that he is knocking his own price
down to where he is no price at all.

But Dancing Dan only laughs ha-ha, and goes on dancing
with Miss Muriel O'Neill any time he gets a chance, and Good
Time Charley says he does not blame him, at that, as Miss
Muriel O'Neill is so beautiful that he will be dancing with her
himself no matter what, if he is five years younger and can get a
Roscoe out as fast as in the days when he runs with Paddy the
Link and other fast guys.

Well, anyway, as Dancing Dan comes in he weighs up the
joint in one quick peek, and then he tosses the package he is
carrying into a corner where it goes plunk, as if there is
something very heavy in it, and then he steps up to the bar
alongside of Charley and me and wishes to know what we are
drinking.

Naturally we start boosting hot Tom and Jerry to Dancing
Dan, and he says he will take a crack at it with us, and after one
crack, Dancing Dan says he will have another crack, and Merry
Christmas to us with it, and the first thing anybody knows it is
a couple of hours later and we are still having cracks at the hot
Tom and Jerry with Dancing Dan, and Dan says he never drinks
anything so soothing in his life. In fact, Dancing Dan says he
will recommend Tom and Jerry to everybody he knows, only he
does not know anybody good enough for Tom and Jerry, except
maybe Miss Muriel O'Neill, and she does not drink anything
with drugstore rye in it.

Well, several times while we are drinking this Tom and Jerry,
customers come to the door of Good Time Charley's little
speakeasy and knock, but by now Charley is commencing to be
afraid they will wish Tom and Jerry, too, and he does not feel
we will have enough for ourselves, so he hangs out a sign which

says "Closed on Account of Christmas," and the only one he will let in is a guy by the name of Ooky, who is nothing but an old rum-dum, and who is going around all week dressed like Santa Claus and carrying a sign advertising Moe Lewinsky's clothing joint around in Sixth Avenue.

This Ookey is still wearing his Santa Claus outfit when Charley lets him in, and the reason Charley permits such a character as Ooky in his joint is because Ookey does the porter work for Charley when he is not Santa Claus for Moe Lewinsky, such as sweeping out, and washing the glasses, and one thing and another.

Well, it is about nine-thirty when Ookey comes in, and his puppies are aching, and he is all petered out generally from walking up and down and here and there with his sign, for any time a guy is Santa Claus for Moe Lewinsky he must earn his dough. In fact, Ooky is so fatigued, and his puppies hurt him so much that Dancing Dan and Good Time Charley and I all feel very sorry for him, and invite him to have a few mugs of hot Tom and Jerry with us, and wish him plenty of Merry Christmas.

But old Ooky is not accustomed to Tom and Jerry and after about the fifth mug he folds up in a chair, and goes right to sleep on us. He is wearing a pretty good Santa Claus make-up, what with a nice red suit trimmed with white cotton, and a wig, and false nose, and long white whiskers, and a big sack stuffed with excelsior on his back and if I do not know Santa Claus is not apt to be such a guy as will snore loud enough to rattle the windows, I will think Ooky is Santa Claus sure enough.

Well, we forget Ooky and let him sleep, and go on with our hot Tom and Jerry, and in the meantime we try to think up a few songs appropriate to Christmas, and Dancing Dan finally renders My Dad's Dinner Pail in a nice baritone and very loud, while I do first rate with Will You Love Me in December As You Do in May? But personally I always think Good Time Charley Bernstein is a little out of line trying to sing a hymn in Jewish on such an occasion, and it causes words between us.

While we are singing many customers come to the door and

knock, and then they read Charley's sign, and this seems to cause some unrest among them, and some of them stand outside saying it is a great outrage, until Charley sticks his noggin out the door and threatens to bust somebody's beezer if they do not go on about their business and stop disturbing peaceful citizens.

Naturally the customers go away, as they do not wish their beezers busted, and Dancing Dan and Charley and I continue drinking our hot Tom and Jerry, and with each Tom and Jerry we are wishing one another a very Merry Christmas, and sometimes a very Happy New Year, although of course this does not go for Good Time Charley as yet, because Charley has his New Year separate from Dancing Dan and me.

By and by we take to waking Ooky up in his Santa Claus outfit and offering him more hot Tom and Jerry, and wishing him Merry Christmas, but Ooky only gets sore and calls us names, so we can see he does not have the right holiday spirit in him, and let him alone until along about midnight when Dancing Dan wishes to see how he looks as Santa Claus.

So Good Time Charley and I help Dancing Dan pull off Ooky's outfit and put it on Dan, and this is easy as Ooky only has this Santa Claus outfit and on over his ordinary clothes, and he does not even wake up when we are undressing him of the Santa Claus uniform.

Well, I wish to say I see many a Santa Claus in my time, but I never see a better looking Santa Claus than Dancing Dan, especially after he gets the wig and white whiskers fixed just right, and we put a sofa pillow that Good Time Charley happens to have around the joint for the cat to sleep on down his pants to give Dancing Dan a nice fat stomach such as Santa Claus is bound to have.

In fact, after Dancing Dan looks at himself in a mirror awhile he is greatly pleased with his appearance, while Good Time Charley is practically hysterical, although personally I am commencing to resent Charley's interest in Santa Claus, and Christmas generally, as he by no means has any claim on these matters. But then I remember Charley furnishes the hot Tom and Jerry, so I am more tolerant toward him.

"Well," Charley finally says, "it is a great pity we do not know where there are some stockings hung up somewhere, because then," he says, "you can go around and stuff things in these stockings, as I always hear this is the main idea of a Santa Claus. But," Charley says, "I do not suppose anybody in this section has any stockings hung up, or if they have," he says, "the chances are they are so full of holes they will not hold anything. Anyway," Charley says, "even if there are any stockings hung up we do not have anything to stuff in them, although personally," he says, "I will gladly donate a few pints of Scotch."

Well, I am pointing out that we have no reindeer and that a Santa Claus is bound to look like a terrible sap if he goes around without any reindeer, but Charley's remarks seem to give Dancing Dan an idea, for all of a sudden he speaks as follows:

"Why," Dancing Dan says, "I know where a stocking is hung up. It is hung up at Muriel O'Neill's flat over here in West Forty-ninth Street. This stocking is hung up by nobody but a party by the name of Gammer O'Neill, who is Miss Muriel O'Neill's grandmamma," Dancing Dan says. "Gammer O'Neill is going on ninety-odd," he says "and Miss Muriel O'Neill tells me she cannot hold out much longer, what with one thing and another, including being a little childish in spots.

"Now," Dancing Dan says, "I remember Miss Muriel O'Neill is telling me just the other night how Gammer O'Neill hangs up her stocking on Christmas Eve all her life, and," he says, "I judge from what Miss Muriel O'Neill says that the old doll always believes Santa Claus will come along some Christmas and fill the stocking full of beautiful gifts. But," Dancing Dan says, "Miss Muriel O'Neill tells me Santa Claus never does this, although Miss Muriel O'Neill personally always takes a few gifts home and pops them into the stocking to make Gammer O'Neill feel better.

"But, of course," Dancing Dan says, "these gifts are nothing much because Miss Muriel O'Neill is very poor, and proud, and also good, and will not take a dime off of anybody, and I can lick the guy who says she will, although," Dancing Dan says, "between me, and Heine Schmitz, and a raft of other guys I can mention, Miss Muriel O'Neill can take plenty."

Well, I know that what Dancing Dan states about Miss Muriel O'Neill is quite true, and in fact it is a matter that is often discussed on Broadway, because Miss Muriel O'Neill cannot get more than twenty bobs per week working in the Half Moon, and it is well known to one and all that this is no kind of dough for a doll as beautiful as Miss Muriel O'Neill.

"Now," Dancing Dan goes on, "it seems that while Gammer O'Neill is very happy to get whatever she finds in her stocking on Christmas morning, she does not understand why Santa Claus is not more liberal, and," he says, "Miss Muriel O'Neill is saying to me that she only wishes she can give Gammer O'Neill one real big Christmas before the old doll puts her checks back in the rack.

"So," Dancing Dan states, "here is a job for us. Miss Muriel O'Neill and her grandmamma live all alone in this flat over in West Forty-ninth Street, and," he says, "at such an hour as this Miss Muriel O'Neill is bound to be working, and the chances are Gammer O'Neill is sound asleep, and we will just hop over there and Santa Claus will fill up her stocking with beautiful gifts."

Well, I say, I do not see where we are going to get any beautiful gifts at this time of night, what with all the stores being closed, unless we dash into an all-night drug store and buy a few bottles of perfume and a bum toilet set as guys always do when they forget about their ever-loving wives until after store hours on Christmas Eve, but Dancing Dan says never mind about this, but let us have a few more Tom and Jerrys first.

So we have a few more Tom and Jerrys, and then Dancing Dan picks up the package he heaves into the corner, and dumps most of the excelsior out of Ooky's Santa Claus sack, and puts the bundle in, and Good Time Charley turns out all the lights but one, and leaves a bottle of Scotch on the table in front of Ooky for a Christmas gift, and away we go.

Personally, I regret very much leaving the hot Tom and Jerry, but then I am also very enthusiastic about going along to help

Dancing Dan play Santa Claus, while Good Time Charley is practically overjoyed, as it is the first time in his life Charley is ever mixed up in so much holiday spirit. In fact, nothing will do Charley but that we stop in a couple of spots and have a few drinks to Santa Claus' health, and these visits are a big success, although everybody is much surprised to see Charley and me with Santa Claus, especially Charley, although nobody recognizes Dancing Dan.

But of course there are no hot Tom and Jerrys in these spots we visit, and we have to drink whatever is on hand, and personally I will always believe that the noggin I have on me afterwards comes of mixing the drinks we get in these spots with my Tom and Jerry.

As we go up Broadway, headed for Forty-ninth Street, Charley and I see many citizens we know and give them a large hello, and wish them Merry Christmas, and some of these citizens shake hands with Santa Claus, not knowing he is nobody but Dancing Dan, although later I understand there is some gossip among these citizens because they claim a Santa Claus with such a breath on him as our Santa Claus has is a little out of line.

And once we are somewhat embarrassed when a lot of little kids going home with their parents from a late Christmas party somewhere gather about Santa Claus with shouts of childish glee, and some of them wish to climb up Santa Claus' legs. Naturally, Santa Claus gets a little peevish, and calls them a few names, and one of the parents comes up and wishes to know what is the idea of Santa Claus using such language, and Santa Claus takes a punch at the parent, all of which is no doubt most astonishing to the little kids who have an idea of Santa Claus as a very kindly old guy. But of course they do not know about Dancing Dan mixing the liquor we get in the spots we visit with his Tom and Jerry, or they will understand how even Santa Claus can lose his temper.

Well, finally we arrive in front of the place where Dancing Dan says Miss Muriel O'Neill and her grandmamma live, and it is nothing but a tenement house not far back of Madison Square Garden, and furthermore it is a walk-up, and at this time there are no lights burning in the joint except a gas jet in the main hall, and by the light of this jet we look at the names on the letter boxes, such as you always find in the hall of these joints, and we see that Miss O'Neill and her grandmamma live on the fifth floor.

This is the top floor, and personally I do not like the idea of walking up five flights of stairs, and I am willing to let Dancing Dan and Good Time Charley go, but Dancing Dan insists we must all go, and finally I agree because Charley is commencing to argue that the right way for us to do is to get on the roof and let Santa Claus go down a chimney, and is making so much noise I am afraid he will wake somebody up.

So up the stairs we climb and finally we come to a door on the top floor that has a little card in a slot that says O'Neill, so we know we reach our destination. Dancing Dan first tries the knob, and right away the door opens, and we are in a little two- or three-room flat, with not much furniture in it, and what furniture there is is very poor. One single gas jet is burning near a bed in a room just off the one the door opens into, and by this light we see a very old doll is sleeping on the bed, so we judge this is nobody but Gammer O'Neill.

On her face is a large smile, as if she is dreaming of something very pleasant. On a chair at the head of the bed is hung a long black stocking, and it seems to be such a stocking as is often patched and mended, so I can see that what Miss Muriel O'Neill tells Dancing Dan about her grandmamma hanging up her stocking is really true, although up to this time I have my doubts.

Well, I am willing to pack in after one gander at the old doll, especially as Good Time Charley is commencing to prowl around the flat to see if there is a chimney where Santa Claus can come down, and is knocking things over, but Dancing Dan stands looking down at Gammer O'Neill for a long time.

Finally he unslings the sack on his back, and takes out his package, and unties this package, and all of a sudden out pops a raft of big diamond bracelets, and diamond rings, and diamond brooches, and diamond necklaces, and I do not know what all else in the way of diamonds, and Dancing Dan and I begin stuffing these diamonds into the stocking and Good Time Charley pitches in and helps us.

There are enough diamonds to fill the stocking to the muzzle, and it is no small stocking, at that, and I judge that Gammer O'Neill has a pretty fair set of bunting sticks when she is young. In fact, there are so many diamonds that we have enough left over to make a nice little pile on the chair after we fill the stocking plumb up, leaving a nice diamond-studded vanity case sticking out the top where we figure it will hit Gammer O'Neill's eye when she wakes up.

And it is not until I get out in the fresh air again that all of a sudden I remember seeing large headlines in the afternoon papers about a five-hundred-G's stick-up in the afternoon of one of the biggest diamond merchants in Mainden Lane while he is sitting in his office, and I also recall once hearing rumors that Dancing Dan is one of the best lone-hand git-'em-up guys in the world.

Naturally, I commence to wonder if I am in the proper company when I am with Dancing Dan, even if he is Santa Claus. So I leave him on the next corner arguing with Good Time Charley about whether they ought to go and find some more presents somewhere, and look for other stockings to stuff, and I hasten on home, and go to bed.

The next day I find I have such a noggin that I do not care to stir around, and in fact I do not stir around much for a couple of weeks.

Then one night I drop around to Good Time Charley's little speakeasy, and ask Charley what is doing.

"Well," Charley says, "many things are doing, and personally," he says, "I am greatly surprised I do not see you at Gammer O'Neill's wake. You know Gammer O'Neill leaves this wicked old world a couple of days after Christmas," Good Time Charley says, "and," he says, "Miss Muriel O'Neill states that Doc Moggs claims it is at least a day after she is entitled to go, but she is sustained," Charley says, "by great happiness on finding her stocking filled with beautiful gifts on Christmas morning.

"According to Miss Muriel O'Neill," Charley says, "Gammer O'Neill dies practically convinced that there is a Santa Claus, although of course," he says, "Miss Muriel O'Neill does not tell her the real owner of the gifts, an all-right guy by the name of Shapiro leaves the gifts with her after Miss Muriel O'Neill notifies him of the finding of same.

"It seems," Charley says, "this Shapiro is a tenderhearted guy, who is willing to help keep Gammer O'Neill with us a little longer when Doc Moggs says leaving the gifts with her will do it.

"So," Charley says, "everything is quite all right, as the coppers cannot figure anything except that maybe the rascal who takes the gifts from Shapiro gets conscience stricken, and leaves them the first place he can, and Miss Muriel O'Neill receives a ten-G's reward for finding the gifts and returning them. And," Charley says, "I hear Dancing Dan is in San Francisco and is figuring on reforming and becoming a dancing teacher, so he can marry Miss Muriel O'Neill, and of course," he says, "we all hope and trust she never learns any details of Dancing Dan's career."

Well, it is Christmas Eve a year later that I run into a guy by the name of Shotgun Sam, who is mobbed up with Heine Schmitz in Harlem, and who is a very, very obnoxious character indeed.

"Well, well, well," Shotgun says, "the last time I see you is another Christmas Eve like this, and you are coming out of Good Time Charley's joint, and," he says, "you certainly have your pots on."

"Well, Shotgun," I say, "I am sorry you get such a wrong impression of me, but the truth is," I say, "on the occasion you speak of, I am suffering from a dizzy feeling in my head."

"It is all right with me," Shotgun says. "I have a tip this guy Dancing Dan is in Good Time Charley's the night I see you, and Mockie Morgan, and Gunner Jack and me are casing the joint, because," he says, "Heine Schmitz is all sored up at Dan over some doll, although of course," Shotgun says, "it is all right now, as Heine has another doll.

"Anyway," he says, "we never get to see Dancing Dan. We watch the joint from six-thirty in the evening until daylight Christmas morning, and nobody goes in all night but old Ooky the Santa Claus guy in his Santa Claus make-up, and," Shotgun says, "nobody comes out except you and Good Time Charley and Ooky.

"Well," Shotgun says, "it is a great break for Dancing Dan he never goes in or comes out of Good Time Charley's, at that, because," he says, "we are waiting for him on the second-floor front of the building across the way with some nice little sawed-offs, and are under orders from Heine not to miss."

"Well, Shotgun," I say, "Merry Christmas."

"Well, all right," Shotgun says, "Merry Christmas."

Mr. K*A*P*L*A*N and the Magi

LEONARD Q. ROSS

Also in Manhattan, at Christmastime and the year around, but some spiritual distance away from Damon Runyon's Broadway, immigrants from all over Europe were struggling in the 1930s with what H. L. Mencken called "the American language." On paper, it was English, the same tongue that "foreigners" around the globe had been facing up to from the onset of the British Empire. But more than that, it was the gradual simmering, at times almost to boiling, of a cultural broth that has turned out to be unique. Not words alone, their meaning and pronunciation, were being learned, but attitudes, styles, and values, ways of thinking and looking; ways, for example, of keeping Christmas; like—in the case of the class at the American Night Preparatory School for Adults—how to form a committee and how to pick out the right Christmas present for the teacher. Leonard Q. Ross's stories of men and women in this learning process, droll and poignant as they are, point up how much the immigrants themselves were putting of their own substance and seasoning into the new cultural mix—perhaps

Leonard Q. Ross, "Mr. K*A*P*L*A*N and the Magi," in *The Education of H*Y*M*A*N K*A*P*L*A*N* (New York: Harcourt, Brace and World, 1937), 66–69. Permission to reprint this excerpt has been obtained from Harcourt Brace Jovanovich.

180

more than they took out. In addition to sympathizing with the heartfelt efforts of newcomers like Hyman Kaplan, anyone who has ever tried to write in dialect is moved as well by this author's strivings to put down on paper the speech of new Americans in the making.

When Mr. Parkhill saw that Miss Mitnick, Mr. Bloom, and Mr. Hyman Kaplan were absent, and that a strange excitement pervaded the beginners' grade, he realized that it was indeed the last night before the holidays and that Christmas was only a few days off. Each Christmas the classes in the American Night Preparatory School for Adults gave presents to their respective teachers. Mr. Parkhill, a veteran of many sentimental Yuletides, had come to know the procedure. That night, before the class session had begun, there must have been a hurried collection; a Gift Committee of three had been chosen; at this moment the Committee was probably in Mickey Goldstein's Arcade, bargaining feverishly, arguing about the appropriateness of a pair of pajamas or the color of a dozen linen handkerchiefs, debating whether Mr. Parkhill would prefer a pair of fleece-lined slippers to a set of mother-of-pearl cuff links.

"We shall concentrate on—er—spelling drill tonight," Mr. Parkhill announced.

The students smiled wisely, glanced at the three empty seats, exchanged knowing nods, and prepared for spelling drill. Miss Rochelle Goldberg giggled, then looked ashamed as Mrs. Rodriguez shot her a glare of reproval.

Mr. Parkhill always chose a spelling drill for the night before the Christmas vacation: it kept all the students busy simultaneously; it dampened the excitement of the occasion; above all, it kept him from the necessity of resorting to elaborate pedagogical efforts in order to hide his own embarrassment.

Mr. Parkhill called off the first words. Pens and pencils scratched, smiles died away, eyes grew serious, preoccupied, as the beginners' grade assaulted the spelling of "Banana . . . Romance . . . Groaning." Mr. Parkhill sighed. The class seemed incomplete without its star student, Miss Mitnick, and barren without its most remarkable one, Mr. Hyman Kaplan. Mr. Kaplan's most recent linguistic triumph had been a fervent speech extolling the D'Oyly Carte Company's performance of an operetta by two English gentlemen referred to as "Goldberg and Solomon."

"Charming . . . Horses . . . Float," Mr. Parkhill called off.

Mr. Parkhill's mind was not really on "Charming . . . Horses . . . Float." He could not help thinking of the momentous event which would take place that night. After the recess the students would come in with flushed faces and shining eyes. The Committee would be with them, and one member of the Committee, carrying an elaborately bound Christmas package, would be surrounded by several of the largest students in the class, who would try to hide the parcel from Mr. Parkhill's eyes. The class would come to order with uncommon rapidity. Then, just as Mr. Parkhill resumed the lesson, one member of the Committee would rise, apologize nervously for interrupting, place the package on Mr. Parkhill's desk, utter a few half-swallowed words, and rush back to his or her seat. Mr. Parkhill would say a few halting phrases of gratitude and surprise, everyone would smile and fidget uneasily, and the lesson would drag on, somehow, to the final and distant bell.

"*Accept . . . Except . . . Cucumber.*"

And as the students filed out after the final bell, they would cry "Merry Christmas, Happy New Year!" in joyous voices. The Committee would crowd around Mr. Parkhill with tremendous smiles to say that if the present wasn't *just right* in size or color (if it was something to wear) or in design (if it was something to use), Mr. Parkhill could exchange it. He didn't *have* to abide by the Committee's choice. He could exchange the present for *any*thing. They would have arranged all that carefully with Mr. Mickey Goldstein himself.

That was the ritual, fixed and unchanging, of the last night of school before Christmas.

"Nervous . . . Goose . . . Violets."

The hand on the clock crawled around to eight. Mr. Parkhill

could not keep his eyes off the three seats, so eloquent in their vacancy, which Miss Mitnick, Mr. Bloom, and Mr. Kaplan ordinarily graced with their presences. He could almost see these three in the last throes of decision in Mickey Goldstein's Arcade, harassed by the competitive attractions of gloves, neckties, an electric clock, a cane, spats, a "lifetime" fountain pen. Mr. Parkhill grew cold as he thought of a fountain pen. Three times already he had been presented with "lifetime" fountain pens, twice with "lifetime" pencils to match. Mr. Parkhill had exchanged these gifts: he had a fountain pen. Once he had chosen a woollen vest instead; once a pair of mittens and a watch chain. Mr. Parkhill hoped it wouldn't be a fountain pen. Or a smoking jacket. he had never been able to understand how the Committee in '32 had decided upon a smoking jacket. Mr. Parkhill did not smoke. He had exchanged it for fur-lined gloves.

Just as Mr. Parkhill called off "Sardine . . . *Ex*quisite . . . Palace" the recess bell rang. The heads of the students bobbed up as if propelled by a single spring. There was a rush to the door, Mr. Sam Pinsky well in the lead. Then, from the corridor, their voices rose. Mr. Parkhill began to print "Banana" on the blackboard, so that the students could correct their own papers after recess. He tried not to listen, but the voices in the corridor were like the chatter of a flock of sparrows.

"Hollo, Mitnick!"

"Bloom, Bloom, vat is it?"

"So vat did you gat, Keplen? Tell!"

Mr. Parkhill could hear Miss Mitnick's shy "We bought—" interrupted by Mr. Kaplan's stern cry, "Mitnick! Don' say! Plizz, faller-students! Come *don* mit de voices! Titcher vill awreddy hearink, you hollerink so lod! Still! Order! Plizz!" There was no question about it: Mr. Kaplan was born to command.

"Did you bought a Tsheaffer's Fontain Pan Sat, guarantee for de whole life, like *I* said?" one voice came through the door. A Sheaffer Fountain Pen Set, Guaranteed. That was Mrs. Moskowitz. Poor Mrs. Moskowitz, she showed so little imagination, even in her homework. "Moskovitz! Mein Gott!" the stentorian whisper of Mr. Kaplan soared through the air. "Vy you don' open op de door Titcher should *positivel* hear? Ha! Let's goink to odder and fromm de hall!"

The voices of the beginners' grade died away as they moved to the "odder and" of the corridor, like the chorus of "Aida" vanishing into Egyptian wings.

Mr. Parkhill printed "Charming" and "Horses" on the board. For a moment he thought he heard Mrs. Moskowitz's voice repeating stubbornly, "Did—you—bought—a—Tsheaf-fer—Fontain—Pan—Sat—*Guarantee?*"

Mr. Parkhill began to say to himself, "Thank you, all of you. It's *just* what I wanted," again and again. One Christmas he hadn't said "It's just what I wanted" and poor Mrs.Oppenheimer, chairman of the Committee that year, had been hounded by the students' recriminations for a month.

It seemed an eternity before the recess bell rang again. The class came in *en masse*, and hastened to the seats from which they would view the impending spectacle. The air hummed with silence.

Mr. Parkhill was printing "Cucumber." He did not turn his face from the board as he said, "Er—please begin correcting your own spelling. I have printed most of the words on the board."

There was a low and heated whispering. "Stend op, Mit-nick!" he heard Mr. Kaplan hiss. "You should stend op *too!*:

"The *whole* Committee," Mr. Bloom whispered. "Stand op!"

Apparently Miss Mitnick, a gazelle choked with embarrass-ment, did not have the fortitude to "stend op" with her col-leagues.

"A fine raprezantitif *you'll* gonna make!" Mr. Kaplan hissed scornfully. "Isn't for *mine* sek I'm eskink, Mitnick. Plizz *stend op!*"

There was a confused, half-muted murmur, and the an-guished voice of Miss Mitnick saying, "I *can't*." Mr. Parkhill printed "Violets" on the board. Then there was a tense silence.

And then the voice of Mr. Kaplan rose, firmly, clearly, with a decision and dignity which left no doubt as to its purpose.

"Podden me, Mr. Pockheel!"

It had come.

"Er—yes?" Mr. Parkhill turned to face the class.

Messrs. Bloom and Kaplan were standing side by side in front of Miss Mitnick's chair, holding between them a large, long package, wrapped in cellophane and tied with huge red ribbons. A pair of small hands touched the bottom of the box, listlessly. The owners of the hands, seated in the front row, was hidden by the box.

"De hends is Mitnick," Mr. Kaplan said apologetically.

Mr. Parkhill gazed at the tableau. It was touching.

"Er—yes?" he said again feebly, as if he had forgotten his lines and was repeating his cue.

"Hau Kay!" Mr. Kaplan whispered to his confreres. The hands disappeared behind the package. Mr. Kaplan and Mr. Bloom strode to the platform with the box. Mr. Kaplan was beaming, his smile rapturous, exalted. They placed the package on Mr. Parkhill's desk, Mr. bloom dropped back a few paces, and Mr. Kaplan said, "Mr. Pockheel! Is mine beeg honor, becawss I'm Chairman fromm de Buyink an' Deliverink to You a Prazent Committee, to givink to you dis fine peckitch."

Mr. Parkhill was about to stammer, "Oh, thank you," when Mr. Kaplan added hastily, "Also I'll sayink a few voids."

Mr. Kaplan took an envelope out of his pocket. He whispered loudly, "Mitnick, *you still got time to comm op mit de Committee*," but Miss Mitnick only blushed furiously and lowered her eyes. Mr. Kaplan sighed, straightened the envelope, smiled proudly at Mr. Parkhill, and read.

"Dear Titcher—dat's de beginnink. Ve stendink on de adge fromm a beeg holiday." He cleared his throat. "Ufcawss is all kinds holidays in U. S. A. Holidays for politic, for religious, an' *plain* holidays. In Fabrary, ve got Judge Vashington's boitday, a *fine* holiday. Also Abram Lincohen's. In May ve got Memorable Day, for dad soldiers. In July comms, netcheral, Fort July. Also ve have Labor Day, Denksgivink, for de Peelgrims, an' for de feenish fromm de Voild Var, *Armistress* Day."

Mr. Parkhill played with a piece of chalk nervously.

"But arond dis time year ve have a *difference* kind holiday, a spacial, movvellous time. Dat's called—Chrissmas."

Mr. Parkhill put the chalk down.

"All hover de voild," Mr. Kaplan mused, "is pipple cele-braking dis vunderful time. Becawss for som pipple is Chrissmas like for *odder* pipple is Passover. Or Chanukah, batter. De most fine, de most beauriful, de most *secret* holiday fromm de whole bunch!"

("'Sacred,' Mr. Kaplan, 'sacred,' " Mr. Parkhill thought, ever the pedagogue.)

"Ven ve valkink don de stritt an' is snow on de floor an' all kinds tarrible cold!" Mr. Kaplan's hand leaped up dramatically, like a flame. "Ven ve see in de vindows trees mit rad an' grin' laktric lights boinink! Ven is de time for tellink de fancy-tales abot Sandy Claws commink fromm Naut Pole on rainenimals, an' climbink don de jiminies mit *stockings* for all de leetle kits! Ven ve hearink abot de beauriful toughts of de Tree Vise Guys who vere follerink a star fromm de dasert! Ven pipple sayink, 'Oh, Mary Chrissmas! Oh, Heppy Noo Yiss! Oh, bast regotts!' Den ve *all* got a varm fillink in de heart for all humanity vhich should be brodders!"

Mr. Feigenbaum nodded philosophically at this profound thought; Mr. Kaplan, pleased, nodded back.

"*You* got de fillink, Mr. Pockheel. *I* got de fillink, dat's no qvastion abot! Bloom, Pinsky, Caravello, Schneiderman, even Mitnick"—Mr. Kaplan was punishing Miss Mitnick tenfold for her perfidy—"got de fillink! An' vat is it?" There was a momen-tous pause. "De Chrissmas Spirits!"

(" 'Spir*it*,' Mr. Kaplan, 'spir*it*,' " the voice of Mr. Parkhill's conscience said.)

"Now I'll givink de prazent," Mr. Kaplan announced sub-tly. Mr. Bloom shifted his weight. "Becawss you a foist-cless titcher, Mr. Pockheel, an' learn abot gremmer an' spallink an' de hoddest pots pernonciation—ve know is a planty hod jop mit soch students—so ve fill you should havink a sample fromm our—fromm our—" Mr. Kaplan turned the envelope over hastily—"aha! Fromm our santimental!"

Mr. Parkhill stared at the long package and the huge red ribbons.

"Fromm de cless, to our lovely Mr. Pockheel!"

Mr. Parkhill started. "Er—?" he asked involuntarily.

"Fromm de cless, to our lovely Mr. Pockheel!" Mr. Kaplan repeated with pride.

(" *Beloved*,' Mr. Kaplan, *'beloved.'* ")

A hush had fallen over the room. Mr. Kaplan, his eyes bright with joy, waited for Mr. Parkhill to take up the ritual. Mr. Parkhill tried to say, "Thank you, Mr. Kaplan," but the phrase seemed meaningless, so big, so ungainly, that it could not get through his throat. Without a word Mr. Parkhill began to open the package. He slid the big red ribbons off. He broke the tissue paper inside. For some reason his vision was blurred and it took him a moment to identify the present. It was a smoking jacket. It was black and gold, and a dragon with a green tongue was embroidered on the breast pocket.

"Horyantal style," Mr. Kaplan whispered delicately.

Mr. Parkhill nodded. The air trembled with the tension. Miss Mitnick looked as if she were ready to cry. Mr. Bloom peered intently over Mr. Kaplan's shoulder. Mrs. Moskowitz sat entranced, sighing with behemothian gasps. She looked as if she were at her daughter's wedding.

"Thank you," Mr. Parkhill stammered at last. "Thank you, all of you."

Mr. Bloom said, "Hold it op everyone should see."

Mr. Kaplan turned on Mr. Bloom with an icy look. "*I'm* de chairman!" he hissed.

"I—er—I can't tell you how much I appreciate your kindness," Mr. Parkhill said without lifting his eyes.

Mr. Kaplan smiled. "So now you'll plizz hold op de prazent. Plizz."

Mr. Parkhill took the smoking jacket out of the box and held it up for all to see. There were gasps—"Oh!"'s and "Ah!"'s and Mr. Kaplan's own ecstatic "My! Is beauriful!" The green tongue on the dragon seemed alive.

"Maybe ve made a mistake," Mr. Kaplan said hastily. "Maybe you don' smoke—dat's how *Mitnick* tought." The scorn dripped. "But I said, 'Ufcawss is Titcher smokink! Not in de cless, netcheral. At home! At least a *pipe*!' "

"No, no, you didn't make a mistake. It's—it's *just* what I wanted!"

The great smile on Mr. Kaplan's face became dazzling. "Hooray! Vear in de bast fromm helt!" he cried impetuously. "Mary Chrissmas! Heppy Noo Yiss! You should have a *hondert* more!"

This was the signal for a chorus of acclaim. "Mary Chrissmas!" "Wear in best of health!" "Happy New Year!" Miss Schneiderman burst into applause, followed by Mr. Scymzak and Mr. Weinstein. Miss Caravello, carried away by all the excitement, uttered some felicitations in rapid Italian. Mrs. Moskowitz sighed once more and said, "Soch a *sveet* ceremonia." Miss Mitnick smiled feebly, blushing, and twisted her handkerchief.

The ceremony was over. Mr. Parkhill began to put the smoking jacket back into the box with fumbling hands. Mr. Bloom marched back to his seat. But Mr. Kaplan stepped a little closer to the desk. The smile had congealed on Mr. Kaplan's face. It was poignant and profoundly earnest.

"Er—thank you, Mr. Kaplan," Mr. Parkhill said gently.

Mr. Kaplan shuffled his feet, looking at the floor. For the first time since Mr. Parkhill had known him, Mr. Kaplan seemed to be embarrassed. Then, just as he turned to rush back to his seat, Mr. Kaplan whispered, so softly that no ears but Mr. Parkhill's heard it, "Maybe de spitch I rad vas too *formmal*. But avery void I said—it came fromm *below mine heart*!"

Mr. Parkhill felt that, for all his weird, unorthodox English, Mr. Kaplan had spoken with the tongues of the Magi.

The Last Christmas Tree

WILLIAM L. WHITE

December 25, 1939. Although our nation was still almost two years away from the Japanese attack on Pearl Harbor, the hearts and minds (and in many cases the sons and brothers) of Americans were overseas with the British, who had joined France in September of that year to try to stop Hitler's invasive sweep of Europe. William L. White, son of the renowned Progressive and Emporia Gazette publisher William Allen White, was the most famous of America's early war correspondents. For CBS radio on Christmas night in 1939, he broadcast a report from the Finnish-Russian front. He was in Finland, which he described with touching irony as "the country where our legend of Santa Claus and his reindeer first began." Finding his way to the front by following the "sound of big guns from far off," tracing a woodland trail through the deep snow, White dispatched a report that moved the nation and inspired the playwright Robert Sherwood (a dramatist who was himself a member of FDR's administration) to write the drama, There Shall Be No Night.

William L. White, "The Last Christmas Tree," text supplied by Columbia Broadcasting System from radio broadcast of 25 December 1939. Gratitude is extended to Mrs. William L. White of Emporia, Kansas, for assistance in securing the text as originally aired.

W. L. White speaking to you on this Christmas night from Finland, the country where our legend of Santa Claus and his reindeer first began. Reindeer still pull sleighs in the north of Finland tonight, carrying supplies to the little nation's army which is fighting to press back the great army which would come in. But if part of our Christmas story began in Finland, this is also the country where Christmas ends, for beyond the line of its armies lies that great land where there is no Christmas any more, and where the memory of its stories is dimming fast. And this is why, since I have come from a front line post-of-command of this Finnish army, I can tell you tonight about the last Christmas tree. And although you have many finer ones in America tonight, tall trees gay with tinsel, proud with sparkling colored balls, and rich with presents underneath wrapped in pretty papers and tied with silver cords, I think you would like these even better when you know about that brave and sad little Christmas tree at the very edge of the land where Christmas ends.

Even without our guide we might have found the last Christmas tree by following the sound of big guns from far off. Presently when they were close, we left our cars and followed a trail in the deep snow which wound toward the guns through a tall spruce forest, the snow on their branches glistening in the moonlight. The trail led past the second line dugouts on through the woods toward the guns, and sometimes we stepped aside to let pass a horse drawn sleigh, fitted to carry warm boilers of steaming hot soup up to the men ahead. We were told to walk quietly now. Talking in whispers, we passed places where the white snow had been gashed deep by shell craters, and at last we came to the front line post-of-command. The officer here greeted us in a tired voice saying we should go no further, as this forest had only yesterday been retaken from the Russians whose lines were a few hundred yards ahead, and his men had not had time to dig safe trenches. Beyond us was no real front line but only machine gun nests, dugouts and a few shallow trenches, a place where it was not safe for any man to crawl who had not first seen the country by clear light of day. But perhaps we would like to go down into his front line command post dugout, talk to his men and see their Christmas tree.

The dugout was deep beneath snow and earth, and warmed from the zero weather by a tiny stove. Tired men were lying on the straw-strewn floor, and when they rose to greet us we could see by the light of the shaded lantern that their faces were weary and unshaven. The officer explained for this, saying fighting had been very hard, the enemy had greatly outnumbered them, so when there was no fighting there was time for little but sleep.

We asked him what the men would have for Christmas dinner and he told us their mess kits would be filled with thick warm pea soup, rich with pieces of mutton and pork, with plenty of bread spread thick with butter, and for dessert porridge with sugar. And then, because it was Christmas, the army had sent up four Christmas hams, which would be sliced and eaten with the bread.

He said we should remember that several sledges had come laden with Christmas presents for the men—warm sweaters and socks knitted by their wives, or Christmas cookies and tarts baked by them, and there would be something for each man.

We asked when the men up ahead in the last machine gun posts and dugouts would get their presents, and he said not until tomorrow, but they would not mind, because each man knew why he must be there, and what must be done, and not one would wish himself in any other place, and because the people of this country love Christmas so much, each one could carry it with him in his heart.

Then we asked if, at our own risk, we might not crawl up and give them some of the cigarets and sweets and tobacco we had brought. He shook his head saying that if we made a noise and attracted Russian artillery there might be losses among his men, and this was not good to happen on Christmas night.

But tomorrow those men would get their presents in this dugout, and also the Christmas tree would be saved for them to see. The tiny tree was standing near the stove. Little red and white wax candles had been tied by men's clumsy fingers to its branches. The officer said the candles could not be lit, because this might be seen by bombers through the dugout's canvas roof. Also tied to the green spruce twigs were a few gum drops—the kind you buy twisted in colored wax papers. At the very top was tied not a sparkling glass star but a cheap cardboard image of Santa Claus, and this was all. No strips of tinsel, no shining balls, no winking electric lights—. You can be very glad that the Christmas tree in your home tonight is so much finer.

We asked the officer who sent these ornaments and he smiled kindly and said that they came from a very small girl whose father was out on the last line tonight, and with them a note from her mother explaining that the child was very young, and could not understand why he could not come back to them even on Christmas, and had cried bitterly until they let her send him these little things so that at least he could have his own Christmas tree. So the tree would be kept as it was in the dugout until he came back from his outpost tomorrow.

So when you take your last look at your own fine tree tonight before turning out its lights, I think you will like it even better since you know about the last sad little Christmas tree of all, which could not even have its poor candles lit because it faces the land where there is no Christmas. Returning you now to Columbia in New York. . . .

The Homecoming

EARL HAMNER, JR.

While most individuals think of the Great Depression in America as a modern economic tragedy, it also was a time when family life was at its closest. In "The Homecoming" Earl Hamner recalls some of his youthful experiences in the Blue Ridge Mountains. In this episode, Olivia and her eight children await the return of her husband, Clay, who had been working as a machinist in Waynesboro. A bitter winter blizzard on Christmas Eve complicates Clay's arrival, leaving the family at home time to contemplate the real meaning of the holiday. This story had much to do with creating the television series, "The Waltons," which now has grown from an American to an international classic.

All day the cold Virginia sky had hung low over Spencer's Mountain. It was a leaden, silent, moist presence. It promised snow before the fall of night.

Looking from her kitchen window, Olivia Spencer observed the ashen sky. It did not *feel* like Christmas. That moment that had always come in other years, that mingled feeling of excite-

Earl Hamner, Jr., *The Homecoming: A Novel About Spencer's Mountain* (New York: Random House, 1973), 123–29. Reprinted with the permission of Gerald Summer, Random House.

ment and promise that she called "The Christmas Spirit," had evaded her. She had no patience with holiday frivolity. She wished for spring.

This year, if it were not for the children, she might even be tempted to treat Christmas as just another day. Prospects being what they were, it could well turn out to be just another day, no matter how hard she tried to make it festive.

As Olivia watched from her window, the snow began. It arrived in a thin curtain that appeared at the edge of the barn, then swept down across the yard and over the house.

"Y'all children want to see somethen pretty?" she called.

The children, all eight of them, converged on the window and crowded their red heads around their mother. They looked out toward the barn and past it across field and woodland to where Spencer's Mountain was growing dim, softly outlined through the cold, gently drifting whiteness.

On the tallest limb of the crab-apple tree perched a cardinal.

"That redbird is goen to freeze tonight," observed Luke. Luke was ten, the handsome one with hair almost the same shade as the redbird in the crab-apple tree.

"He won't freeze," said Olivia. "A redbird has got the knack of surviven winter. Otherwise he'd of headed South."

"I wish my daddy could fly," said Shirley solemnly. Shirley was the sensitive one.

Her wish that her father could fly like a bird was met with howls of laughter. Shirley pouted prettily and looked at her brothers and sisters with an injured air.

"Y'all leave Shirley alone," warned Olivia. She hugged the little girl to her and said, "Don't you worry about your daddy. He's goen to be home for Christmas."

"He won't be here if he stops off at Miss Emma and Miss Etta's," said Becky, who was 13 and had a mind of her own.

"Huh!" said Olivia, with the contempt she reserved for alcohol, those who sold it and those who had a weakness for it. "The day your daddy spends Christmas Eve with two old lady bootleggers is the day I walk out of this house."

"Where'll we go, Mama?" asked Pattie-Cake.

"Your daddy's goen to be home," Olivia assured Pattie-Cake. "Y'all just stop worryen."

Clay Spencer could only be with his family on weekends. When something called "the Depression" had happened in Washington or New York or some distant place, the soapstone plant had closed down, and all the men in the village had to find other jobs. Clay had found work as a machinist at the Du Pont Company in Waynesboro, which was 40 miles away. He had no car, so every Friday night he would take the Trailways bus to Charlottesville and transfer to the southbound bus that let him off at Hickory Creek on Route 29. From there Clay would walk the remaining six miles or hitchhike if a car happened to go past.

He wouldn't stop at the Staples place tonight, Olivia thought. Not on Christmas Eve. She sometimes thought she would enjoy setting sticks of dynamite under Miss Emma and Miss Etta Staples' house and blowing it sky-high. She enjoyed the vision of the stately, decayed old house and its shelves of Mason jars filled with the notorious "Recipe" the old ladies distilled being blown right off the map.

Olivia realized that the children were still gazing at her with concern.

"Come on," she said. "There's work to do. Who's goen to crack walnuts for my applesauce cake?"

Everybody wanted to crack walnuts. Olivia realized their willingness stemmed from the fact that it would be an excuse to get out into the snow.

"You look after everybody, Clay-Boy," called Olivia as the children filed out. "You're the oldest."

"Yes, ma'am," answered Clay-Boy, a thin boy of 15 with a serious, freckled face. If Clay-Boy had any wish in life, it was that his mother would stop reminding him that he was the oldest.

I'm like some old mother duck, he thought as he made his way through the new snow to the barn, followed by Matt, Becky, Shirley, Mark, Luke, John and Pattie-Cake.

All of the children had red hair, but on each head the shade was a little different. Some had the brown eyes of their father, and some had their mother's green eyes, but on each of them there was a stamp of grace in build and movement. It was this their father voiced when he said, as he often did, "Every one of my babies is a thoroughbred."

Reaching the barn, Clay-Boy lifted the latch and opened the door to the storeroom. The children flowed in past him like heedless, impatient baby chicks. Clay-Boy pulled the burlap sack filled with black walnuts from the bin where he had stored them in October, slung the sack over his shoulder and started back toward the house.

As they worked, Pattie-Cake, who was eight, announced proudly, "I wrote a letter to Santa Claus."

John, who was nine and practical, said, "It won't do you a speck of good. How you goen to get it to him? No letter goen to get to the North Pole by tonight."

"What'll I do, Clay-Boy?" asked Pattie-Cake anxiously.

"You give it to me, honey," said Clay-Boy. "Ill take it down to the post office and send it special delivery."

"What did you ask Santa Claus to bring you, honey?" asked Matt, who was the industrious one and had already cracked six walnuts.

"One whole page in the Sears, Roebuck catalogue," replied Pattie-Cake. "A whole page of dolls."

"I been thinken about writen to him myself," said John. "For a piano and a pair of ice skates."

"Huh!" said Becky in a superior way.

"What's that 'huh' for?" asked Clay-Boy.

"Everybody's so ignorant around here, believen in Santa Claus," snorted Becky. "There's no such thing. It's just somethen Mama and Daddy made up."

"I don't believe you," said Pattie-Cake, and began to weep. Large, salty tears flowed down her cheeks and fell on the one walnut she still struggled to crack.

"You're bad, Becky," said Matt, and gave her a push that sent her sprawling off the porch. Becky rose from the ground, clenched her fists and walked grimly back to Matt.

"Son, you're goen to be sorry you did that," she threatened.

"You watch it, young lady," warned Clay-Boy. "You just watch that biggity talk."

"I'm not goen to have anything to do with any of you," said Becky. She stuck her nose up in the air and walked off into the yard, catching snowflakes on the tip of her tongue. Why did they always give her nothing but trouble?

On the porch the other children had nearly filled the cup with walnuts.

"There is too a Santa Claus, isn't there, Clay-Boy?" asked Pattie-Cake.

"Sho'," answered Clay-Boy reassuringly. "Wait'll in the mornen. You'll see."

Clay-Boy wished he had not spoken so affirmatively. He knew that his mother had not had the money to buy any presents for the children. Their only chance for presents from Santa Claus was if their father brought them, and Clay-Boy had learned enough to know the many temptations that lay in the path of a man who had labored hard all week and who had just received his pay.

Olivia had already started her applesauce cake when the children trooped in with the walnuts. The kitchen steamed with the aroma of cloves, cinnamon and nutmeg. At the old wood-burning cooking range Olivia was stirring the applesauce and singing "O Little Town of Bethlehem."

"Mama's got The Christmas Spirit!" exclaimed John.

"Just come up on me all of a sudden," declared Olivia. "Clay-Boy, you go get the tree!"

Two applesauce cakes were on display in the middle of the kitchen table when Clay-Boy walked in. He breathed in the spicy aroma appreciatively. Something had happened during his absence. There was some quickening of excitement, a sense of Christmas rushing inexorably down upon them, but in spite of the two proud cakes he knew that his mother was not really prepared for the day.

"Did you get the tree?" she asked.

"Yes, ma'am," he answered. "It's out on the porch."

"I sent the children over to ask Mama and Papa to come have supper with us."

Clay-Boy noticed that the ham had been pared down to the bone and that every edible slice had been removed.

"Mama, what are we goen to have for the Christmas dinner?"

"I don't know, boy," answered Olivia. "Maybe I'll wring Gretchen's neck and make stew and dumplens."

"Gretchen's a layen hen," objected Clay-Boy. "What'll we do for eggs if we make a stew out of her?"

"I don't know that either," replied Olivia. "I'm feelen reckless. Let tomorrow take care of itself."

"What about Santa Claus for the kids?" he asked.

"I made some little things," answered Olivia. "Dresses for each of the girls. Warm pajamas for you boys."

"They'll know you made them," observed Clay-Boy. "They'll know they're not from Santa Claus. They'll stop believen."

"Maybe it's time they did," said Olivia soberly. "In hard times like these maybe it's silly to let children go on believen in foolishness."

"You reckon the Depression will last forever, Mama?"

"I don't know, boy," answered Olivia wearily. "Mr. Roosevelt says it won't. Now stop worryen about things you can't help. Go put up the Christmas tree. At least we'll have somethen pretty to look at."

Just then there was a great stomping of feet on the back porch. The children had arrived home. Olivia rushed to the kitchen door, hoping they might have encountered Clay, but there were only the children and their grandparents.

"Merry Christmas, daughter," boomed Homer Italiano.

"Come on in, Papa," cried Olivia. "How are you, Mama?"

"I think I got a crick in my back," replied Ida. Homer's wife was a thin wraith of a woman who, unlike her husband, spoke in a thin near-whisper.

Alone with his wife, Homer was tender and dependent, an

indulged child as much as a husband, but when they were in the presence of others he found it necessary to deride Ida's talents and personality.

"That woman is crazy," remarked Homer with a wondering shake of his head. "Been streaken all over the hills taken orders for the Larkin Company. Old woman like her ought to be home 'stead of scooten 'round like a snowplow!"

"I made three dollars," protested Ida. "And that's three dollars we wouldn't have if I hadn't been out taken orders."

"Where's Clay, daughter?" asked Homer.

"Somewhere between here and Waynesboro," answered Olivia. "Be here soon, I reckon."

"I wouldn't count on it," observed Ida. "I'll bet you he's down yonder drinken whisky with those Staples women right this second." Ida was a pillar of the Baptist Church and she lost no opportunity to remind her daughter that she had married a heathen.

"Mama, I won't have you talken about Clay that way," objected Olivia.

"He drinks, don't he?" snapped Ida.

"He *takes* a drink," said Olivia. "There's a difference. Anyway it's Christmas Eve. Clay'll want to be with his family."

"At least he's worken," said Homer. "That's more'n can be said for the rest of us. I was listenen to the radio. They're doen right smart talken about this New Deal."

"I hear 'em talken about it all the time, but I don't know what it means," said Ida.

"It means we got a man in the White House that's goen to do somethen," announced Homer. "Roosevelt says he's goen to open the banks, and I believe he'll do it."

"I don't care what they do as long as they get the mill open and Clay can come home to work again," said Olivia.

Just then they heard the sounds of footsteps, stomping off snow on the back porch.

"There's Daddy," several voices shouted in unison, but standing on the back porch was Charlie Sneed. Before the Depression he had worked beside Clay in the machine shop.

Since the mill had closed, he had become a backwoods Robin
Hood, poaching game, some of which he sold in Charlottesville
for cash money; the rest he gave to friends or families he knew
to be in special need.

"Where's Clay?" asked Charlie as he entered the kitchen and
closed the door behind him.

"He's late tonight," said Olivia.

"Hey there, Mr. Homer, Miss Ida. How y'all?" asked Charlie. "Ep Bridges been around tonight?"

Ep Bridges was the local sheriff and game warden.

"I saw his truck go by once today," answered Olivia. "But
he hasn't been around here."

Now Charlie turned to the children, who regarded him
curiously. "Can you kids keep your mouths shut if I let you in
on a secret?"

"Sure, Charlie," they answered.

With an air of mystery but yet taking pleasure in what he
was doing, Charlie opened the kitchen door and stepped outside. When he came back in he carried a wild turkey gobbler.

"I knew Clay wouldn't have a chance to go hunten this
Christmas so I thought he'd appreciate a little meat on the
table."

Tears welled up in Olivia's eyes. She had worried all day
about what she would serve for Christmas dinner. Now she
envisioned the turkey, roasted a rich brown, sitting in the middle
of the table on her blue-willow platter.

"We're much obliged to you, Charlie," said Olivia, taking
the turkey from him and carrying it to the sink. "This turkey is
the answer to my prayers. I declare, I think I'll cook it tonight!
Won't Clay Spencer be surprised when he walks in that door
and finds a Christmas turkey roasten in the oven!"

The storm outside seemed less threatening now. Christmas
dinner, if nothing else, was assured. If only Clay were here she
could ignore completely the snow-laden wind that roared in
baffled rage at the windows and doors.

Homer and Ida had gone home and Olivia was feeding wood to
the old cooking range. She felt better now that she had a plan. It

was a village custom that if the man of the house did not return home at some reasonable hour the oldest child in the family would go looking for him. Olivia had taken some pride that she had never had to send Clay-Boy to look for Clay, but tonight she would sacrifice pride. Quietly she called Clay-Boy into the kitchen.

"I didn't want to say it in front of anybody, but I'm worried about your daddy."

"I expect his bus is late. It's a right snowy night."

"Could be any one of a thousand things. Bus could of slid off the road. Maybe he's already at Hickory Creek and the snow's too thick for him to walk the six miles home."

"I could go look for him, I reckon," said Clay-Boy.

"I thought maybe if you could find Charlie Sneed. He's got that old truck. You tell him I said to ride you over to Hickory Creek and see if there's any sign of Clay walken."

"Charlie's down at the pool hall, or was. I saw his truck."

"You try to catch him. Tell Charlie we'll pay for the gas."

Charlie Sneed's truck was still parked in front of the pool hall when Clay-Boy staggered up through the blizzard. He was uncertain of his reception here. There was an unwritten law that no children and no decent woman ever entered. It was strictly a man's preserve and a jealously guarded one.

"Hey," said a voice that came from Ike Godsey, the bald, round-faced owner, bartender, chef and bouncer combined. "You know I can't serve you, Clay-Boy."

"I know that, Mr. Godsey," answered Clay-Boy. "I'm looken for Charlie Sneed."

Ike peered into the adjoining room, his face clouded with disgust. He beckoned Clay-Boy closer.

"Is your daddy home from Waynesboro yet?"

"No, sir," answered Clay-Boy, "but we're looken for him any minute."

"I wish he'd get here. Maybe he'd talk sense into Ep Bridges."

"What's Ep done now?"

"Arrested Charlie Sneed for hunten out of season. Got him handcuffed in yonder. Claims he goen to throw him in the jail up in Lovingston."

As sympathetic as he was to Charlie's misfortune, Clay-Boy regretted it for personal reasons. He knew of no one else he could ask for a ride to Hickory Creek. Clay-Boy started back toward the door past the entrance to the poolroom. He had not intended to peer in, but when he did, he stopped full in his tracks at the sight of Charlie, sitting forlornly on the bench he was handcuffed to.

"Lord God, Charlie!" exclaimed Clay-Boy sympathetically. "How'd it happen?"

"I run over a calf up yonder on the road a piece. Throwed him in the back of the truck instead of letten him lay there and go to waste."

"First calf I ever seen had ten-point antlers," laughed Ep Bridges from the pool table.

"Ep, be a Christian and let me off," pleaded Charlie. "Christmas ain't no time to throw a man in that Lovingston jail. It's cold and drafty. I'm liable to catch pneumonia and die before mornen. You want it on your conscience I died of pneumonia on Christmas Day?"

"You should of thought about that when you dropped that buck. Come on, Charlie, let's go to Lovingston," said Ep. He crossed to the bench where he had handcuffed his prisoner and unlocked the side that held Charlie to the bench.

"Wait a minute, Ep," said Charlie, and turned to Clay-Boy. "You run and tell your daddy about the fix I'm in."

"Daddy ain't home yet," said Clay-Boy. "We still setten up for him."

"What boy is this, Charlie?" asked the sheriff.

"He's Clay Spencer's boy," said Charlie.

"Last time I laid eyes on Clay Spencer was when I raided that old colored church. They had a poker game goen."

"That's probably where he is right this minute," said Charlie wistfully.

"One thing's sure. You ain't goen to be joined up with him," said the sheriff, and led Charlie to the door.

"Mr. Bridges," called Clay-Boy.

The sheriff turned and looked back at the boy curiously. Clay-Boy hesitated. He hated to ask a favor of a man who was taking Charlie Sneed to jail, but he was desperate.

"You'll be goen by the colored church on your way to Lovingston, won't you?"

"Sho'," replied Ep.

"You wouldn't give me a ride, would you?" asked Clay-Boy. "I just want to see if my daddy happens to be there."

"I ain't supposed to carry riders," said Ep, considering. "But what the hell! It's Christmas! Come on!"

The blizzard had abated somewhat, but the snow still fell heavily, making it difficult for Ep Bridges to find the road and, when he found it, to stick to it. There had been no cars in or out of the village, so there were no tracks for him to follow. Coming to some place where there was a question, he would get out of the car, shine his powerful torchlight around until he was sure of the direction he should take, and then take it.

When he came to the turnoff to the First Abyssinian Baptist Church, he paused briefly to let the boy out of the car.

"You tell your daddy to come go my bail," called Charlie just before Ep Bridges reached over, slammed the door shut and moved off down the road.

Watching the glow of Ep Bridges' headlights swiftly disappear into the soft sibilant snow, Clay-Boy wished he had brought a flashlight. The First Abyssinian Baptist Church was a quarter of a mile down an unpaved road; the snow was already nearly a foot deep and he had no light to guide him. Blindly, Clay-Boy started down the road.

Somewhere above the screaming wind and the biting whine of snow, Clay-Boy heard singing voices. The voices grew stronger, and by the time he came to the graveyard behind the church, Clay-Boy knew that no white men were playing a clandestine game of poker in the church tonight. The rightful tenants had occupied it, and a service was in progress.

Clay-Boy entered the vestibule, which was separated from the main church room by folding doors. He had intended to rest there for a moment and warm himself, but as he opened the outer door the wind forced the folding doors open and row after row of startled dark faces turned toward him.

He stood there for a moment, uncomfortable that he had interrupted the service, seeing in the eyes that gazed at him that he had no right there and was not welcome. A wave of resentment flowed through the congregation. He wanted to speak, to tell them that he was not one of the white men who desecrated their church with their poker playing, but he could not find the words to say it.

"Is that you, Clay-Boy?"

The speaker was a man standing at the foot of the center aisle. He was a man in his 50s, a vigorous, muscular, tall man whose hair was just beginning to be touched with gray. Because the man was dressed in a black suit, white shirt and black tie, Clay-Boy had not recognized Hawthorne Dooly, a farmer whose land Clay-Boy and his father had often gone to to hunt and fish, a leader in the Negro community.

"Hey, Hawthorne," said Clay-Boy.

"What you doen out here?"

"I was lost," said Clay-Boy.

"Come on and warm yourself," said Hawthorne.

"I don't want to get in the way," said Clay-Boy.

"Come on up to the fire," said Hawthorne, and met Clay-Boy halfway down the aisle of wooden benches and led him to where the pot-bellied stove glowed red and hot. Clay-Boy was conscious of the watching eyes turning from resentment to acceptance, and he was relieved.

"Scrunch over," Hawthorne called to a family on the bench nearest the fire. Obliging, smiling now that he was a welcome guest, the family moved together to make room for Clay-Boy at the end of the bench.

Hawthorne returned to his position in front of the congregation, looked out over his flock and announced, "We'll continue the service."

A powerful voice, controlled, tremulous, reverent, began to sing, and when Clay-Boy looked he saw that it was Hawthorne, his face lifted to heaven, his eyes closed.

> *"O holy night! The stars are brightly shining,*
> *It is the night of the dear Savior's birth!*
> *Long lay the world in sin and error pining,*
> *Till he appeared and the soul felt its worth."*

Shivers went down Clay-Boy's back. He had heard the hymn since he was a baby, carried to church in his mother's arms, but he had never heard it sung this way before. Hawthorne crooned the song, stroked and caressed it with tenderness, letting his voice cling to the melody, until the feeling and the events the song described seemed to be taking place now and here and not two thousand years ago in some distant Biblical storybook place.

The song ended; the congregation in a single voice spoke, "Glory Hallelujah!"

Hawthorne bowed his head. "We thank Thee, Father, for the Gift of Thy Son. Help us to be worthy of Thy sacrifice, and to walk in Thy light all the days of our lives. Amen."

"Amen," answered the congregation.

Hawthorne Dooly glanced toward the rear of the church and nodded a signal.

"Ho-ho-ho!" came a booming voice from the vestibule. Every head turned and the children's eyes widened with awe as a roly-poly Santa Claus came marching up the aisle.

"Merry Christmas! Merrrry Christmas!" he called as he stopped to pinch some youngster's cheek.

Clay-Boy started for the door while families rose and visited with each other.

As he made his way past the Negro faces, it came to him that he did not really know any Negroes. He knew those in the village, but he had never been in one of their homes and did not know what they yearned for or what their dreams were. He felt a sense of loss that an entire community existed within the larger community and he did not know one of them beyond his name and face.

When he reached the door, Hawthorne Dooly was waiting for him.

"You out looken for your daddy?" asked Hawthorne.

"I reckon so," answered Clay-Boy.

"Have you tried the Staples place?"

"No, I didn't. So far out there."

"It ain't all that far if you've got transportation," said Hawthorne. "You come and ride on General with me."

Gratefully Clay-Boy accepted the offer and a short while later was riding through the silver night on a white horse with a black man guiding the way. Once the snow lifted, the moon shone sulkily through scudding clouds. Clay-Boy could see their shadow moving along with them in the glittering luster that blanketed the world. We could be two of the wise men, hurrying after the star, thought Clay-Boy.

In observance of Christmas Eve, Miss Emma and Miss Etta Staples had gotten out of the overalls they usually wore and changed into finery. It was Emma's idea. Etta was a ninny and never had an idea of her own. It would have been just like her to have forgotten Christmas altogether and worked right through to New Year's. But Emma remembered, and it was she who cut the tree and set it up, laid the fire in the seldom-used front room.

While Etta decorated the tree, Emma arranged the crèche on the old walnut end table beside the horsehair sofa. She had placed the Jesus figure in the manger and was reaching for a lamb when there came a knocking at the front door.

"Someone has run out of Recipe!" said Etta.

"I was sure everybody had laid in a good supply," said Emma and opened the door.

"Who is it?" asked Emma doubtfully, observing the snow-covered figure just beyond the door.

"Clay-Boy Spencer," answered the boy through lips that were numb with cold.

"What a treat!" cried Miss Emma. "Company, Etta!" she called gaily over her shoulder. "It's Clay Spencer's son!"

"Why, you're just caked with snow!" said Miss Etta, taking his jacket and hanging it on the clothes rack.

"You look frozen to death," cried Miss Emma. "Come by the fire and warm yourself."

Clay-Boy had been in the kitchen of the Staples' house, but he had never seen the front room. It was grand beyond his imagining. Tasseled lamps rested on heavy hand-carved tables. Two horsehair love seats flanked the fireplace. In a corner an ancient grandfather's clock was stopped at 12 minutes past two, and Miss Etta beamed at him from beside a Christmas tree that shimmered with glowing ornaments.

"Etta, this boy is frozen through and through. Take off your shoes, Clay-Boy, and let them dry while you visit. Etta, bring some eggnog and put some Recipe in it."

"Don't go to any trouble," said Clay-Boy, but Miss Etta was already on her way. "I can't stay but a minute."

"Nonsense," said Miss Emma. "Take off those wet shoes before you come down with lung trouble. The socks, too."

Now Miss Emma left the room also and Clay-Boy sat down on the love seat and held his feet out toward the warmth of the fireplace. He felt silly, but he was grateful as the numbing cold began to seep out of his fingers and toes.

Miss Emma and Miss Etta returned together. Miss Emma carried a large, steaming pan of water.

"Soak your feet in this hot water," she commanded. "It will ward off lung disease."

Now Miss Etta came forward carrying a tray on which she had arranged a silver pitcher and three silver mugs.

"This will warm you up," she promised. Clay-Boy accepted one of the mugs, which was filled with eggnog lightly sprinkled with cinnamon. Something in it warmed him all the way to the pit of his stomach and, once it rested there, radiated throughout the rest of his body. Miss Emma and Miss Etta waited expectantly for some reaction from him.

"It's powerful good," said Clay-Boy. "What's in it?"

"It's Papa's Recipe," explained Miss Emma. "Papa used to make it all the time and then when he passed on we used to get so many calls for it that Sister and I just kept on making it. It gives us something to do in our old age, and it makes people happy. Etta, help Clay-Boy to some more eggnog."

Miss Etta poured, and Clay-Boy accepted the refilled cup gratefully. He was warm now from head to toe, and he was beginning to feel so light-headed and relaxed that it seemed the most natural thing in the world to be sitting with two antique ladies, sipping eggnog while his feet soaked in a pan of hot water.

"How are your mother and all those dear children?" inquired Miss Etta.

"Everybody's just fine," said Clay-Boy.

"Your father never comes but what he says for us to come over and visit," observed Miss Emma, "but we never seem to get out any more."

"We're getting old," said Miss Etta proudly. "Hard to get around when you're old."

"Your daddy says you make good grades at school," said Miss Emma, looking at Clay-Boy appraisingly.

"Yes, ma'am."

"What are you going to do with your life?"

"I don't know yet."

"If you had your choice, what would you be?"

Clay-Boy had never confessed his secret yearning to anyone in the world before, but the eggnog while warming him had also released his inhibitions.

"You know these Big Five tablets?" he asked. "Like you do homework in?"

Miss Emma nodded interestedly.

"I keep one under my mattress."

"You're just like Etta," said Miss Emma. "She hides things under her mattress too."

"Just letters from my beaux," said Miss Etta, then turned accusingly to her sister. "And now that I know you've been snooping I'm going to hide them somewhere else."

"Her beaux!" cried Miss Emma to no one in particular and, for a while, each of them was alone with her separate thoughts.

"Etta, put a record on the Victrola," said Miss Emma.

Miss Etta rose and floated to the Victrola. She searched about in the storage cabinet beneath the machine, found a record and placed it on the turntable.

"It probably needs winding," advised Miss Emma. "It hasn't been used since the last time we had a party."

"That was before Papa died," said Miss Etta as she cranked the handle of the Victrola.

The two old women and the boy listened silently as Enrico Caruso sang "It Came Upon the Midnight Clear."

For a moment, when the carol was over, they remained still.

"The nice thing about life," said Miss Etta, "is you never know when there's going to be a party."

"It wouldn't of been if Clay-Boy Spencer hadn't taken it in mind to stop in," said Miss Emma.

When Clay-Boy realized that they thought the object of his trip had been to pay a call, he decided not to tell them otherwise. His father was obviously not there, nor had he been there, for the old ladies would surely have mentioned it.

But now when he looked there were four old ladies, a twin Miss Emma and a twin Miss Etta, their images blurring and wavering into each other. He roused himself and with some difficulty managed to stand upright, although the rest of the room swam unsteadily.

"I certainly appreciate everything," he said in the general direction of his hostesses.

"Oh, you mustn't go yet," cried Miss Etta. "It's still the shank of the evening!"

"No, ma'am, I expect it's getten along toward eleven o'clock."

"How are you traveling, Clay-Boy?" asked Miss Emma.

"On foot, ma'am," he replied.

Suddenly Miss Etta rose and crossed to her sister and whispered something in her ear. She looked back to Clay-Boy briefly. "Excuse my bad manners," she said, and then the two ladies held a brief whispered conference.

At the end of it, Miss Emma rose, fixed an eye on Clay-Boy and said, "Wait here."

When her sister left the room, Miss Etta smiled at Clay-Boy and said, "We've arranged a surprise for you." Clay-Boy looked worriedly after Miss Emma as he heard a door slam at the back of the house.

"I really ought to be getten home."

"Oh, you'll be home before you know it," said Miss Etta. "Now get into your things while I get the blankets!"

Clay-Boy felt he had fallen into the clutches of two old Christmas witches, and he was tempted to slip out of the front door before either of them returned with whatever insane plan they had for getting him home.

He felt his socks, which had been hanging by the fireplace, and, grateful that they were almost dry, he slipped them on. His shoes were stiff from having dried so close to the fire, but he slipped them on his feet and was lacing them up when Miss Etta appeared at the foot of the stairway. She had put on an old fur coat with a hat to match and she carried several lap robes in her arms.

From somewhere outside the house came the silver jingle of bells.

"There she is!" cried Miss Etta. "Come!" she called and rushed toward the front door.

Clay-Boy drew in his breath at the magic landscape beyond the door. The snow had stopped and the sky was a deep blue without a cloud in sight. A full moon shone down on an expanse of virgin snow, and waiting in the driveway was Miss Emma Staples in a horse-drawn sleigh.

"It's Papa's sleigh," explained Miss Etta. "We've kept it polished all these years. Just waiting for an occasion!"

"Hurry up before Lady Esther falls asleep again," called

Miss Emma. Lady Esther, an old black mare, was the only one who showed no enthusiasm for the journey.

Clay-Boy helped Miss Etta into the sleigh, then climbed in after her.

"Gee hup!" called Miss Emma while Miss Etta arranged blankets over everybody's knees.

Lady Esther moved forward through the snow, and once she discovered the ease with which the sleigh flowed gently behind her, she broke into a lively canter.

"Oh, my!" exclaimed Miss Etta as each turning of the road revealed a new white landscape that glittered and sparkled in the moonlight.

"What a treat!" exclaimed Miss Emma as she listened to the merrily jingling bells pealing out across the still night.

Oh, God, thought Clay-Boy. Good manners decreed that he should ask the two old sisters in when they arrived at his home. Mama would hit the roof!

The children had been sitting drowsily around the living-room table, but when they heard the sounds of sleigh bells they jumped up with cries of astonishment.

"It's Santa Claus!"

Even Olivia rushed to the living-room window and brushed aside the curtains to look down at the front gate. There, clearly in the cold white light, was a sleigh, drawn by a horse that stamped its hooves and blew clouds of vapor into the air. Someone detached himself from the sleigh, stood for a moment and waved. "Merry Christmas," came the words across the yard, and then the horse turned smartly and drew the sleigh away from the gate.

"It's Clay-Boy," said Olivia, as the figure turned and walked up the front walk. Her heart went cold with disappointment. He had not found his father, and the time was racing toward midnight. Fear for Clay, and anger with him too, rose in her throat.

She followed the children to the kitchen and waited there until Clay-Boy opened the door and entered. He looked to

Olivia questioningly and she shook her head. The children caught the exchange, sensed what it implied and fell silent. The roasted turkey, still warm from the oven, rested in the center of the table beside the two applesauce cakes, but the joy was gone from them now. They had been the trappings of a festival. Now they were simply food.

"Who was that let you off at the gate?" asked Olivia.

"It was Miss Emma and Miss Etta," said Clay-Boy, holding out a mason jar of Recipe. "They sent this. Said it was Christmas Cheer."

"It's bootleg whisky, is what it is," observed Olivia.

"What do you want me to do with it, Mama?"

"I'll take it," said Olivia, accepting the jar. "I can use some to make frosting for my applesauce cakes."

The children had gone reluctantly to bed. Olivia and Clay-Boy sat in the living room. Olivia had been drowsing, but now when she woke and saw that it was one o'clock, she called softly, "Clay-Boy."

"Hum?" he asked sleepily.

"You go on to bed now."

"Where you reckon he is, Mama?"

"I don't know any more than you do, son."

"I'll go up and lay down, but I'll keep my clothes on, just in case any word comes."

"I don't expect to hear a word before mornen," said Olivia.

"Good night, Mama," he said at the landing.

"Good night, son."

He was about to call "Merry Christmas," but it was obviously going to be anything but merry so he held his tongue. Tiptoeing, carefully, he made his way to the top of the stairs.

"What time is it, Clay-Boy?" called Becky in a whisper.

"Time for you to be asleep," he whispered.

He was on the way down the hall to the boys' room when there came an enormous crash on the roof. At the same moment from somewhere in the backyard someone could be heard shouting and cursing. Again the thudding noise came on the roof and in the next moment the stairway was alive with pounding feet and cries of alarm as each child scrambled downstairs to find his mother.

Olivia was already on her way to the back door when Clay-Boy, followed the by the children, ran into the kitchen.

"What in God's name is it?" he cried.

His mother's face was twisted with worry.

"It sounds like your daddy, but I don't know!"

The children stopped their onrush and huddled together at the living-room door as Olivia unlocked the back door and apprehensively swung it open. Framed in the doorway was Clay Spencer, half frozen, an impish grin on his face, his arms overflowing with bundles.

"I've been worried sick about you," said Olivia, but the voice broke, and she buried her face in her hands and wept.

"Mama, don't cry," said Clay-Boy. "He's home!"

Struggling with packages, Clay entered. He placed his bundles down on the table, knelt and opened his arms and immediately they were filled with children, brushing the snow from his face, hugging him around the neck, crushing his chest with their frantic embraces.

Now he rose and the children watched with delight as he crossed the floor to Olivia. He kissed her tenderly on the cheek, but then, and this was what the children were waiting for, he picked her up and danced about the kitchen shouting joyously, "God, what a woman I married!" while Olivia shouted indignantly, "Put me down, you old fool!"

Finally he placed her back on her feet. Olivia adjusted her clothing with mock annoyance and demanded, "Where in the world have you been?"

"I missed the last bus out of Charlottesville, so I hitchhiked to Hickory Creek. From there it was every blessed step of the way on foot."

"Well, you must be nearly frozen. I've been keepen coffee warm." Olivia went to get cup and saucer, and poured the coffee. Clay took his seat at the table and grinned as he saw the children casting appraising glances at the packages.

"What's in them bundles, Daddy?" asked Luke.

"Well, I'll tell you," said Clay, lowering his voice confidentially. "I was comen up the walk there a minute ago, when all of a sudden somethen come flyen across the sky and landed right on top of the house."

"We heard it!" cried Mark and John.

"Well, I looked up and there was a team of some kind of animals about the size of a year-old calf. Somethen kind of pointy on their heads."

"Reindeer," supplied Pattie-Cake.

"I never saw one, but that's what it was, all right. Well, it kind of stopped me in my tracks, and I just stood there watchen. First thing I see, this old son-of-a-gun jumped out, all dressed up in boots and a red suit trimmed with fur."

"Santa Claus!" whispered John.

"Well, I never laid eyes on the old poot before. Didn't know who he was. I just thought it was somebody tryen to break into the house, so I picked up the biggest rock I could find, and . . ."

Horror stared back at him. "You hit him with a rock!"

"Not exactly, but I scared him so that the sleigh started slippen off the roof and landed right out there in the backyard. The old man in the red suit started cracken the whip and called for them reindeer to take off, but I caught up with him just before that sleigh left the ground."

"You talked to him?" asked Pattie-Cake wonderingly.

"No, but I wrassled him, and just before he got away I grabbed a big armful of stuff from the sleigh and there it is right on the table."

"You see!" said Pattie-Cake victoriously to Becky. "He's real!"

"You're right, honey," nodded Becky with a smile. "You're double-durned right."

"Which one is mine?" asked Pattie-Cake, touching the packages shyly.

"Try that one," said Clay, pointing to a package. "And this one's for you, and this one's for you," he said until all the bundles had been passed out, except one.

Cries and shrieks of joy filled the room as Pattie-Cake removed a brand-new golden-haired doll that cried and opened and closed its eyes. Becky and Shirley were holding up brand-new dresses, and each of the children uncovered treasure after treasure as they went deeper and deeper into their packages: monkeys that magically climbed up strings, teddy bears with soft fur and button noses, banks in the form of mules that kicked when a penny was inserted, cookie cutters and tea sets, catcher's mitts and footballs, and boxes of puzzles and oranges and nuts and candies and still the bottoms of the bags were not yet reached.

"Open yours, son," said Clay to Clay-Boy, who held his package in his arms while he watched his brothers and sisters exclaim with breathless astonishment as they discovered each new treasure.

Self-consciously Clay-Boy tore the wrapper open and he looked at his father with confusion and gratitude and questioning eyes as he found five tablets of good writing paper and a brand-new fountain pen.

"I wonder how news got all the way to the North Pole that you wanted to be a writer," said Clay with a grin.

"I guess he's a right smart man," said Clay-Boy, his throat almost too full to speak.

"This one must be for you," said Clay to Olivia, pointing to the one package still remaining on the table.

"What in the world could it be?"

"You been wishen for springtime," said Clay, and placed the package in her hands.

"Oh, Clay," cried Olivia and gazed down at a flowerpot containing three hyacinths, one blue, one white and one rose, and all in full bloom.

Pattie-Cake, cradling her doll in her arms, suddenly became aware of something that saddened her.

"You didn't get nothen, Daddy," she said. Gently Clay lifted the little girl in his arms and looked around the room at his family.

"Sweetheart," he said, "I've got Christmas every day of my

life in you kids and your mama." He turned to Olivia. "Did you ever see such thoroughbreds?"

"I see some sleepy children," said Olivia. "Off to bed now. You can play in the mornen."

"Can't I shoot just one firecracker, Mama?" pleaded Matt.

Olivia considered, but then she smiled and unexpectedly answered, "Yes." It'll wake everybody within ten miles, she thought, but she didn't care. Let the world know that Clay Spencer was home.

As the children filed out onto the back porch to watch Matt light the firecracker, Olivia came and sat across from Clay. She looked at him and then at the hyacinths, and reproach would not come.

"You must have spent every cent of the paycheck," she said. She tried to sound cross but she didn't succeed.

"Just about," he admitted cheerfully.

"What are we goen to live on this comen week?" she asked.

"Love, woman," he said, and this time he did not seize her in his arms and waltz madly about the room, but kissed her gently and took her hand in his.

"BOOM!" went the five-inch firecracker, and "boom" it resounded across the hills, falling away into the distance like thunder. Now the children came running into the house, their faces alight with the excitement of it all.

"Bedtime," said their father, and with only a few objections the children marched upstairs and pulled the covers once more over their heads.

But nobody went to sleep.

They waited until they heard the familiar sound of lights being turned off downstairs, the passage of their mother and father down the hall to their bedroom and the click of the light being switched off.

From the girls' room Becky called, "Good night, Luke," and Luke answered, "Good night, Becky; good night, Pattie-Cake." And Pattie-Cake called, "Good night, Luke; good night, Mama."

Other voices joined in a round song of good-nights until all the people in the house had said so many good-nights that they could not remember whom they had said good night to and whom they had not. To keep the whole good-night chorus from starting all over again, Clay called, "Good night, everybody, and Merry Christmas!" and gave a long sleepy yawn, which was the signal that everyone had been bidden a proper good-night. The house fell silent.

Around the house the world lay bright as day. The moon blazed down its cold light on an earth that was touched with magic. An ancient wind sighed along the ridges of crusted snow. Angels sang, and the stars danced in the sky.

The Invisible Christmas Trees

WILLIAM BARTHEL

Germany surrendered in May and Japan in August, and World War II was over in the summer of 1945. By the following Christmas, the more fortunate of American families were reunited, and returning GI's, like veterans of every war, were groping and sometimes grasping for their place in society. Doers of great deeds abroad did not always come across as heroes at home; veterans were not necessarily an elite in everyday democratic society. The returning soldier in this story had spent the previous Christmas in Bastogne, France, in the Battle of the Bulge. For his first Yuletide season at home he faced the prospect of being a small-time entrepreneur in New York City. The simple account reminds us that imagination, resolve, and a bit of understanding can turn nothing much into something of durable value.

A few days after the Thanksgiving of 1945, my wife's Uncle Bob Stevens bundled 230 Christmas trees into an old truck and headed from Maine to New York City to make his fortune. That was the way he put it, but what he meant was he wanted to earn enough money to give his mother and three sisters a very

William Barthel, "The Invisible Christmas Trees," *Reader's Digest,* December 1975, 75–78. Permission to reprint this essay has been obtained from *Reader's Digest.*

merry Christmas—the first peacetime one in four years. His father had died at sea early in the war, and Bob had spent the previous Christmas in a woods near Bastogne, in the Battle of the Bulge.

He reached New York on a dark and windy afternoon. As he drove up and down the avenues, what he noticed most was all the fir trees nodding to his fir trees from street corners, storefronts and parking lots. It seemed that a great many people were out to make their fortunes selling Christmas trees that year.

It was dusk when he arrived, by chance, in Greenwich Village. He parked and, tucking a large, flat parcel under his arm, began wandering through the meandering streets with their colorful shops and lively people. Down one narrow street he discovered a small Italian delicatessen, brightly lit, with a narrow concrete patio in front that was probably used for outdoor tables in summer. It would be a great place to sell trees.

Inside, the air was warm and fragrant. Salamis, sausages, cheeses hung in festive rows above the counter. Holiday cookies filled a glass case, and crusty breads were piled in straw baskets. Bob inhaled and grinned and stated his business, offering Old Joe, the owner, a percentage on every tree sold.

Old Joe conferred with Young Joe and Mamma, a solemn woman in a black dress and white apron who regarded Bob with a mixture of suspicion and curiosity about the package under his arm.

"Let me show you my sign," Bob said. He tore away the wrapping to reveal a homemade wooden panel with CHRIST-MAS TREES FOR SALE in shiny red and green letters.

But Bob hadn't stopped at that. The sign was filled to overflowing with exuberant scenes of a New England Christmas. Carolers and shoppers strolled between the letters. The O in FOR was a skating pond alive with children. There was a snowy barn with a Christmas tree on the roof, a horse-drawn sleigh ride, a church. On the left of the sign, it was Christmas Eve; on the right Christmas Morning. At the top, Santa and all his reindeer rode the moonlit sky. Bob had created an American primitive, touched with innocence and joy.

Young Joe and Mamma were smiling when Old Joe held out his hand to Bob. "You will sell your Christmas trees here," he said.

Bob left his sign with Old Joe and went back to where he'd parked the truck, tired but happy. But there was only a bough in the gutter at his feet. The truck was gone!

Somebody directed him to the police station on Charles Street. The sergeant on duty didn't seem at all surprised to hear about a stolen truck full of Christmas trees.

"Now that might qualify as perishable cargo," he said. "I sure hope you find them before Christmas, because you don't get much call for them after."

Bob thought the sergeant had the pronoun wrong. He was hoping *they* were going to find them. "Shouldn't be so hard to locate an old truck with a Maine license, loaded with Christmas trees," he said.

"Fourth of July, maybe, but right now—figure it out, buddy."

Bob had only a few dollars in his pocket, and the bank had loaned him the money to buy the trees. He had a bad night's sleep in a rooming house and went back to the police station early in the morning. No luck.

He walked glumly to the store and saw the two Joes hanging his sign outside on the patio. Soon they were draping a string of Christmas lights along the top and sides. It looked terrific.

When Old Joe heard the story, he patted Bob's shoulder and took Young Joe inside. Bob was still staring at the sign. He had no idea that something right out of O. Henry was about to happen to him.

It was only nine o'clock in the morning, but down the street came a dapper gentleman, walking very slowly, taking time to avoid objects in his path which he alone could see. He was already tipsy at that early hour, and at his heel was a limousine driven by an anxious chauffeur. The man saw Bob's Christmas tree sign. He read it carefully, then turned to regard the empty patio.

"Best Christmas trees I ever saw," he said.

Bob grinned. "State of Maine trees," he said. "Can't beat 'em."

The man kept staring. "Wonderful trees," he said. "Can't make up my mind. I'll take them all."

The chauffeur had stopped the car and was holding the rear door open. "Burton," the man said, "put those trees in the back." Then he turned to Bob and put something in his jacket pocket. "That should cover it," he said.

In spite of his troubles, Bob laughed as the car pulled away. Then he put his hand in his pocket and felt a crumpled ball of paper. It was a $20 bill. It was against Bob's nature to get something for nothing. He ran to the corner, but the limousine was already out of sight.

When he returned to the sign, a tall, dark-haired girl was studying it intently. Her cheeks were colored by the cold and her eyes were smiling.

"Did you paint this?" she asked. Bob nodded. "It's marvelous. But where are the Christmas trees?"

"Just sold every last one of 'em." Bob found himself telling her what had happened. "I guess I can afford to wait around another day or so," he said, "but then I'll have to take a bus home."

"Oh, don't *quit*. You don't have to stop selling Christmas trees just because you haven't got any!"

The girl was hurrying away. "Wait," Bob called after her. "My name's Bob. What's yours?"

She looked back with a laugh. "You may not believe me, but my name is Holly." She disappeared around the corner, leaving Bob to wonder what her words meant. *You don't have to stop selling Christmas trees just because . . .*

Bob bounded into the store. "Hey Joe, would a town like this have a lumber yard?"

There was a lumber yard on East 12th Street. Bob spent

most of the $20 getting a hundred pieces of clear pine cut on a jigsaw. They were six inches tall and looked like this:

He bought brushes and quick-drying paints at an art store, and worked all day and most of the night. The next morning he had Christmas trees for sale, all "trimmed" in his primitive style—with tiny ornaments and candy canes, toy drums and horns, Christmas stars and angels.

Old Joe brought the outdoor tables up from the cellar, and Mamma covered them with bright-green cloths to display Bob's trees. He sold them for stocking stuffers, ornaments, table decorations and he used the profits for supplies to make new trees. And he kept looking for the girl.

He didn't see her again until the middle of December. She came by in a rush, her arms full of books, even prettier than before. She looked at Bob's trees and flashed him the V for Victory sign. "They're wonderful, Bob. Now personalize them."

"What?"

"Just decorate one side. Paint the other a pretty color, but leave it blank. Then you can put a girl's or boy's name on it— or anybody's—to order."

"Say," Bob laughed, "who are you anyway?"

"Just a schoolgirl." She told him the name of the university she was attending and then was gone before he could ask her address.

The personalized Christmas trees were even more popular than the others. What everybody liked best, though, was the Christmas-tree sign. Several people wanted to buy it, and the owner of an art gallery on Eighth Street offered him $75 for it. Bob said he'd sure think about that. He began taking the sign to his room at night, saying he wanted to work on it some more.

The day before Christmas Eve, Bob got a present from the New York City Police Department. They'd found his truck behind a deserted warehouse in Brooklyn. the trees were gone, but nothing had happened to the truck. There was even half a tank of gas.

It was time to head home. Bob personalized trees for Old Joe and Young Joe and Mamma. Then he settled up accounts.

"What about the sign, Bob?" Old Joe said. "You take it over to Eighth Street, you got yourself 75 bucks."

Bob took the sign down and polished it lightly with his sleeve. My luck, he thought.

"It's the end of an era," a voice said behind him.

"Holly! I was just going to give this to Joe to keep for you—I knew you'd be by." He turned the sign over and handed it to her. "I personalized it," he said.

On the back of the sign was the word HOLLY, surrounded by pictures of a dark-haired girl celebrating Christmas in New York. She dashed in and out of the letters with her arms full of presents. She run up to a sidewalk Santa, bustled into a Village toy shop, hurried past the tree in Rockefeller Center. She was on a dozen holiday errands, East Side, West Side, all around the town.

I'll love it all my life, Bob."

"Holly, let's have lunch before I go." He saw her hesitate and knew she was expected somewhere. "You know how you always look?" he said. "You always look like you're double-parked."

"All right, wise guy. Just let me make a phone call."

They had lunch in a restaurant owned by Old Joe's cousin, a Christmas feast complete with wine. Bob told Holly a little about the war, how it was good being back home in Maine. But jobs were scarce, and he had no idea what he was going to do with the rest of his life.

"What would you be," Holly asked, "if you could be anything?"

Bob hesitated. "I spent some time at a Battalion Aid Station," he said. "Nothing serious. I was what you call 'walking wounded,' and a doctor commandeered me to assist him. He worked for a stretch of 60 hours before he keeled over. If I could be anything . . ."

Holly leaned across the table and touched his arm. "You certainly have the hands for it," she said. Then her eyes flashed fire. "Well, don't think you can't do it just because you don't think you can do it!" It was another of her curious pronouncements, and the words were already stuck in his mind.

Bob spent the rest of the day Christmas shopping, then headed home, his truck a Santa's sleigh. The family celebrated Christmas for days. When Bob stopped in at the bank to repay his loan and open a savings account for $216, the bank president was impressed. He asked Bob his future plans, and the words spilled out as Bob told him how much he wanted to go back to New York to medical school. That night, the banker talked with two other citizens of the town. Some long-term loans were offered to supplement Bob's G.I. benefits.

It turned out to be a great investment for Maine. Today, 30 years later, my wife's Uncle Bob Stevens is a Maine doctor in the old-fashioned sense of the word, working too many days and nights. But he still finds time for painting, and his style remains deceptively simple and clear.

Some of his most treasured paintings are of weddings and receptions. All of Bob's sisters are married, and at reunions they tease him because now he has just the right touch of gray at the temples, and because his tailor-made clothes hang so well on his lanky frame. Sometimes Bob's mother joins in the kidding, saying he'll soon be setting up practice on Park Avenue.

The truth is, Bob does look as if he's been a distinguished doctor all his life. If he said he was once a penniless painter selling Christmas trees in Greenwich Village, I don't know who'd believe him.

Except my wife's Aunt Holly.

A Christmas Story

ALEXANDER WOOLLCOTT

Alexander Woollcott, in the 1940s a superb radio critic and commentator on literature, the arts, and quirks of human behavior, chose for his Christmas broadcast in 1946 to relate a tender and benign joke on a pair of young people who were struggling to succeed in the theater. Postwar America faced issues that were not only enormous but newer than most things under the sun: the birth of the United Nations, the unlikely possibility of both developing and containing atomic energy, the obligation to help restore Europe and Asia in lands devastated as never before by the twentieth-century engines of battle. Much as all of these might affect our lives, they were, nevertheless, matters of state. Individual Americans were concentrated as ever on the daily rounds of life: domestic needs, jobs, careers, food and shelter. In the world of the performing arts—one in which even very concentrated folk do not always succeed in earning a living—the time and place of the next job were often shrouded in mystery, and the makings of a Christmas dinner could be a challenge.

Alexander Woollcott, "A Christmas Story," in *The Portable Woollcott* (New York: Viking Press, 1946), 646–50. Permission to reprint has been obtained from Eileen Godlis of Viking Penguin.

This is Woollcott speaking. This is Woollcott breaking all precedent by venturing to tell here this afternoon a true story which he never happens to have told before. It is a Christmas story, a melancholy Christmas story concerning two young people who were once closely interlocked but who, in the intervening years, have gone their separate ways. I refer to Dorothy Dickson and Carl Hyson, a young and gracile couple who at one time seemed likely to step into the shoes—the dancing shoes, that is—of Mr. and Mrs. Vernon Castle. I am telling about a Christmas of theirs more than twenty years ago. Since then Dorothy Dickson has had tremendous success in London and even played during one Christmas season the aforesaid role of Peter Pan. At the time of which I tell, they were yet to wheel their first perambulator through the streets of New York. This came a little later and since then, by the way, the smiling occupant of that perambulator has climbed out of it and, under the name of Dorothy Hyson, herself gone on the stage.

During this very season she has achieved on her own account a considerable London success. But twenty years ago her father and mother were just a worried young couple trying to get along and wondering if they could manage it. In a now forgotten December, they were lodged at the Algonquin, a New York hotel where, ever since John Barrymore and Elsie Janis were not particularly humble beginners, people of the theater have ever been especially welcome.

Carl and Dorothy had a room at the Algonquin but once when they had no job nor any job in sight their credit was suspended and they had to face a question which often rises to plague the youngsters of show business. They had no job. While they had to get one, should they accept temporary defeat and retreat to their respective families for shelter—he, to his and she, to hers? Or should they somehow stick it out at that hotel where, at least, the sight of them would keep their names alive in people's minds? Why, even as they got out of the elevator next day or strutted this very evening in an elaborately carefree manner across the lobby, they might catch the roving eye of some manager or playwright who if they had any sense would say "Why, there's Carl Hyson and Dorothy Dickson. We must have them in our next show."

In their room on this night they went into conference. They counted up the money in the treasury and decided they did have enough to see them through another six weeks if they need consider only their room rent. But they must stop eating at the hotel. If they had to eat at all, they must buy odds and ends at the delicatessen around the corner, smuggle them up in the elevator and stay their hunger as best they could while the management wasn't looking. Certain other expenses, they would have, of course. For instance each would have to go to a gymnasium every day to practice the tremendous leaps which, when they tried doing them in their hotel room, brought bitter complaints to the management from all the angry people living on the floor below. Laundry? Well, she could manage that with a little soap and hot water in the bathroom. But food? Well, he must bring some in from time to time under his overcoat. This wouldn't be quite their idea of high life in the great city but there was nothing else for it. "And when," he asked moodily, "do we begin?" "Tomorrow," she replied firmly. "But," he said dolefully, "tomorrow's Christmas." That," she replied, "doesn't matter." Therefore, on the morrow when he came in at twilight he had concealed under his elegant overcoat a loaf of bread and a hunk of sausage.

At best this seemed to them a pretty lean Christmas dinner and they were such amateurs at the game of fending for themselves that only when they unwrapped these dainties did they realize they hadn't a thing to go with them. Not a napkin, not a knife, not a fork, no butter, no salt, no pepper. Not a dish. This was too depressing. It was then she had a bright idea. For this once, until they could provide themselves with these unforeseen extras, they would order one dish from the dining room below. A dish of soup, say. They could count on the strange hotel custom of bringing up a full paraphernalia no matter what you ordered. Even if you sent for one order of soup you'd get a table, enough table linen for a family of five, a small arsenal of knives and forks, several pats of butter sitting uncomfortably in a bowl of cracked ice, salt, pepper, everything a young couple could want. So they telephoned to room service and requisitioned one order of soup. "Just one order of soup?" "Yes, just one." "Nothing else?" "Nothing else." It was a somewhat surprised waiter who eventually staggered up to their room with this meager repast. Sure enough he brought all the lugs with it.

In high glee they waited while he placed it before them and tactfully withdrew. They would pay him later when he came to take the table away. No sooner had the door closed than they leaped to their feet, produced the bread and sausage from under the bed, sliced it up with knives, thus handsomely provided, filled themselves to the brim with soup and bread and sausage and drank toasts to their everlasting success in iced water provided by the management. Of course, the soup would cost fifty cents but the next day they could go around to Woolworth's and with a little carefully spent cash convert the top bureau drawer into a well-stocked sideboard. Finally the last drop of soup was gone, the last crumb of bread, the last bit of sausage. He kissed her. She kissed him. They dug up the price of the soup, decided how much of a tip they could afford to lay out for this one occasion and with this much settled, haughtily telephoned for the waiter to come up and clear away. The waiter had just shrouded the poor debris of their dinner in the tablecloth and was starting to go when, in an elaborately casual manner, Hyson said, "Oh, by the way, waiter, the check please. We have decided to pay cash for everything from now on." The waiter looked puzzled. "The check?" he said. "Yes, yes," milord replied in his most testy manner, "the check please. We wish to settle it." But the waiter said, "There is no check." "No check? What do you mean, no check?" "Why, no," the waiter replied, "there are no checks tonight. This is Christmas. The guests can order anything they like for dinner and it's on the management. You are the only couple who didn't order the whole darn menu. You must be on a diet. Well, good night. Merry Christmas, Mr. Hyson. Merry Christmas Miss Dickson." He started to trundle his table toward the door. The silence, broken by a cascade of

Christmas chimes from the belfry of a church in Fifth Avenue, was concluded, in that room at least only as the waiter vanished over the threshold. The two were looking at each other as they said to him (and to themselves, I suppose) in the feeblest voice in which the phrase was ever uttered, "Merry Christmas."

IV

Contemporary
America

Introduction

America approached mid-century with foreboding. The bombs that had been dropped on Hiroshima and Nagasaki in August of 1945 began a new age as well as a period of incertitude, questioning, national introspection, and widespread fear. Harry Truman did not seem big enough to replace Franklin Roosevelt. In the United States Senate, Joseph McCarthy exploited the emotional vulnerability of the citizenry with an insidious assault on the loyalty of government officials, artists and writers, college professors, and public school teachers. The launching of *Sputnik* in 1957 made the man on the street wonder if the USSR had surpassed the United States in education and technology. In many communities individuals dug shelters in their back yards, stocking them with provisions and making game plans to deal with less prudent neighbors who might try to use these facilities in times of crisis. The 1950s and 1960s brought new wars, both in Asia: first in Korea, then Vietnam. And finally, assassins' bullets at home cut down some of the most popular leaders of the century: Medgar Evers, John Kennedy, Robert Kennedy, Martin Luther King.

In an era of rapid change, the celebration of Christmas could not remain the same. Television, the most regulated of the new mass media, struggled to portray some of the old values: the "Charlie Brown" specials entertained children, but these programs also tried to get adults to question contemporary hype. Classics, such as *A Christmas Carol* and *Miracle on 34th Street*, were shown over and over again on less than prime time. Regular performers often set aside one day during December to introduce the public to their families and those who worked behind the scenes. Specials, such as Earl Hamner's "The Homecoming," scored impressively in the ratings, that particular program going on to become a nostalgic series of its own. "The Grinch Who Stole Christmas" proved so popular that the cartoon character began to vie with Santa Claus as a holiday symbol.

As the 1980s came to a close, it is clear that Christmas remained largely a festival of consumption. For example, a department store might do one-half to two-thirds of its annual sales during the season. These profits, however, have paled in comparison to the revenue generated seasonally by the media and music industry. Some churches have tried to adapt by bringing in contemporary images and music; however, these practices often result in alienating the old instead of enticing the young. The most enduring part of Christmas is that which is celebrated in the traditional home because the holiday is a time of renewal for the generations. In the broken home, conversely, the season may bring discontent and depression, commingled with a belief that somehow tomorrow will be better.

A Christmas Story from Korea

LT. COL. MELVIN BLAIR

Halfway through the twentieth century, American soldiers were once again embattled, almost as far as possible from home. World War II had been fought to end all wars, and to make the world safe for democracy. But now there was the Cold War: a seemingly endless chain of engagements designed to hold back the tide of Communism. On Christmas Eve in 1950, the American Army's Twenty-Fifth Infantry Division, in the frozen time of the Korean year, was encamped near the confluence of the Imjin and Han rivers, waiting for the Chinese Army to attack. This particular frontline report came from an American Intelligence officer on duty with another division of infantry stationed nearby. Sandwiched between the two divisions were thousands of North Korean refugees: women, children, and very old men. On both sides of the line, all of these diverse souls held in common only their tactically indefensible positions. Being Americans, however, the men of the infantry had Christmas on their minds and in their hearts. But once again, the behavioral phenomenon that might be called the Scrooge principle was

Lt. Col. Melvin Russell Blair, "A Christmas Story from Korea," *The Saturday Evening Post* 224, no. 25 (December 22, 1951): 8. Permission to reprint this essay has been obtained from Mary Beth Vahle of *The Saturday Evening Post*.

seen at work in human events, with a curious result of benefit to all concerned.

O n the south bank of the Imjin River, Korea, the 25th (Tropic Lightning) Infantry Division was dug in, waiting for the Chinese Army to attack. Three battle-hardened regiments—the 24th (Eagles), the 27th (Wolfhounds) and 35th (Cacti)—were holding the sector near the confluence of the Imjin and Han rivers where the Chinese were expected to strike. As the soldiers listened to the peculiar, high-pitched wail of the wind that came in from the Yellow Sea, whipping up little twisters of snow as it bit into the north bank where thousands of North Korean refugees were huddled, one GI mirthlessly commented, "Wind's singing us a carol." It was December 24, 1950.

Our biggest nightmare was the refugees. Between the 25th Division and the Chinese were some 40,000 North Korea civilians. It was an ironic paradox that these people feared the Chinese communists—their "allies"—more than death itself, and fled from their approach. They were mostly women, children and very old men—for the North Korean Army had conscripted all of the able-bodied males.

There we were—an outnumbered army in a tactically indefensible position, with thousands of refugees in our line of fire.

What we saw across the river was hard to take. The refugees were starving, and we had no food to give them. They were dressed in cotton rags in weather that dropped to five degrees below zero; yet, if they lit a fire, our patrols were forced to put it out, for fires would attract the enemy.

The meager roads became choked with refugees who crossed the Imjin, creating a security hazard. Finally, 8th Army headquarters ordered that no more North Koreans be permitted to cross the river. The men of the 25th were confused about these people. They had no love for them, for they knew of the savageries perpetrated by North Korean civilians upon our wounded and captured soldiers. Yet, as they silently watched the ragged, starving women and children pass through their lines before the embargo was clamped on, they were reminded of their own women and children back home. They wanted somehow to help. But they didn't know exactly how.

The answer came on this day before Christmas.

It had been a rather special day. We had expected the Chinese attack to come on Christmas Day, so headquarters had ordered that we feed our men Christmas dinner a day early. The quartermaster worked a minor miracle and brought a hot turkey dinner right up to the front-line troops. Turkey and all the trimmings—including stuffing, cranberries, sweet potatoes, rolls and real butter—even candy and mince and pumpkin pie. What really tickled the men, though, was that packages from home came through, just in time for Christmas. Expecting the Chinese to strike, no one heeded "Do Not Open Until Christmas" instructions. Front-line foxholes bulged with cakes, tinned delicacies, socks, mittens and the like.

I happened to be at the front lines that afternoon in connection with my duties as Division G-2 (Intelligence officer). I stopped in the area held by the 35th Infantry, leaned over a foxhole and asked the soldier occupying it who he was and how he was doing. He hopped out and told me he was Pfc. Stanley Crowley, of Birmingham, Alabama, and that he was doing all right. He was a red-haired, freckle-faced rifleman, nineteen years old. He was not particularly chunky, but he looked enormous because of the six layers of clothing he was wearing in the subzero weather.

"Let me show you what I got for Christmas, colonel," Crowley drawled. First, he produced a wool scarf; then, commencing an odd sort of strip-tease, he pulled back layer after layer of clothing, finally coming to the object he had next to his skin. It was a fruit cake. "Got it here to keep it from freezing," he explained.

Just at that moment there was a diversion. A band of refugees, utterly desperate, decided—orders or no orders—to cross the river.

The stampede—and hundreds came across before we could stop it—it was led by a woman with three children. It was low tide. She waded through the ice-clogged water that came about her waist. With one arm, she carried a child of about three; with her other arm, she supported a second child of about five so his head was above water. The third—a boy of about seven—had to make out for himself.

These four were the first to reach the south bank, and they started running right through the 35th's position. When they reached Private First Class Crowley's foxhole, they stopped, for Crowley was standing in their path.

He looked at the woman. She returned the gaze from black, sunken sockets. He looked at the children. Their lips were cracked and bleeding; their fingers bluish with frostbite. The oldest boy had slipped and gone in over his head in crossing; his hair was frozen into icy wisps.

Slowly, from around his neck, the red-haired boy from Alabama unwound his Christmas scarf. "Here, take it," he said to the woman.

She drew back in fear. Crowley kept holding it out, and finally she took it. She looked at her children to see which needed it worst. She settled on the oldest boy, who was shaking so violently he hardly could stand.

Then Crowley again began his curious strip-tease with the six layers of clothing. He brought out his fruit cake and handed it to her. Again she hesitated. Then she took it.

She broke off three small pieces and handed a piece to each of her children. None for herself. She handed the cake back to Crowley. By gestures, he conveyed that she was to keep it all. She stood expressionless, then bowed to Crowley, and motioned for each of her children to bow.

While this was going on, other refugees were watching. So were the men of Private First Class Crowley's company. Silently, spontaneously, a sort of spiritual chain reaction began. Crowley had shown what to do about the refugees.

Out of their foxholes came the soldiers, bearing gifts for the North Koreans. They gave gloves, mufflers, food from their own rations, cakes and delicacies from the U.S.A. Some of the soldiers made second trips and came back with blankets and shoe-pacs; others peeled off jackets and draped them around wet, shivering children.

The whole thing was done almost in dead silence, though some of the boys said things like "Merry Christmas, Joe," or "Happy New Year, little girl," as they passed out their presents.

In the middle of it all, up raced the battalion commander in an open car, ready to chop off heads for the flagrant security breach. What the hell was going on, he wanted to know. He found out. Before he left, he passed out a pocketful of hard candy to Korean kids. He also turned his head when his driver gave away the blankets they had been swathed in when they drove up.

"Sure cold today, colonel," said the driver cheerfully.

"Drive on," said the colonel.

Slowly, Operation Santa Claus subsided. South Korean police stopped the refugee flow. Those who had come over were directed to a railroad track and told to start walking south—fast.

Then the soldiers returned to their foxholes. Materially, they were poorer; militarily, they had done a risky thing. The only thing about it was that the men of the 35th, holding their sector of the 25th Division's battle line, all felt so good that evening. There was no peace, but there was considerable good will, on the south bank of the Imjin on that Christmas Eve, 1950.

(P.S.: In April, 1951, Pfc. Stanley Crowley was reported killed in Action.) (1951)

Simple Santa

LANGSTON HUGHES

By the 1950s, Langston Hughes had come to be regarded as one of the key figures in the Harlem Renaissance, a flowing of literature that followed the great migration of blacks from the rural South to the industrial North. Hughes was a skilled poet, a biting critic, and, at times, a caustic writer. In this story from 1953, Hughes undertakes to teach a Christmas lesson on race relations. The main character, a black man given a job as Santa Claus, fancies himself as the St. Nick who would answer the letters of white children in the deep South. One wonders if Hughes foresaw the chain of assassins' bullets that would bring down Medgar Evers, Martin Luther King, and other black leaders in the era between Korea and Vietnam.

Carlye's wife is pregnant again," said Simple. "What do you reckon they are going to do with two babies in one room?"

"I imagine your landlady is worried about that, too."

"She is," said Simple. "She done swore she won't rent to no more *young* married couples. From now on they have to be

Langston Hughes, "Simple Santa," in *Santa Takes A Wife* (New York: Simon and Schuster, 1953), 202–7. Permission to reprint this selection has been obtained from Tamora Pierce of Harold Ober Associates.

settled folks that works hard—too tired and settled to raise a family in her house."

"Is your landlady really as hard-hearted as that toward children?" I asked.

"No," said Simple. "But she has her rules. Still and yet, she is really crazy about both of them little old babies in the house, spite the fact she objected to them being born. Every time she boils some beef for Trixie, she sends them babies up a cup of hot broth. And if one of them gets the colic, she is more worried than their mamas. Only thing she does not worry about is giving them heat. She says babies is due to stay wrapped up in blankets with booties on their feets. And if a house is too hot, they get overheated. So I asked her to give me an extra blanket since I do not have booties. Do you think she did?"

"Ha! Ha!" I said.

"She come giving me some kind of spiel about what makes men so cold-natured when women, she says, go around in zero weather in open-work shoes on the streets, yet do not catch pneumonia and die. Neither do they freeze. Which is true, I have never heard of a woman having chilblains yet. But if a man went out in his sox-feet in the winter, me for instant, I would be so full of cold the next day I could not draw a decent breath. Women can go low-necked and bare-footed in the snow in party shoes and do not even sneeze. In this New York zero weather, if men dressed like women we would develop galloping consumption and go into decline. Then where would the human race be without mens? For instant, without your father, you would not be here today."

"The same goes for your mother," I said.

"Cut it out," yelled Simple. "I'm not playing the dozens. Listen, I want to borrow a dollar."

"For what?"

"To give a kid."

"What kid?"

"Not my kid, 'cause I ain't got none," said Simple. "but if you was to go across the street with me, you would see what kid. It is a kid who wants to buy his grandma a present for Christmas."

"Do you know his grandma?"

"No. Neither do I know the kid. But he made a mistake. He saw a present a week ago in the West Indian store window, and the sign was written wrong. It said, 'One-twenty-nine cents.' But it was written like this—see: O-N-E-and a dash—and a twenty-nine cent sign. 1–29 cents. The kid thought it meant one for twenty-nine cents. But what it really meant was One Dollar *and* Twenty-Nine Cents."

"For one what?" I asked.

"Dustpan," said Simple.

"What in the world does a kid want to give his grandmother a dustpan for?"

"Because that is what she wants for Christmas," said Simple. "So this kid had been saving up his pennies till he got twenty-nine cents. Now the man wants a *Dollar and Twenty-Nine Cents* for that dustpan."

"I never heard of such a price!" I said. "A Dollar and Twenty-Nine Cents for an ordinary dustpan?"

"It is made of genu-wine metal," said Simple, "and painted red with a white handle. It is a *fine* dustpan! So I want to borrow a dollar off of you to give that kid. He has got his heart set on giving his grandma that dustpan, so he is standing over there crying. See?

"He is only eight-nine years old—and he read that sign wrong. Some people do not know how to paint a sign. Besides, I remember when I was a little kid, I did not ever have any money but a nickel now and then, and I always wanted to buy something that costs more than I had. I have got no kids myself, but if I did have, I would want him to be happy on Christmas and give presents—so I am going to give that kid a dollar to get that there dustpan."

"You are a very sentimental Santa Claus," I said. "You haven't got a dollar and you do not even know the lad."

"No, I do not know that kid," said Simple, "but I know for

a kid to save up Twenty-Nine Cents sometimes is hard. When he wants to give it away in a present to his grandma instead of eating it up in a candy or going to see Humphrey Bogart, I admire that kid. Lend me a dollar!"

"Here! Pay me back Fifty Cents. I will also invest in an unseen dustpan for an unknown boy and his unknown grandmother."

"You are making fun of me and that kid," said Simple.

"I am not," I said. "It just strikes me as funny—a dustpan for a Christmas present! But hurry up across the street and give the youngster the dollar before he is gone."

"If he's gone, I'll be coming back—and we'll drink this dollar up."

"Oh, no!" I cried. "Either give it to the child, or give my money back to me."

"Then I will be broke," said Simple, "and I want to wish you a Merry Christmas ahead of time. How else can I wish you a Merry Christmas except to buy you a drink?"

"With my money?" I said.

"Don't be technical!" said Simple.

When he came back into the bar he was grinning.

"That kid thinks I'm Santa Claus," he said. "Right now I wish I was Santa Claus for just one day so I could open some of that mail he gets up yonder at the North Pole. I would particularly like to latch onto that mail from children down in Alabama, Mississippi, and Florida. I would answer them white kids down there in a way they would never forget."

"Race again, I'll bet! Those kids," I said, "have nothing to do with Jim Crow, and it would be a shame to intrude the race problem into their Christmas thoughts."

"A shame, nothing!" said Simple. "They are growing up to be a problem. And if I was a Santa Claus, being my color, I would teach them a lesson before they got too far gone. Suppose I was to open a letter from some little Johnnie Dixiecrat in Mississippi asking me to bring him a hunting rifle, for instant. I would dip my pen in ink and reply:

North Pole, Santa Claus Land
December the so-and-so
Year Now

Johnnie:

I would call you "Dear Johnnie," but I am a colored
Santa Claus so I am afraid you might be insulted, because
I fears as a white child in the South you have been reared
wrong in regards to race. You say you are seven years old.
Well, I hope you do not want that rifle you wrote me about
to lend your cousin Talbot to shoot a Negro—because
where you live lynchings is frequent, although they do not
call them by that name now. I read in the paper the other
day where eight white mens riddled one black man with
bullets. Johnnie, the grown mens in your place do not act
right. If you don't, I will not bring you a thing after you
grow up. I will bring you this hunting rifle now, little as
you are, because I believe you are still good.

But, listen, Johnnie! When you get up in your teens,
don't let me catch you getting on the bus in front of some
crippled old colored lady just because you are white and
she is black. And don't let me catch you calling her by her
first name, Sarah, and she is old enough to be your
grandma, when you ought to be calling her Mrs. What-
Ever-Her-Name-Is. If you do such, I will not bring you that
bicycle you gonna want to ride to high school. And you
sure won't get that television set if you go around using
bad words about colored folks. As long as Santa Claus
stays black, I will not stand for that!

Also, Johnnie Dixiecrat, sir, if you gets to be a salesman
or a insurance man or a bill collector in Meridian or
Jackson, Mississippi, show your manners and take off your
hat when you go in a colored woman's house. If you don't,
I will not put nothing in your sox on Christmas Eve, not a
doggone thing! And if you get big enough to vote, see to it
that colored folks can vote, too. If you don't, I'm liable to
drop down your chimney a present you don't want—a
copy of the United States Constitution. See how that would
be for your constitution—since it says everybody is free
and equal.

I am signing off now, dear Johnnie, since I have got one

million letters more to answer from Alabama and Georgia, so I cannot take up too much time with you in Mississippi. If you see me on Christmas Eve, you will know me by my white beard and black face. Up North the F.E.P.C. has given a Negro the Santa Claus job this year. Dark as I am, though, I intend to treat you equal.

MERRIE CHRISTMAS! The rifle I will bring when I come. Don't be rowdy.

Cheerio!

JESS SIMPLE SANTA CLAUS

A Christmas Memory

TRUMAN CAPOTE

*"It's fruitcake weather! Fetch our buggy. Help me find my hat"
is the heralding of a Christmas that transports the reader to the
magical southern ambient of Truman Capote's childhood
world. Fictional perhaps in some of the detail, but abounding
in palpable truth, this 1950s account of the companionship
between a "sixty-something" woman and a seven-year-old boy
celebrates not only the Yuletide but all the different creature
forms of sustaining affection that make life worthwhile. After
Tennessee Williams and William Faulkner of Mississippi, Capote of New Orleans became the third in a literary triumvirate
that would not let the deep South forget its heritage. This story
by a talented stylist, however, did not presage a happy life for
the writer. Truman was not able to conquer addiction and his
life ended well short of threescore and ten.*

Imagine a morning in late November. A coming of winter
morning more than twenty years ago. Consider the kitchen
of a spreading old house in a country town. A great black stove
is its main feature; but there is also a big round table and a

Truman Capote, "A Christmas Memory," in *Breakfast at Tiffany's. A Short Novel and
Three Stories* (New York: Signet Book, 1958), 114–27. Permission to reprint this
excerpt has been obtained from Random House.

fireplace with two rocking chairs placed in front of it. Just today the fireplace commenced its seasonal roar.

A woman with shorn white hair is standing at the kitchen window. She is wearing tennis shoes and a shapeless gray sweater over a summery calico dress. She is small and sprightly, like a bantam hen; but, due to a long youthful illness, her shoulders are pitifully hunched. Her face is remarkable—not unlike Lincoln's, craggy like that, and tinted by sun and wind; but it is delicate too, finely boned, and her eyes are sherry-colored and timid. "Oh my," she exclaims, her breath smoking the windowpane, "it's fruitcake weather!"

The person to whom she is speaking is myself. I am seven; she is sixty-something. We are cousins, very distant ones, and we have lived together—well, as long as I can remember. Other people inhabit the house, relatives; and though they have power over us, and frequently make us cry, we are not, on the whole, too much aware of them. We are each other's best friend. She calls me Buddy, in memory of a boy who was formerly her best friend. The other Buddy died in the 1880's, when she was still a child. She is still a child.

"I knew it before I got out of bed," she says, turning away from the window with a purposeful excitement in her eyes. "The courthouse bell sounded so cold and clear. And there were no birds singing; they've gone to warmer country, yes indeed. Oh, Buddy, stop stuffing biscuit and fetch our buggy. Help me find my hat. We've thirty cakes to bake."

It's always the same: a morning arrives in November, and my friend, as though officially inaugurating the Christmas time of year that exhilarates her imagination and fuels the blaze of her heart, announces: "It's fruitcake weather! Fetch our buggy. Help me find my hat."

The hat is found, a straw cartwheel corsaged with velvet roses out-of-doors has faded: it once belonged to a more fashionable relative. Together, we guide our buggy, a dilapidated baby carriage, out to the garden and into a grove of pecan trees. The buggy is mine; that is, it was bought for me when I was born. It is made of wicker, rather unraveled, and the wheels wobble like a drunkard's legs. But it is a faithful object; spring-time, we take it to the woods and fill it with flowers, herbs, wild fern for our porch pots; in the summer, we pile it with picnic paraphernalia and sugar-cane fishing poles and roll it down to the edge of a creek; it has its winter uses, too: as a truck for hauling firewood from the yard to the kitchen, as a warm bed for Queenie, our tough little orange and white rat terrier who has survived distemper and two rattlesnake bites. Queenie is trotting beside it now.

Three hours later we are back in the kitchen hulling a heaping buggyload of windfall pecans. Our backs hurt from gathering them: how hard they were to find (the main crop having been shaken off the trees and sold by the orchard's owners, who are not us) among the concealing leaves, the frosted, deceiving grass. Caarackle! A cheery crunch, scraps of miniature thunder sound as the shells collapse and the golden mound of sweet oily ivory meat mounts in the milk-glass bowl. Queenie begs to taste, and now and again my friend sneaks her a mite, though insisting we deprive ourselves. "We mustn't, Buddy. If we start, we won't stop. And there's scarcely enough as there is. For thirty cakes." The kitchen is growing dark. Dusk turns the window into a mirror: our reflections mingle with the rising moon as we work by the fireside in the firelight. At last, when the moon is quite high, we toss the final hull into the fire and, with joined sighs, watch it catch flame. The buggy is empty, the bowl is brimful.

We eat our supper (cold biscuits, bacon, blackberry jam) and discuss tomorrow. Tomorrow the kind of work I like best begins: buying. Cherries and citron, ginger and vanilla and canned Hawaiian pineapple, rinds and raisins and walnuts and whiskey and oh, so much flour, butter, so many eggs, spices, flavorings: why, we'll need a pony to pull the buggy home.

But before these purchases can be made, there is the question of money. Neither of us has any. Except for skinflint sums persons in the house occasionally provide (a dime is considered very big money); or what we earn ourselves from various activities: holding rummage sales, selling buckets of hand-picked blackberries, jars of homemade jam and apple jelly and peach preserves, rounding up flowers for funerals and weddings. Once we won seventy-ninth prize, five dollars, in a national football contest. Not that we know a fool thing about football. It's just that we enter any contest we hear about: at the moment our hopes are centered on the fifty-thousand-dollar Grand Prize being offered to name a new brand of coffee (we suggest "A.M."; and, after some hesitation, for my friend thought it perhaps sacrilegious, the slogan "A.M.! Amen!"). To tell the truth, our only *really* profitable enterprise was the Fun and Freak Museum we conducted in a back-yard woodshed two summers ago. The Fun was a stereopticon with slide views of Washington and New York lent us by a relative who had been to those places (she was furious when she discovered why we'd borrowed it); the Freak was a three-legged biddy chicken hatched by one of our own hens. Everybody hereabouts wanted to see that biddy: we charged grownups a nickel, kids two cents. And took in a good twenty dollars before the museum shut down due to the decease of the main attraction.

But one way and another we do each year accumulate Christmas savings, a Fruitcake Fund. These moneys we keep hidden in an ancient bead purse under a loose board under the floor under a chamber pot under my friend's bed. The purse is seldom removed from this safe location except to make a deposit, or, as happens every Saturday, a withdrawal; for on Saturdays I am allowed ten cents to go to the picture show. My friend has never been to a picture show, nor does she intend to: "Id rather hear you tell the story, Buddy. That way I can imagine it more. Besides, a person my age shouldn't squander their eyes. When the Lord comes, let me see him clear." In addition to never having seen a movie, she has never: eaten in a restaurant, traveled more than five miles from home, received or sent a telegram, read anything except funny papers and the Bible, worn cosmetics, cursed, wished someone harm, told a lie on purpose, let a hungry dog go hungry. Here are a few things she has done, does do: killed with a hoe the biggest rattlesnake ever seen in this county (sixteen rattles), dip snuff (secretly), tame hummingbirds (just try it) till they balance on her finger, tell ghost stories (we both believe in ghosts) so tingling they chill you in July, talk to herself, take walks in the rain, grow the prettiest japonicas in town, know the recipe for every sort of old-time Indian cure, including a magical wart-remover.

Now, with supper finished, we retire to the room in a faraway part of the house where my friend sleeps in a scrap-quilt-covered iron bed painted rose pink, her favorite color. Silently, wallowing in the pleasures of conspiracy, we take the bead purse from its secret place and spill its contents on the scrap quilt. Dollar bills, tightly rolled and green as May buds. Somber fifty-cent pieces, heavy enough to weight a dead man's eyes. Lovely dimes the liveliest coin, the one that really jingles. Nickels and quarters, worn smooth as creek pebbles. But mostly a hateful heap of bitter-odored pennies. Last summer others in the house contracted to pay us a penny for every twenty-five flies we killed. Oh, the carnage of August: the flies that flew to heaven! Yet it was not work in which we took pride. And, as we sit counting pennies, it is as though we were back tabulating dead flies. Neither of us has a head for figures; we count slowly, lose track, start again. According to her calculations, we have $12.73. According to mine, exactly $13. "I do hope you're wrong, Buddy. We can't mess around with thirteen. The cakes will fall. Or put somebody in the cemetery. Why, I wouldn't dream of getting out of bed on the thirteenth." This is true: she always spends thirteenths in bed. So, to be on the safe side, we subtract a penny and toss it out the window.

Of the ingredients that go into four fruitcakes, whiskey is the most expensive, as well as the hardest to obtain: State laws forbid its sale. But everybody knows you can buy a bottle from Mr. Haha Jones. And the next day, having completed our more prosaic shopping, we set out for Mr. Haha's business address, a "sinful" (to quote public opinion) fish-fry and dancing cafe down by the river. We've been there before, and on the same errand; but in previous years our dealings have been with Haha's wife, an iodine-dark Indian woman with brassy peroxided hair and a dead-tired disposition. Actually, we've never laid eyes on her husband, though we've heard the he's an Indian too. A giant with razor scars across his cheeks. They call him Haha because he's so gloomy, a man who never laughs. As we approach his cafe (a large log cabin festooned inside and out with chains of garish-gay naked light bulbs and standing by the river's muddy edge under the shade of river trees where moss drifts though the branches like gray mist) our steps slow down. Even Queenie stops prancing and sticks close by. People have been murdered in Haha's cafe. Cut to pieces. Hit on the head. There's a case coming up in court next month. Naturally these goings-on happen at night when the colored lights cast crazy patterns and the victrola wails. In the daytime Haha's is shabby and deserted. I knock at the door, Queenie barks, my friend calls: "Mrs. Haha, ma'am? Anyone to home?"

Footsteps. The door opens. Our hearts overturn. It's Mr. Haha Jones himself! And he *is* a giant; he *does* have scars; he *doesn't* smile. No, he glowers at us through Satan-tilted eyes and demands to know: "What you want with Haha?"

For a moment we are too paralyzed to tell. Presently my friend half-finds her voice, a whispery voice at best: "If you please, Mr. Haha, we'd like a quart of your finest whiskey."

His eyes tilt more. Would you believe it? Haha is smiling! Laughing, too. "Which one of you is a drinkin' man?"

"It's for making fruitcakes, Mr. Haha. Cooking."

This sobers him. He frowns. "That's no way to waste good whiskey." Nevertheless, he retreats into the shadowed cafe and seconds later appears carrying a bottle of daisy yellow unlabeled liquor. he demonstrates its sparkle in the sunlight and says: "Two dollars."

We pay him with nickels and dimes and pennies. Suddenly, handling the coins in his hand like a fistful of dice, he face softens. "Tell you what," he proposes, pouring the money back into our bead purse, "just send me one of them fruitcakes instead."

"Well," my friend remarks on our way home, "there's a lovely man. We'll put an extra cup of raisins in *his* cake."

The black stove, stoked with coal and firewood, glows like a lighted pumpkin. Eggbeaters whirl, spoons spin round in bowls of butter and sugar, vanilla sweetens the air, ginger spices it; melting, nose-tingling odors saturate the kitchen, suffuse the house, drift out to the world on puffs of chimney smoke. In four days our work is done. Thirty-one cakes, dampened with whiskey, bask on window sills and shelves.

Who are they for?

Friends. Not necessarily neighbor friends: indeed, the larger share are intended for persons we've met maybe once, perhaps not at all. People who've struck our fancy. Like President Roosevelt. Like the Reverend and Mrs. J. C. Lucey, Baptist missionaries to Borneo who lectured here last winter. Or the little knife grinder who comes through town twice a year. Or Abner Packer, the driver of the six o'clock bus from Mobile, who exchanges waves with us every day as he passes in a dust-cloud whoosh. Or the young Wistons, a California couple whose car one afternoon broke down outside the house and who spent a pleasant hour chatting with us on the porch (young Mr. Wiston snapped our picture, the only one we've ever had taken). Is it because my friend is shy with everyone *except* strangers that these strangers, and merest acquaintances, seem to us our truest friends? I think yes. Also, the scrapbooks we keep of thank-you's on White House stationery, time-to-time communications from California and Borneo, the knife grinder's penny post cards, make us feel connected to eventful worlds beyond the kitchen with its view of a sky that stops.

Now a nude December fig branch grates against the window. The kitchen is empty, the cakes are gone; yesterday we carted the last of them to the post office, where the cost of stamps turned our purse inside out. We're broke. That rather depresses me, but my friend insists on celebrating—with two inches of whiskey left in Haha's bottle. Queenie has a spoonful in a bowl of coffee (she likes her coffee chicory-flavored and strong). The rest we divide between a pair of jelly glasses. We're both quite awed at the prospect of drinking straight whiskey; the taste of it brings screwed-up expressions and sour shudders.

But by and by we begin to sing, the two of us singing different songs simultaneously. I don't know the words to mine, just: *Come on along, come on along, to the dark-town strutter's ball.* But I can dance: that's what I mean to be, a tap dancer in the movies. My dancing shadow rollicks on the walls; our voices rock the chinaware; we giggle: as if unseen hands were tickling us. Queenie rolls on her back, her paws plow the air, something like a grin stretches her black lips. Inside myself, I feel warm and sparky as those crumbling logs, carefree as the wind in the chimney. My friend waltzes round the stove, the hem of her poor calico skirt pinched between her fingers as though it were a party dress: *Show me the way to go home,* she sings, her tennis shoes squeaking on the floor. *Show me the way to go home.*

Enter: two relatives. Very angry. Potent with eyes that scold, tongues that scald. Listen to what they have to say, the words tumbling together into a wrathful tune: "A child of seven! whiskey on his breath! are you out of your mind? feeding a child of seven! must be loony! road to ruination! remember Cousin Kate? Uncle Charlie? Uncle Charlie's brother-in-law? shame! scandal! humiliation! kneel, pray, beg the Lord!"

Queenie sneaks under the stove. My friend gazes at her shoes, her chin quivers, she lifts her skirt and blows her nose and runs to her room. Long after the town has gone to sleep and the house is silent except for the chimings of clocks and the sputter of fading fires, she is weeping into a pillow already as wet as a widow's handkerchief.

"Don't cry," I say, sitting at the bottom of her bed and shivering despite my flannel nightgown that smells of last winter's cough syrup, "don't cry," I beg, teasing her toes, tickling her feet, "you're too old for that."

"It's because," she hiccups, "I *am* too old. Old and funny."

"Not funny. Fun. More fun than anybody. Listen. If you don't stop crying you'll be so tired tomorrow we can't go cut a tree."

She straightens up. Queenie jumps on the bed (where Queenie is not allowed) to lick her cheeks. "I know where we'll find real pretty trees, Buddy. And holly, too. With berries big as your eyes. It's way off in the woods. Farther than we've ever been. Papa used to bring us Christmas trees from there: carry them on his shoulder. That's fifty years ago. Well, now: I can't wait for morning."

Morning. Frozen rime lusters the grass; the sun, round as an orange and orange as hot-weather moons, balances on the horizon, burnishes the silvered winter woods. A wild turkey calls. A renegade hog grunts in the undergrowth. Soon, by the edge of knee-deep, rapid-running water, we have to abandon the buggy. Queenie wades the stream first, paddles across barking complaints at the swiftness of the current, the pneumonia-making coldness of it. We follow, holding our shoes and equipment (a hatchet, a burlap sack) above our heads. A mile more: of chastising thorns, burs and briers that catch at our clothes; of rusty pine needles brilliant with gaudy fungus and molted feathers. Here, there, a flash, a flutter, an ecstasy of shrillings remind us that not all the birds have flown south. Always, the path unwinds through lemony sun pools and pitch vine tunnels. Another creek to cross: a disturbed armada of speckled trout froths the water round us, and frogs the size of plates practice belly flops; beaver workmen are building a dam. On the farther shore, Queenie shakes herself and trembles. My friend shivers, too: not with cold but enthusiasm. One of her hat's ragged roses sheds a petal as she lifts her head and inhales the pine-heavy air. "We're almost there; can you smell it, Buddy?" she says, as though we were approaching an ocean.

And, indeed, it is a kind of ocean. Scented acres of holiday trees, prickly-leafed holly. Red berries shiny as Chinese bells: black crows swoop upon them screaming. Having stuffed our burlap sacks with enough greenery and crimson to garland a dozen windows, we set about choosing a tree. "It should be," muses my friend, "twice as tall as a boy. So a boy can't steal the star." The one we pick is twice as tall as me. A brave handsome brute that survives thirty hatchet strokes before it keels with a creaking rending cry. Lugging it like a kill, we commence the long trek out. Every few yards we abandon the struggle, sit down and pant. But we have the strength of triumphant huntsmen; that and the tree's virile, icy perfume revive us, goad us on. Many compliments accompany our sunset return along the red clay road to town; but my friend is sly and noncommittal when passers-by praise the treasure perched in our buggy: what a fine tree and where did it come from? "Yonderways," she murmurs vaguely. Once a car stops and the rich mill owner's lazy wife leans out and whines: "Give ya two-bits cash for that ol tree." Ordinarily my friend is afraid of saying no; but on this occasion she promptly shakes her head: "We wouldn't take a dollar." The mill owner's wife persists. "A dollar, my foot! Fifty cents. That's my last offer. Goodness, woman, you can get another one." In answer, my friend gently reflects: "I doubt it. There's never two of anything."

Home: Queenie slumps by the fire and sleeps till tomorrow, snoring loud as a human.

A trunk in the attic contains: a shoebox of ermine tails (off the opera cape of a curious lady who once rented a room in the house), coils of frazzled tinsel gone gold with age, one silver star, a brief rope of dilapidated, undoubtedly dangerous candy-like light bulbs. Excellent decorations, as far as they go, which isn't far enough: my friend wants our tree to blaze "like a Baptist window," droop with weighty snows of ornament. But we can't afford the made-in-Japan splendors at the five-and-dime. So we do what we've always done: sit for days at the kitchen table with scissors and crayons and stacks of colored paper. I make sketches and my friend cuts them out: lots of cats, fish too (because they're easy to draw), some apples, some watermelons, a few winged angels devised from saved-up sheets of Hershey-bar tin foil We use safety pins to attach these creations to the three; as a final touch, we sprinkle the branches with shredded cotton (picked in August for this purpose). My friend, surveying the effect, clasps her hands together. "Now honest, Buddy. Doesn't it look good enough to eat?" Queenie tries to eat an angel.

After weaving and ribboning holly wreaths for all the front windows, our next project is the fashioning of family gifts. Tie-dye scarves for the ladies, for the men a home-brewed lemon and licorice and aspirin syrup to be taken "at the first Symptoms of a Cold and after Hunting." But when it comes time for making each other's gift, my friend and I separate to work secretly. I would like to buy her a pearl-handled knife, a radio, a whole pound of chocolate-covered cherries (we tasted some once and she always swears: "I could live on them, Buddy, Lord yes I could—and that's not taking His name in vain"). Instead, I am building her a kite. She would like to give me a bicycle (she's said so on several million occasions: "If only I could, Buddy. It's bad enough in life to do without something *you* want; but confound it, what gets my goat is not being able to give somebody something you want *them* to have. Only one of these days I will, Buddy. Locate you a bike. Don't ask how. Steal it, maybe"). Instead, I'm fairly certain that she is building me a kite—the same as last year, and the year before: the year before that we exchanged slingshots. All of which is fine by me. For we are champion kite-fliers who study the wind like sailors; my friend, more accomplished than I, can get a kite aloft when there isn't enough breeze to carry clouds.

Christmas Eve afternoon we scrape together a nickel and go to the butcher's to buy Queenie's traditional gift, a good gnaw-able beef bone. The bone, wrapped in funny paper, is placed high in the tree near the silver star. Queenie knows it's there. She squats at the foot of the tree staring up in a trance of greed: when bedtime arrives she refuses to budge. Her excitement is equaled by my own. I kick the covers and turn my pillow as though it were a scorching summer's night. Somewhere a rooster crows: falsely, for the sun is still on the other side of the world.

"Buddy, are you awake?" It is my friend, calling from her room, which is next to mine; and an instant later she is sitting on my bed holding a candle. "Well, I can't sleep a hoot," she declares. "My mind's jumping like a jack rabbit. Buddy, do you think Mrs. Roosevelt will serve our cake at dinner?" We huddle in the bed, and she squeezes my hand I-love-you. "Seems like your hand used to be so much smaller. I guess I hate to see you grow up. When you're grown up, will we still be friends?" I says always. "But I feel so bad, Buddy. I wanted so bad to give you a bike. I tried to sell my cameo Papa gave me. Buddy—" she hesitates, as though embarrassed—"I made you another kite." Then I confess that I made her one, too; and we laugh. The candle burns too short to hold. Out it goes, exposing the starlight, the stars spinning at the window like a visible caroling that slowly, slowly daybreak silences. Possibly we doze; but the beginnings of dawn splash us like cold water: we're up, wide-eyed and wandering while we wait for others to waken. Quite deliberately my friend drops a kettle on the kitchen floor. I tap-dance in front of closed doors. One by one the household emerges, looking as though they'd like to kill us both; but its Christmas, so they can't. First, a gorgeous breakfast: just every-thing you can imagine—from flapjacks and fried squirrel to hominy grits and honey-in-the-comb. Which puts everyone in a good humor except my friend and I. Frankly, we're so impatient to get at the presents we can't eat a mouthful.

Well, I'm disappointed. Who wouldn't be? With socks, a Sunday school shirt, some handkerchiefs, a hand-me-down sweater and a year's subscription to a religious magazine for children. *The Little Shepherd*. It makes me boil. It really does.

My friend has a better haul. A sack of Satsumas, that's her best present. She is proudest, however, of a white wool shawl knitted by her married sister. But she *says* her favorite gift is the kite I built her. And it *is* very beautiful; though not as beautiful as the one she made me, which is blue and scattered with gold and green Good Conduct stars; moreover, my name is painted on it, "Buddy."

"Buddy, the wind is blowing."

The wind is blowing, and nothing will do till we've run to a pasture below the house where Queenie has scooted to bury her bone (and where, a winter hence, Queenie will be buried, too.) There, plunging through the healthy waist-high grass, we unreel our kites, feel them twitching at the string like sky fish as they swim into the wind. Satisfied, sun-warmed, we sprawl in the grass and peel Satsumas and watch our kites cavort. Soon I forget the socks and hand-me-down sweater. I'm as happy as if we'd already won the fifty-thousand-dollar Grand Prize in that coffee-naming contest.

"My, how foolish I am!" my friend cries, suddenly alert, like a woman remembering too late she has biscuits in the oven. "You know what I've always thought?" she asks in a tone of discovery, and not smiling at me but a point beyond. "I've always thought a body would have to be sick and dying before they saw the Lord. And I imagined that when He came it would be like looking at the Baptist window: pretty as colored glass with the sun pouring through, such a shine you don't know it's getting dark. And it's been a comfort: to think of that shine taking away all the spooky feeling. But I'll wager it never happens. I'll wager at the very end a body realizes the Lord has already shown Himself. That things as they are"—her hand circles in a gesture that gathers clouds and kites and grass and Queenie pawing earth over her bone—"just what they've always seen, was seeing Him. As for me, I could leave the world with today in my eyes."

This is our last Christmas together.

Life separates us. Those who Know Best decide that I belong in a military school. And so follows a miserable succession of bugle-blowing prisons, grim reveille-ridden summer camps. I have a new home too. But it doesn't count. Home is where my friend is, and there I never go.

And there she remains, puttering around the kitchen. Alone with Queenie. Then alone. ("Buddy dear," she writes in her wild hard-to-read script, "yesterday Jim Macy's horse kicked Queenie bad. Be thankful she didn't feel much. I wrapped her in a Fine Linen sheet and rode her in the buggy down to Simpson's pasture where she can be with all her Bones . . ."). For a few Novembers she continues to bake her fruitcakes single-handed; not as many, but some: and, of course, she always sends me "the best of the batch." Also, in every letter she encloses a dime wadded in toilet paper: "See a picture show and write me the story." But gradually in her letters she tends to confuse me with her other friend, the Buddy who died in the 1880's; more and more thirteenths are not the only days she stays in bed: a morning arrives in November, a leafless birdless coming of winter morning, when she cannot rouse herself to exclaim: "Oh my, it's fruitcake weather!"

And when that happens, I know it. A message saying so merely confirms a piece of news some secret vein had already received, severing from me an irreplaceable part of myself, letting it loose like a kite on a broken string. That is why, walking across a school campus on this particular December morning, I keep searching the sky. As if I expected to see, rather like hearts, a lost pair of kites hurrying toward heaven.

Stubby Pringle's Christmas

JACK WARNER SCHAEFER

In Shane, *Jack Schaefer wrote the book for the most viewed western film of all time, superseding even* Stagecoach *by Ernest Haycox. (Both writers, incidentally, often wrote stories, such as "The Raiders of Saint Nicholas" and "Canyon Passage" for* The Saturday Evening Post.*) Simplicity of story and theme gives westerns a timelessness that will continue to make them popular for generations to come. In this selection, Stubby Pringle, who had been on his way to spend the Christmas holiday in town, stops to help a family who is down on its luck.*

High on the mountainside by the little line cabin in the crisp clean dusk of evening Stubby Pringle swings into saddle. He has shape of bear in the dimness, bundled thick against cold. Double socks crowd scarred boots. Leather chaps with hair out cover patched corduroy pants. Fleece-lined jacket with wear of winters on it bulges body and heavy gloves blunt fingers. Two gay red bandannas folded together fatten throat under chin. Battered hat is pulled down to sit on ears and in side pocket of

Jack Warner Schaefer, "Stubby Pringle's Christmas" in *The Collected Stories of Jack Schaefer* (Boston: Houghton Mifflin, 1966), 508–20. Permission to reprint this essay has been obtained from Mary Ann Flynn of Don Congdon Associates.

jacket are rabbit-skin earmuffs he can put to use if he needs them.

Stubby Pringle swings up into saddle. He looks out and down over worlds of snow and ice and tree and rock. He spreads arms wide and they embrace whole ranges of hills. He stretches tall and hat brushes stars in sky. He is Stubby Pringle, cowhand of the Triple X, and this is his night to howl. He is Stubby Pringle, son of the wild jackass, and he is heading for the Christmas dance at the schoolhouse in the valley.

Stubby Pringle swings up and his horse stands like rock. This is the pride of his string, flop-eared ewe-necked cat-hipped strawberry roan that looks like it should have died weeks ago but has iron rods for bones and nitroglycerin for blood and can go from here to doomsday with nothing more than mouthfuls of snow for water and tufts of winter-cured bunch-grass snatched between drifts for food. It stands like rock. It knows the folly of trying to unseat Stubby. It wastes no energy in futile explosions. It knows that twenty-seven miles of hard winter going are foreordained for this evening and twenty-seven more of harder uphill return by morning. It has done this before. It is saving the dynamite under its hide for the destiny of a true cowpony which is to take its rider where he wants to go—and bring him back again.

Stubby Pringle sits his saddle and he grins into cold and distance and future full of festivity. Join me in a look at what can be seen of him despite the bundling and frosty breath vapor that soon will hang icicles on his nose. Those are careless haphazard scrambled features under the low hatbrim, about as handsome as a blue boar's snout. Not much fuzz yet on his chin. Why, shucks, is he just a boy? Don't make that mistake, though his twentieth birthday is still six weeks away. Don't make the mistake Hutch Handley made last summer when he thought this was young unseasoned stuff and took to ragging Stubby and wound up with ears pinned back and upper lip split and nose mashed flat and the whole of him dumped in a rainbarrel. Stubby has been taking care of himself since he was orphaned at thirteen. Stubby has been doing man's work since he was fifteen. Do you think Hardrock Harper of the Triple X would have anything but an all-around hard-proved hand up here at his farthest winter line camp siding Old Jake Hanlon, toughest hard-bitten old cowman ever to ride range?

Stubby Pringle slips gloved hand under rump to wipe frost off the saddle. No sense letting it melt into patches of corduroy pants. He slaps rightside saddlebag. It contains a burlap bag wrapped around a two-pound box of candy, of fancy chocolates with variegated interiors he acquired two months ago and has kept hidden from Old Jake. He slaps leftside saddlebag. It holds a burlap bag wrapped around a paper parcel that contains a close-folded piece of dress goods and a roll of pink ribbon. Interesting items, yes. They are ammunition for the campaign he has in mind to soften the affections of whichever female of the right vintage among those at the schoolhouse appeals to him most and seems most susceptible.

Stubby Pringle settles himself firmly into the saddle. He is just another of far-scattered poorly-paid patched-clothes cowhands that inhabit these parts and likely marks and smells of his calling have not all been scrubbed away. He knows that. But this is his night to howl. He is Stubby Pringle, true-begotten son of the wildest jackass, and he has been riding line through hell and highwater and winter storms for two months without a break and he has done his share of the work and more than his share because Old Jake is getting along and slowing some and this is his night to stomp floorboards till schoolhouse shakes and kick heels up to lanterns above and whirl a willing female till she is dizzy enough to see past patched clothes to the man inside them. He wriggles toes deep into stirrups and settles himself firmly in the saddle.

I could of et them choc'lates," says Old Jake from the cabin doorway. "They wasn't hid good," he says. "No good at all."

"An' be beat like a drum," says Stubby. "An' wrung out like a dirty dishrag."

"By who?" says Old Jake. "By a young un like you? Why, I'd of tied you in knots afore you knew what's what iffen you tried it. You're a dang-blatted young fool," he says. "A ding-busted dang-blatted fool. Riding out a night like this iffen it is Chris'mas eve. A dong-bonging ding-busted dang-blatted fool," he says. "But iffen I was your age agin, I reckon I'd be doing it too." He cackles like an old rooster. "Squeeze one of 'em for me," he says and he steps back inside and he closes the door.

Stubby Pringle is alone out there in the darkening dusk, alone with flop-eared ewe-necked cat-hipped roan that can go to the last trumpet call under him and with cold of wicked winter wind around him and with twenty-seven miles of snow-dumped distance ahead of him. "Wahoo!" he yells. "Skip to my Loo!" he shouts. "Do-si-do and round about!"

He lifts reins and the roan sighs and lifts feet. At easy warming-up amble they drop over the edge of benchland where the cabin snugs into tall pines and on down the great bleak expanse of mountainside.

Stubby Pringle, spurs a jingle, jogs upslope through crusted snow. The roan, warmed through, moves strong and steady under him. Line cabin and line work are far forgotten things back and back and up and up the mighty mass of mountain. He is Stubby Pringle, rooting tooting hard-working hard-playing cowhand of the Triple X, heading for the Christmas dance at the schoolhouse in the valley.

He tops out on one of the lower ridges. He pulls rein to give the roan a breather. He brushes an icicle off his nose. He leans forward and reaches to brush several more off sidebars of old bit in the bridle. He straightens tall. Far ahead, over top of last and lowest ridge, on into the valley, he can see tiny specks of glowing allure that are schoolhouse windows. Light and gaiety and good liquor and fluttering skirts are there. "Wahoo!" he yells. "Gals an' women an' grandmothers!" he shouts. "Raise your skirts and start askipping! I'm acoming!"

He slaps spurs to roan. It leaps like mountain lion, out and down, full into hard gallop downslope, rushing, reckless of crusted drifts and ice-coated bush-branches slapping at them. He is Stubby Pringle, born with spurs on, nursed on tarantula juice, weaned on rawhide, at home in the saddle of a hurricane in shape of horse that can race to outer edge of eternity and back, heading now for high-jinks two months overdue. He is ten feet tall and the horse is gigantic, with wings, iron-boned and dynamite-fueled, soaring in forty-foot leaps down the flank of the whitened wonder of a winter world.

They slow at the bottom. They stop. They look up the rise of the last low ridge ahead. The roan paws frozen ground and snorts twin plumes of frosty vapor. Stubby reaches around to pull down fleece-lined jacket that has worked a bit up back. He pats rightside saddlebag. He pats leftside saddlebag. He lifts reins to soar up and over last low ridge.

Hold it, Stubby. What is that? Off to the right.

He listens. He has ears that can catch snitch of mouse chewing on chunk of bacon rind beyond the log wall by his bunk. He hears. Sound of ax striking wood.

What kind of dong-bonging ding-busted dang-blatted fool would be chopping wood on a night like this and on Christmas Eve and with a dance underway at the schoolhouse in the valley? What kind of chopping is this anyway? Uneven in rhythm, feeble in stroke. Trust Stubby Pringle, who has chopped wood enough for cookstove and fireplace to fill a long freight train, to know how an ax should be handled.

There. That does it. That whopping sound can only mean that the blade has hit at an angle and bounced away without biting. Some dong-bonged ding-busted dang-blatted fool is going to be cutting off some of his own toes.

He pulls the roan around to the right. He is Stubby Pringle, born to tune of bawling bulls and blatting calves, branded at birth, cowman raised and cowman to the marrow, and no true cowman rides on without stopping to check anything strange on range. Roan chomps on bit, annoyed at interruption. It remembers who is in saddle. It sighs and obeys. They move quietly in dark of night past boles of trees jet black against dim greyness of crusted snow on ground. Light shows faintly ahead. Lantern light through a small oiled-paper window.

Yes. Of course. Just where it has been for eight months now. The Henderson place. Man and woman and small girl and waist-high boy. Homesteaders. Not even fools, homesteaders. Worse than that. Out of their minds altogether. All of them. Out here anyway. Betting the government they can stave off starving for five years in exchange for one hundred sixty acres of land. Land that just might be able to support seven jack-rabbits and two coyotes and nine rattlesnakes and maybe all of four thin steers to a whole section. In a good year. Homesteaders. Always out of almost everything, money and food and tools and smiles and joy of living. Everything. Except maybe hope and stubborn endurance.

Stubby Pringle nudges the reluctant roan along. In patch-light from the window by a tangled pile of dead tree branches he sees a woman. Her face is grey and pinched and tired. An old stocking-cap is pulled down on her head. Ragged man's jacket bumps over long woolsey dress and clogs arms as she tried to swing an ax into a good-sized branch on the ground.

Whopping sound and ax bounces and barely misses an ankle.

"Quit that!" says Stubby, sharp. He swings the roan in close. He looks down at her. She drops ax and backs away, frightened. She is ready to bolt into two-room bark-slab shack. She looks up. She sees that haphazard scrambled features under low hatbrim are crinkled in what could be a grin. She relaxes some, hand on door latch.

"Ma'am," says Stubby. "You trying to cripple yourself?" She just stares at him. "Man's work," he says. "Where's your man?"

"Inside," she says; then, quick, "He's sick."

"Bad?" says Stubby.

"Was," she says. "Doctor that was here this morning thinks he'll be all right now. Only he's almighty weak. All wobbly. Sleeps most of the time."

"Sleeps," says Stubby, indignant. "When there's wood to be chopped."

"He's been almighty tired," she says, quick, defensive. "Even afore he was took sick. Wore out." She is rubbing cold hands together, trying to warm them. "He tried," she says, proud.

"Only a while ago. Couldn't even get his pants on. Just fell flat on the floor."

Stubby looks down at her. "An' you ain't tired?" he says.

"I ain't got time to be tired," she says. "Not with all I got to do."

Stubby Pringle looks off past dark boles of trees at last row ridgetop that hides valley and schoolhouse. "I reckon I could spare a bit of time," he says. "Likely they ain't much more'n started yet," he says. He looks again at the woman. He sees grey pinched face. He sees cold-shivering under bumpy jacket. "Ma'am," he says. "Get on in there an' warm your gizzard some. I'll just chop you a bit of wood."

Roan stands with dropping reins, ground-tied, disgusted. It shakes head to send icicles tinkling from bit and bridle. Stopped in midst of epic run, wind-eating, mile-gobbling, iron-boned and dynamite-fueled, and for what? For silly chore of chopping.

Fifteen feet away Stubby Pringle chops wood. Moon is rising over last low ridgetop and its light, filtered through trees, shines on leaping blade. He is Stubby Pringle, moonstruck maverick of the Triple X, born with ax in hands, with strength of stroke in muscles, weaned on whetstone, fed on cordwood, raised to fell whole forests. He is ten feet tall and ax is enormous in moonlight and chips fly like stormflakes of snow and blade slices through branches thick as his arm, through logs thick as his thigh.

He leans ax against a stump and he spreads arms wide and he scoops up whole cords at a time and strides to door and kicks it open . . .

Both corners of front room by fireplace are piled full now, floor to ceiling, good wood, stout wood, seasoned wood, wood enough for a whole wicked winter week. Chore done and done right, Stubby looks around him. Fire is burning bright and well-fed, working on warmth. Man lies on big old bed along opposite wall, blanket over, eyes closed, face grey-pale, snoring long and slow. Woman fusses with something at old woodstove. Stubby steps to doorway to backroom. He pulls aside hanging cloth.

Faint in dimness inside he sees two low bunks and in one, under an old quilt, a curly-headed small girl and in the other, under other old guilt, a boy who would be waist-high awake and standing. He sees them still and quiet, sleeping sound. "Cute little devils," he says.

He turns back and the woman is coming toward him, cup of coffee in hand, strong and hot and steaming. Coffee the kind to warm the throat and gizzard of chore-doing hard-chopping cowhand on a cold cold night. He takes the cup and raises it to his lips. Drains it in two gulps. "Thank you, ma'am," he says. "That was right kindly of you." He sets cup on table. "I got to be getting along," he says. He starts toward outer door.

He stops, hand on door latch. Something is missing in two-room shack. Trust Stubby Pringle to know what. "Where's your tree?" he says. "Kids got to have a Christmas tree."

He sees the woman sink down on chair. He hears a sigh come from her. "I ain't had time to cut one," she says.

"I reckon not," says Stubby. "Man's job anyway," he says. "I'll get it for you. Won't take a minute. Then I got to be going."

He strides out. He scoops up ax and strides off, upslope some where small pines climb. He stretches tall and his legs lengthen and he towers huge among trees swinging with ten-foot steps. He is Stubby Pringle, born an expert on Christmas trees, nursed on pine needles, weaned on pine cones, raised with an eye for size and shape and symmetry. These. A beauty. Perfect. Grown for this and for nothing else. Ax blade slices keen and swift. Tree topples. He strides back with tree on shoulder. He rips leather whangs from his saddle and lashes two pieces of wood to tree bottom, crosswise, so tree can stand upright again.

Stubby Pringle strides into shack, carrying tree. He sets it up, center of front-room floor, and it stands straight, trim and straight, perky and proud and pointed. "There you are, ma'am," he says. "Get your things out an' start decorating. I got to be going." He moves toward outer door.

He stops in outer doorway. He hears the sigh behind him.

"We got no things," she says. "I was figuring to buy some but sickness took the money."

Stubby Pringle looks off at last low ridgetop hiding valley and schoolhouse. "Reckon I still got a bit of time," he says. "They'll be whooping it mighty late." He turns back, closing door. He sheds hat and gloves and bandannas and jacket. He moves about checking everything in the sparse front room. He asks for things and the woman jumps to get those few of them she has. He tells her what to do and she does. He does plenty himself. With this and with that magic wonders arrive. He is Stubby Pringle, born to poverty and hard work, weaned on nothing, fed on less, raised to make do with least possible and make the most of that. Pinto beans strung on thread brighten tree in firelight and lantern light like strings of store-bought beads. Strips of one bandanna, cut with shears from sewing-box, bob in bows on branch-ends like gay red flowers. Snippets of fleece from jacket-lining sprinkled over tree glisten like fresh fall of snow. Miracles flow from strong blunt fingers through bits of old paper-bags and dabs of flour paste into link chains and twisted small streamers and two jaunty little hats and two smart little boats with sails.

"Got to finish it right," says Stubby Pringle. From strong blunt fingers comes five-pointed star, triple-thickness to make it stiff, twisted bit of old wire to hold it upright. He fastens this to topmost tip of topmost bough. He wraps lone bandanna left around throat and jams battered hat on head and shrugs into now-skimpy-lined jacket. "A right nice little tree," he says. "All you got to do now is get out what you got for the kids and put it under. I really got to be going." He starts toward the door.

He stops in open doorway. He hears the sigh behind him. He knows without looking around the woman has slumped into old rocking chair. "We ain't got anything for them," she says. "Only now this tree. Which I don't mean it isn't a fine grand tree. It's more'n we'd of had 'cept for you."

Stubby Pringle stands in open doorway looking out into cold clean moonlit night. Somehow he knows without turning head two tears are sliding down thin pinched cheeks. "You go on along," she says. "They're good young uns. They know how it is. They ain't expecting a thing."

Stubby Pringle stands in open doorway looking out at last ridgetop that hides valley and schoolhouse. "All the more reason," he says soft to himself. "All the more reason something should be there when they wake." He sighs too. "I'm dong-bonging ding-busted dang-blatted fool," he says. "But I reckon I still got a mite more time. Likely they'll be sashaying around till it's most morning."

Stubby Pringle strides on out, leaving door open. He strides back, closing door with heel behind him. In one hand he has burlap bag wrapped around paper parcel. In other hand he has squarish chunk of good pine wood. He tosses bag-parcel into lap-folds of woman's apron.

"Unwrap it," he says. "There's the makings for a right cute dress for the girl. Needle-and-threader like you can whip it up in no time. I'll just whittle me out a little something for the boy."

Moon is high in cold cold sky. Frosty clouds drift up there with it. Tiny flakes of snow float through upper air. Down below by a two-room shack droops a disgusted cowpony roan, ground-tied, drooping like statute snow-crusted. It is accepting the inescapable destiny of its kind which is to wait for its rider, to conserve deep-bottomed dynamite energy, to be ready to race to the last margin of motion when waiting is done.

Inside the shack fire in fireplace cheerily gobbles wood, good wood, stout wood, seasoned wood, warming two-rooms well. Man lies on bed, turned n side, curled up some, snoring slow and steady. Woman sits in rocking chair, sewing. Her head nods slow and drowsy and her eyelids sag weary but her fingers fly, stitch-stitch-stitch. A dress has shaped under her hands, small and flounced and with little puff-sleeves, fine dress, fancy dress, dress for smiles and joy of living. She is sewing pink ribbon around collar and down front and into fluffy bow on back.

On a stool nearby sits Stubby Pringle, piece of good pine wood in one hand, knife in other hand, fine knife, splendid knife, all-around-accomplished knife, knife he always has with him, seven-bladed knife with four for cutting from little to big and corkscrew and can opener and screwdriver. Big cutting blade has done its work. Little cutting blade is in use now. He is Stubby Pringle, born with feel for knives in hand, weaned on emery wheel, fed on shavings, raised to whittle·his way through the world. Tiny chips fly and shavings flutter. There in his hands, out of good pine wood, something is shaping. A horse. Yes. Flop-eared ewe-necked cat-hipped horse. Flop-eared head is high on ewe neck, stretched out, sniffing wind, snorting into distance. Cat-hips are hunched forward, caught in crouch for forward leap. It is a horse fit to carry a waist-high boy to uttermost edge of eternity and back.

Stubby Pringle carves swift and sure. Little cutting blade makes final little cutting snitches. Yes. Tiny mottlings and markings make no mistaking. It is a strawberry roan. He closes knife and puts it in pocket. He looks up. Dress is finished in woman's lap. But woman's head has dropped down in exhaustion. She sits slumped deep in rocking chair and she too snores slow and steady.

Stubby Pringle stands up. He takes dress and puts it under tree, fine dress, fancy dress, dress waiting now for small girl to wake and wear it with smiles and joy of living. He sets wooden horse beside it, fine horse, proud horse, snorting-into-distance horse, cat-hips crouched, waiting now for waist-high boy to wake and ride it around the world.

Quietly he piles wood on fire and banks ashes around to hold it for morning. Quietly he pulls on hat and wraps bandanna around and shrugs into skimpy-lined jacket. He looks at old rocking chair and tired woman slumped in it. He strides to outer door and out, leaving door open. He strides back, closing door with heel behind. He carries other burlap bag wrapped around box of candy, of fine chocolates, fancy chocolates with variegated interiors. Gently he lays this in lap of woman. Gently he takes big old shawl from wall nail and lays this over her. He stands by big old bed and looks down at snoring man. "Poor devil," he says. "Ain't fair to forget him." He takes knife from pocket, fine knife, seven-bladed knife, and lays this on blanket on bed. He picks up gloves and blows out lantern and swift as sliding moon shadow he is gone.

High high up frosty clouds scuttle across face of moon. Wind whips through topmost tips of tall pines. What is it that hurtles like hurricane far down there on upslope of last low ridge, scattering drifts, smashing through brush, snorting defiance at distance? It is flop-eared ewe-necked cat-hipped roan, iron-boned and dynamite-fueled, ramming full gallop through the dark of night. Firm in saddle is Stubby Pringle, spurs ajingle, toes atingle, out on prowl, ready to howl, heading for the dance at the schoolhouse in the valley. He is ten feet tall, great as a grizzly, and the roan is gigantic, with wings, soaring upward in thirty-foot leaps. They top out and roan rears high, pawing stars out of sky, and drops down, cat-hips hunched for fresh leap out and down.

Hold it, Stubby. Hold hard on reins. Do you see what is happening on out there in the valley?

Tiny lights that are schoolhouse windows are winking out. Tiny dark shapes moving about are horsemen riding off, are wagons pulling away.

Moon is dropping down the sky, haloed in frosty mist. Dark grey clouds dip and swoop and sweep of horizon. Cold winds weave rustling through ice-coated bushes and trees. What is that moving slow and lonesome up snow-covered mountainside? It is a flop-eared ewe-necked cat-hipped roan, just that, nothing more, small cowpony, worn and weary, taking its rider back to clammy bunk in cold line cabin. Slumped in saddle is Stubby Pringle, head down, shoulders sagged. He is just another of far-scattered poorly-paid patched-clothes cowhands who inhabit these parts. Just that. And something more. He is the biggest thing there is in the whole wide roster of the human race. He is a man who has given of himself, of what little he has and is, to bring smiles and joy of living to others along his way.

He jogs along, slump-sagged in saddle, thinking of none of

this. He is thinking of dances undanced, of floorboards un-stomped, of willing women left unwhirled.

He jogs along, half-asleep in saddle, and he is thinking now of bygone Christmas seasons and of a boy born to poverty and hard work and make-do poring in flicker of firelight over ragged old Christmas picturebook. And suddenly he hears something. The tinkle of sleigh bells.

Sleigh bells?

Yes. I am telling this straight. He and roan are weaving through thick-clumped brush. Winds are sighing high overhead and on up the mountainside and lower down here they are whipping mists and snow flurries all around him. He can see nothing in mystic moving dimness. But he can hear. The tinkle of sleigh bells, faint but clear, ghostly but unmistakable. And suddenly he sees something. Movement off to the left. Swift as wind, glimmers only through brush and mist and whirling snow, but unmistakable again. Antlered heads high, frosty breath streaming, bodies rushing swift and silent, floating in flash of movement past, seeming to leap in air alone needing no touch of ground beneath. Reindeer? Yes. Reindeer strong and silent and fleet out of some far frozen northland marked on no map. Reindeer swooping down and leaping past and rising again and away, strong and effortless and fleeting. And with them, hard on their heels, almost lost in swirling snow mist of their passing, vague and formless but there, something big and bulky with runners like sleigh and flash of white beard whipping in wind and crack of long whip snapping.

Startled roan has seen something too. It stands rigid, head up, staring left and forward. Stubby Pringle, body atingle, stares too. Out of dark of night ahead, mingled with moan of wind, comes a long-drawn chuckle, deep deep chuckle, jolly and cheery and full of smiles and joy of living. And with it long-drawn words.

We-e-e-l-l-l do-o-o-ne . . . pa-a-a-artner!

Stubby Pringle shakes his head. He brushes an icicle from his nose. "An' I didn't have a single drink," he says. "Only coffee an' can't count that. Reckon I'm getting soft in the head."

But he is cowman through and through, cowman through to the marrow. He can't ride on without stopping to check anything strange on his range. He swings down and leads off to the left. He fumbles in jacket pocket and finds a match. Strikes it. Holds it cupped and bends down. There they are. Unmistakable. Reindeer tracks.

Stubby Pringle stretches up tall. Stubby Pringle swings into saddle. Roan needs no slap of spurs to unleash strength in upward surge, up up up steep mountainside. It knows. There in saddle once more is Stubby Pringle, moonstruck maverick of the Triple X, all-around hard-proved hard-boned cowhand, ten feet tall, needing horse gigantic, with wings, iron-boned and dynamite-fueled, to take him home to little line cabin and some few winks of sleep before another day's hard work . . .

Stubby Pringle slips into cold clammy bunk. He wriggles vigorous to warm blanket under and blanket over.

"Was it worth all that riding?" comes voice of Old Jake Hanlon from other bunk on other wall.

"Why, sure," says Stubby. "I had me a right good time."

All right, now. Say anything you want. I know, you know, any dong-bonged ding-busted dang-blatted fool ought to know, that icicles breaking off branches can sound to drowsy ears something like sleigh bells. That blurry eyes half-asleep can see strange things. That deer and elk make tracks like those of reindeer. That wind sighing and soughing and moaning and maundering down mountains and through piny treetops can sound like someone shaping words. But we could talk and talk and it would mean nothing to Stubby Pringle.

Stubby is wiser than we are. He knows, he will always know, who it was, plump and jolly and belly-bouncing, that spoke to him that night out on wind-whipped winter-worn mountainside.

We-e-e-l-l-l do-o-o-ne . . . pa-a-a-rt-ner!

Merry Christmas,
All Authorized Personnel?

JOHN STEINBECK IV

*To young Americans who fought in or against the Vietnam War,
the traditional spirit of loving communication and optimism
must have appeared remote. One of those combatants was John
Steinbeck IV, who here tracks his own growing feeling of
cynicism through a frontline Christmas and an equally disen-
chanting one back home in postwar America. Yet, on a return
visit to Southeast Asia, the writer's cumulative disappointments
somehow resolve in a new understanding of Christmas as an
occasion endowed with humanistic meaning for all people.*

As I write this, it's not Christmas yet, and thinking now of the
coming event stirs only my memories of a Christmas in
Vietnam, of Tet, the Vietnamese new year celebration, and a
few fragments from my childhood holidays. It would be wonderful to be able to say that this Christmas will be the best
Christmas in my life, and to feel the moment as something
thrilling or perfectly Christian, and I mean that in the most

meek and ethereal sense of the word. But since I was sixteen, Christmas has often passed nearly unnoticed except for the commercial aspects of the holiday, which seemed always to overshadow everything.

On the eve of 1970, when you're too old to be singing boy soprano, despite the childhood memory of choiring in the high church, what does Christmas mean anymore? In America, beyond the platitudes of a secular fiesta of grotesque proportions in dollars and cents, what is Christmas? What will the festivities mean to my contemporaries? Most people are too jaded for Santa Claus by the time they're twelve. Judging from the way things are today, the whole concept of Christmas would have died fifty years ago but that Charles Dickens and O. Henry and a few poets breathed some life into it, which helped what remained of the warmth of the holiday to get this far.

No doubt there are millions of older Americans who have memories of Christmas with goose and turkey and cranberry sauce, and sleigh rides, and forages deep into the forest to get a prize tree, but unfortunately very little of this remains to cheer the children and youth of today. Department stores are the nuances of Christmas today with cocktail parties and big tips as the gestures of good will.

I remember my Christmas in Vietnam, when I was there in the Army, in an isolated outpost near Pleiku. For three weeks before Christmas, mail delivery had been regular and there were a lot of packages of crumbled chocolate chip cookies, fairly sturdy fruit cakes, and various kinds of gluey homemade candy. My friends and I ate it all immediately after it arrived, and began to grow nostalgic in the evenings when Armed Forces Radio began to broadcast more and more Christmas carols every evening from Saigon. We felt this holiday was exclusively our own, and it suddenly became a sad one because we were in an Asian land. It was hard to imagine Santa Claus, even without the war, bounding down the tin smokestack of a thatched hut.

On Christmas Eve there was a cease-fire, although guard duty on our mountain-top post was still mandatory. We felt that though we might not be the picture of mufflered, snow-flecked carolers, we at least had the chance of not having to endure the nightly rocket attack. Inside the low-ceilinged tents surrounded by sandbags, the pinups and family pictures near each cot were peppered with bright-colored Christmas cards from home. It was so hot most of us had our shirts off. We'd piled the goodies from that day's mail in the middle of the room on the table with the tree made out of a pyramid combination of barded wire and bayonets; the tree was trimmed with grenades and machine gun ammo belts for tinsel. We had our extra C rations of canned date pudding, chocolate bars, and crackers, and several cases of rapidly warming beer. We'd also pooled some money to get some Scotch from the black market in the town at the foot of the mountain.

I remember feeling that I was almost sorry Christmas had to be celebrated. We sat in a neon pool of light, drinking, eating, and sweating while the transistor radio reeled out Mel Torme singing "Chestnuts Roasting by the Open Fire" and repeated greetings sent to us boys out there in Vietnam by the President, various USO girl-voices, the Commanding General, and the Army announcer in Saigon, who was the only one who laughed when he said "Merry Christmas!"

Certainly for the GI, Christmas in Vietnam was what any Ernie Pyle fan would have loved. It gave us all a chance to feel like the great heroes of all the war movies we had grown up with. On Christmas Eve, marijuana or booze helped us all fantasize just what we would be doing if we were home right that instant. This was the great Christmas game, and by filibuster, you could tell the story as long as you could keep talking, but if you once tired, or paused to grab a beer, someone else would jump in with, "Well, that's pretty good, but that ain't nothing. Why if I was home, well let me see, right now it's almost Christmas morning. But back home in Massachusetts it's still the day before Christmas, and right now I'd be just driving my Chevy . . . did I ever tell you about the way I have my Chevy set up? . . . well, anyway, I'd just right now, right this instant be picking up my girl from her folks' house to take her over to my house to start putting the presents under the tree . . ." and the voices of fantasy would drift on the open Christmas caucus while everybody dreamed his own dream about where they would be at that precise moment if they weren't in a hole in the ground in the Nam.

The tragedy of those who would never see another Christmas was a terrible weight on the happiness of those of us who made it back; but for those who did, despite terrible homesickness, our Christmas in war gave some of our shabby lives a drama and pathos that was much better than watching war movies. Why, here we were starring in *Guadalcanal Diary* with much more guts and fortitude than Anthony Quinn or William Bendix ever gave to the role. For maybe the first Christmas, we were our parents' heroes to the man. You could almost hear them at their Christmas party and how they would be saying right now, "Merry Christmas everybody, and a toast and a prayer for our Billie away in Vietnam . . . that's him on the piano just after he got out of Basic."

But anyway you looked at it, Christmas remained pretty much a contrived affair. With these images and memories swirling in my brain. I cannot wonder that my generation has chosen to rebel against society, or to conclude that Christmas is meaningless. My generation is faced, seemingly, with two possibilities: either to hang on desperately and try to believe in the reality of the "old-fashioned" Christmas that the magazines give such great picture space to every year: or to accept the fact that Christmas is meaningless, especially in Vietnam burned out by almost thirty years of war.

These possibilities, and many more frightening ones, spurred me to go back to Vietnam as a civilian, after my discharge from the army. The country fascinated me, and I wanted to go there without a uniform, be vulnerable to a way of life and thought I had only been able to be nourished by at a distance.

As a civilian in Saigon, I saw another aspect of Christmas. At first, watching the little kids move among the tables on the terrace of the Continental cafe selling Vietnamese Christmas cards to the officers and newsmen, I still thought of Christmas

being an American, a Western celebration, and that the Vietnamese were only trying to make another quick dollar by
catering to the round-eyes' whimsies. But as I walked down Tu
Do street or Nguyen Hue street, I saw that all the stores and
stalls were crammed with green plastic fir trees, gee-gaws that
bristled and tinkled in the air, huge paper stars with a light
inside them, box upon box and row after row of toys from
Japan, France, and America, Hong Kong and Singapore. On a
side street I saw maybe thirty different vendors of real fir trees
as beautiful as I'd ever seen. They were brought down in trucks
from the mountains of Dalat.

My impression still was that all this must be a further sign
of the Americans' tendency to impose their cultural traditions
as well as their technology, upon the tiny country.

But I learned that this is not the case with Christmas. It is a
big holiday in Vietnamese cities because of the large Catholic
population. The Catholics represent fifth generation believers,
for one of France's justifications for colonizing Vietnam well
over one hundred years ago was not unlike that of Spain's in
Latin America: It was a mission to convert the heathen into the
true faith.

The Jesuits came and conquered, but, as in every other case
of foreign imposition on the Vietnamese, the people absorbed
the Catholic religion and made it into something uniquely
Vietnamese. It is possible to make endless comparisons between
Vietnamese Catholicism, Vietnamese folk religion, and pure
Buddhism if the purpose is to establish what is strict Roman
law and what is the actual Vietnamese interpretation of it. One
needs to remember that the origin of Christian symbols to
identify the various psychic or spiritual phenomena between
man and his universe have exact parallels in Taoist and Buddhist
thought. For the very reason that the Vietnamese bring to the
drama of Christ their own background containing their organic
suffering, there is a reinforcement of the divinity and authority
of that drama and Buddha's drama as well. The Hindu sacred
texts say: Worship, the worshiper, and the worshiped—these
three are one.

A couple of months after Christmas came Tet, which is a high holiday time of the year for everyone throughout Vietnam. Tet is still very much associated with the motif of spring—planting, budding, fertility. Truckloads of fresh flowers are brought into the cities from Dalat, and the people buy them in great quantities to decorate their homes, shrines, churches, and pagodas. Large branches from certain kinds of flowering fruit trees are for sale. A single one of these branches costs about forty dollars, but a great many of them are purchased for the home, where they are considered much more than mere decoration. If the buds on the branches blossom out during Tet, this is a mark of good fortune for the whole year. Particular emphasis is made on prayers, offerings, devotions to ancestors during Tet, and the Catholics and Buddhists all respond to the mood of this period.

The Americans are not quite sure what to do about Tet because there is a tension of excitement in the air then that carries with it the force and impact of what is truly, mysteriously Vietnamese, what cannot be molded and shaped to fit America's notion of what would be best for Vietnam. But to my mind, which is attracted more to the spiritual than the political, the mystery and excitement of the spring festival of Tet and the fervor of their Christmas gave me new feeling about my own idea of Christmas, new hope for my own country, America. That is: Tet, Christmas, or what have you, are manifestations of man's spiritual imagination. That aspect of man's nature will never die. Christmas commemorates a day that historically might have happened 2,000 years ago, though its place in space and time is immaterial. On that day, the infinite consciousness of God mingled and interchanged with the consciousness of man; in this particular case, it was Jesus Christ. This is not to say it couldn't have happened countless times before and after to men of love and charity. Every culture and its religion has its own way of helping you open the real Christmas gift, the potentiality of our own divinity. As new generations arise in America, with their peculiar rebellions and kinds of things they find enjoyment in, today's idea of Christmas may change in form and custom. But the change will always revolve around that fundamental truth: God is in man, and man, as he rediscovers this over and over, finding myriad doors opening in his soul, will find just as many ways to celebrate his joy.

The Talisman

MARGARET COUSINS

Margaret Cousins, a successful editor for Doubleday and later for a prominent women's magazine, often wrote Christmas stories for publication. Here she deals with a businesswoman who has been much too busy for marriage. She meets and falls in love with a married man and soon a decision must be reached about the future of the relationship. The solution to her dilemma comes from a talisman that was given to her by an elderly spinster long ago. Will the heroine follow her heart or will she turn back to the values of her youth? That is the central question of the following story about a New York Christmas in the early 1960s.

When I consider the events I am about to relate, I am aware that they contain elements of the ludicrous and that the interpretation placed on them may be a matter of personal whimsy. There must be more telling intimations that life is a grand design and that the unwitting seed, dropped in another time and place, still produces the straw that breaks the camel's back. But to simple people, whose crises (as far as they know) do not bulk large in the world's history, the instrument of

Margaret Cousins, "The Talisman," *McCall's Magazine*, December 1962. Permission to reprint this essay has been obtained from Anne Soorikian of *McCall's Magazine*.

decision should be in keeping, no more important or prepossessing than Mattie Stroud's pincushion.

Miss Mattie was not a woman you could rank with the archangels in either looks or personality. She was a sandy, irritating *femme seule* of indeterminate years, brusque in manner, long of tongue, whose chief distinction lay in the fact that she was solitary in a town where nobody ever knew what it was to be alone. The last of a dwindled line of grocery merchants, Miss Mattie subsisted on the remnants of an income in the old Stroud house on Warburton Street and was, therefore, not even a denizen of the deserving poor. She had never married, and my father, in relaxed moments, indicated that this was because she acted as if she had been weaned on a pickle. My mother pursed her mouth at such a heresy, insisting that Miss Mattie was a dear good soul, and changed the subject, to keep anybody from bringing up the legend that Miss Mattie was the victim of some sorry, backstreet romance, which had addled her life.

For 364 days of the year, Miss Mattie got along perfectly all right, minding her own business, which seemed to be chiefly gossip and needlework of the vintage of yellowing lines, marked with florid monograms, edgings of tatting and crochet and buttonholing, French knots and silken roses, moldering in a dowry cedar chest in the Warburton Street attic. Between the devising of doilies, fanciful with drawnwork, or dresser sets, which everybody had long since ceased to use, Miss Mattie practiced her eccentricities, which consisted of publicly washing her car, an ancient, high-waisted Buick she rarely drove, writing angry letters to the newspaper reporting any indiscretions of youth she was able to observe, and teasing small children, most of whom gave her wide berth. It was only at Christmas that she became my mother's burning responsibility. The thought of Miss Mattie, alone in the old Stroud house, without kith, kin, or turkey on the Lord's Birthday, reduced my mother, already staggering under the physical load of the annual pre-Christmas holocaust, to near hysteria.

"I think we should ask Mattie to come for breakfast this year," my mother said tentatively, about December fifteenth.

"Why?" my father inquired, straight to the point.

"In time for the tree," my mother said. "Gardner and Lucy will be bringing little Gardner, and Kenneth and Jody will be coming home from school and it's going to be unusually exciting."

"I don't see what that has to do with Mattie," my father answered obtusely.

"Oh, Walter," my mother said, tears springing to her delphinium eyes. "You know Mattie hasn't got anybody!" My mother, to whom any relation five times removed, be he blackguard, wastrel, or indigent crumb-bum, was a jewel to be cherished above rubies, found Miss Mattie's relationless situation more than human spirit could bear.

"But I never know what it is she has given me," my father complained. "How can I say, 'Thank you for the thingumabob'?" He had been gifted the season before with a pale-blue silk pillow three inches long, embroidered with forget-me-nots and his initials. Considerable delicate probing disclosed that this was a sachet to go in his collar box. Since my father had never worn a detachable collar in his life, even with a dinner jacket, he did not own a collar box; but he let it pass.

"You ought to be ashamed," my mother rebuked now. "Mattie works all year long on her presents for us."

"There ought to be a law," my father muttered. "Have you used up your hand-embroidered fly swatter?"

"It's a charming conceit," my mother stated primly.

"A fly approached with that swatter would drop dead of its own accord," my father said.

"Well," said my mother, as if that proved something.

"I wish she would get hep to the fact that I am past the age of mittens," Teddy, a senior in high school, chimed in.

I was about to put in my two cents worth about my lack of use for a combing jacket, with my haircut when my mother drew herself up. "Not another word," she said. "It's not the gift, it's the spirit of the thing. I want you always to remember that!" She then thought up enough chores to keep us all lashing in her wake until dark. Everybody knew, without knowing how or why, she had won her point. . .

It is hard to know whether Christmas in those days is hallowed in the mind's eye by time and distance or whether it was actually the glistening season of wonderment it seemed to be. Has the world, in its acceleration, in its new confusions, its teetering on the horizon of infinity, its incredible inventions fomenting toward the stars, lost the power of innocent merriment? Or will some youth of today, a decade or so from now, be retracing his footsteps through the same old continents of the heart?

Christmas was such a time—such a triumph of housewifery, such a contest of culinary skill, such a bell-wether for clan gathering, for the drawing in of that ancient and respected unit of society, the family. They gathered around the communal hearth, and there was a melding of the generations in one day of armed truce; a welcoming of prodigals and a burying of old hatchets. Nobody bothered to consult the seed of these miracles or knew whether it was the mince pies cooling in toothsome ranks on the back porch, the turkey turning brown in the oven, the table laid in ironed damask splendor, the rustle of red ribbons, or the shining eyes of satiated childhood that engendered good will or that made of diverse individuals an indestructible entity. But it was something to do with the women, ruling their little season, basking in the reflected glory of the Queen of Heaven. It was somehow concerned with the fantasy and imagination to which women are prone. It was the time in which women, for a little space, got their way.

Miss Mattie came for breakfast.

It is beside the point that she stayed through dinner. There was nothing new about that. At Christmas, Miss Mattie, who didn't have anybody, had all of us. She wheeled up in her Buick at eight in the morning, with her freight of handmade delicacies, neatly tied with last year's well-pressed ribbons, and under the stern eye of my mother, was welcomed by all and sundry. Removing her weathered tweed coat and blowing her red nose, Miss Mattie adjusted her spectacles and remarked that the tree had a hole on that side. My father, who had selected the tree, apologized. Throughout the day—the wild fray of exchanging gifts as the tree showered down its loot, the breakfast scramble, the eggnog when the neighbors dropped in—Miss Mattie lived up to her reputation of pebble in the shoe and kept happiness from getting out of hand.

My brother Gardner's little boy, delirious with joy over a new puppy, was advised by Miss Mattie that that particular breed of dog required to have his tail cut off and would probably bleed to death. Miss Mattie took issue with one neighbor's politics and told Mrs. Braden, from next door, that she seemed to be gaining weight. She suggested that Kenneth would never pass his midterms and would be booted out of college. She advised me, in transports over a slave bracelet presented to me by Barry Westfall, my current heart interest, that there was bad blood in the Westfall line and that I had best watch my step. She prophesied that my younger brother, Ted, was too weedy to make the football team, and she quizzed Jody about her love life. Jody was in boarding school and didn't have a love life.

My mother, between her manifold duties, was constantly smoothing over the depredations of poor old Miss Mattie and keeping us in check, like a team of wild horses, and such were the blandishments of the season that mayhem was not done.

As the day wore on and we finally sat down to dinner in the glimmer of candlelight, even Miss Mattie had subsided to a state of grace. I can remember looking around the table—laid with the gold-banded china and the best glasses, with little Gardner, Junior, raised to table level with three thick volumes, my father at the head, my mother at the foot, and all the familiar family faces up and down the groaning board—thinking that I was perfectly happy, that nothing could add to that moment of Christmas. As my father mumbled his immemorial grace, which he seemed to feel God already knew all about, I counted my blessings—my new squirrel bolero, my new slave bracelet, and all the old love that had sheltered my life like a sturdy roof. It was then that my heart went out to each of them, forgiving them every little abrasion of human association and willing them to forgive me. I even forgave Miss Mattie.

In the solstice that follows overeating, there was the stir of leaving, as Miss Mattie tooled off, satisfied with her unoriginal loot of hosiery and toilet water and scarves and slippers (which I daresay suited her as ill as her gifts to us) and for having told us how the cow ate the cabbage. Kenneth went to get his girl, and Barry Westfall, to my intense pleasure, dropped by. My father and mother (her eyes shining with success) went off to a party. Lucy put little Gardner down for a nap in the spare room, and the rising generation sat around the fire—the boys experimenting with illicit Martinis, and the girls experimenting with illicit cigarettes—and yearned toward the future and sophistication and the great world, since this one left little to be desired.

It was during this aftermath that we also experimented with cruelty and held poor old Miss Mattie and her offerings up to ridicule. We had all received our customary mementos—hand-embroidered shoe rags for Kenneth and Teddy and Gardner; doilies for Lucy; and camisoles, which Jody and I didn't recognize and didn't know what to do with, for us. My father had been the recipient of half a dozen knitted miniature bootees, designed to cover golf clubs, except that my father didn't play golf.

But for my mother, Miss Mattie had gone all the way.

"But what *is* it?" Ted demanded, holding up the masterpiece. It was a green velvet bullfrog, with shoe-button eyes, posed on a flat pad and surrounded with white lace ruffles, quite obviously intended to simulate the petals of a water lily. The frog's spots had been meticulously embroidered with yellow silk thread, along with a legend on the lily pad, which read: "Look before you leap."

It was easily one of the most hideous objects I have ever seen. There was something malevolent about the homemade frog, covered with his spots and nestled in lace ruffles, and the bossy injunction. Artist Miss Mattie was not, but a woman's reach must exceed her grasp!

"Maybe it's a hat," Gardner said, snatching it and putting it on his crew cut. We all roared.

"Or a corsage," Jody cried, holding it to her bosom.

We all tried it on various aspects of our anatomy and managed to be faintly obscene.

"I think it's a pincushion," I said. "Something for someone who has everything!"

"I'd like to stick some pins in *her*," Kenneth said, still sulking over Miss Mattie's twitting about his never passing his midterms. "Speaking of toads."

It was at this moment of unspoken consent that the tradition began. When Kenneth went back to Amherst, Jody and I, giggling like children, concealed the pincushion in his luggage. Kenneth, who passed his examinations with flying colors, never admitted to the plant, and my mother never asked for the pincushion.

We did not see it again until the following Christmas, when Lucy rushed to the hospital prematurely to bear her second baby, found it reposing on the dressing gown in her suitcase.

The next year, Kenneth and Ted were in the war. Ted was in Malta with the Navy, and Kenneth was sweating it out with the Air Force in Florida. When Ted opened his Christmas parcel, sometime in February, Miss Mattie's frog confronted him, with suitable sneer. Ted posted it back from Malta with his presents to the family the next Christmas having preserved it in his foot locker through a long year of war.

Our circle had narrowed, and my mother's eyes were shadowed with absence, but she laughed when the saw it. "Wherever has that thing been?" she asked. "Poor old Miss Mattie's frog." Miss Mattie had been gathered to her reward some time before.

When Jody phoned me from Northampton to say that she was determined to marry an unknown soldier before he put out for North Africa, I had time to buy her a nightgown and enclose the talisman. Later, she called to say that the soldier's leave was canceled and she was keeping the nightgown; but she never saw him again. When Gardner and Lucy had a falling out and Lucy took the children and went home to her mother for a visit, Gardner received it by parcel post, in a plain wrapper.

The years wore on, and I stopped wearing my slave bracelet and moved to New York and got a job at Lord & Taylor's. Kenneth married a girl from Seattle and went to work at Boeing Aircraft. Ted studied law at Harvard and settled in Lincoln, Nebraska, where he married, and Jody got involved in television and married a producer, who moved to California. They all procreated and presented me with a string of nieces and nephews. As long as my father and mother lived, some of us straggled home for Christmas, as many as could afford it or could manage the time, often at great inconvenience. But even as the ranks thinned, we kept our Christmas merry still. After a while, there was no reason to go home.

With the passage of time, I moved up in merchandising, which I found enthralling. I suppose I acquired the kind of gloss of sophistication that a country girl considers necessary. The fashion business traded up my clothes, and since I had a homing instinct, I had a pretty apartment and a part-time maid, and I gave stylish little parties and sat in dark little bars and talked knowledgeably about the market with important businessmen. I went to Europe and dabbled in culture and joined organizations and sat on boards and bought an abstract painting. I had hundreds of acquaintances and two or three friends and some off-again-on-again beaux, who weren't serious. I was terribly busy.

At first, we made some effort to get together at Christmas after we no longer had a family home. Once I flew to California to be with Jody and my brother-in-law. They were both dears, but it was a strange time and a strange place, and I felt all at sea. Then Gardner and Lucy brought the children to New York one Christmas. They were already teen-agers, and we had a harassed season of sight-seeing and whipped up jollity; but the apartment suddenly seemed too small. We parted with mutual relief. I met Ted and his family in Miami one winter; but Christmas in a hotel is never the best thing, especially with young children, and the weather turned cold and gray, so it was expensive and a sort of frost. Kenneth was simply too far away. After these efforts, we all relaxed and pursued our separate ways.

Christmas in New York can be quite pleasant. I got in the habit of giving a brunch for waifs and strays who couldn't get away to go home or didn't have one to go to. This became a tradition and was occasionally mentioned in a column. I went to three or four cocktail parties a day all during the season and began to look forward to the New Year, when I would have time to worry about the bills I had run up. I was showered with undeserved loot of the most extravagant sort, and the apartment was always massed with red roses, which I was known to favor. Needless to say, I was on a diet, so that an old-fashioned spread was something I wouldn't have approached with a ten-foot pole. The thought of the calories in one eggnog turned me pale. The telephone rang all the time, and the cards and notes accumulated, and I was a big operator. Christmas was an operation. Everything was an operation.

Eventually, however, I fell in love. I met a husband, but he wasn't mine. He wasn't exactly a husband, but he wasn't divorced, and he was the father of two. He had moved to a hotel long before he hove over my horizon, and he saw his family only on Sundays. There is no way for me to describe Bradley, since I saw him only with the eyes of infatuation. I doubt that I know what he was really like. At the time, he seemed to me to be a cross between Benjamin Franklin and Apollo, but I doubt that. He was a man, and in some aspects, they all have something in common, especially as far as womankind goes. Beauty, character, quality, intelligence—all are in the eye of the beholder at such a time. In any event, Bradley never got to Rye except on Sundays, and the rest of the week he was on the town. He was good company, I'll say that. I met him in the summer, and we had a marvelous time. We experienced a resurgence of immaturity and acted like teenagers, though the clock was already striking the nether hours. I never meant to fall in love with him, if I did. Somewhere in the back of my well-schooled brain a signal always kept bonging: "Keep it light." I don't think he ever intended to fall in love with me. He just hated to eat alone.

It's a curious thing about being a woman in business. You learn so many disciplines, and you handle so many problems, and you think as much through that it makes you brave. You achieve a kind of arrogance and know-how that convince you you can cope, and usually you *can* cope with everything that doesn't really matter. The ability to block out the nagging doubt, or deal with the instinctive reaction tomorrow, or accept, without turning a hair, a situation that would once have made your blood run cold comes with practice. Not only do you accept it, but everybody else accepts it, with the possible exception of the man's wife and children, and they are people you never meet. They live in another world, and you live in yours, which has its own rules. There was never any thought about my being the other woman; I was just Bradley's girl. That armor, which enables you to survive in the contemporary jungle, never indicates to you that it has a fissure somewhere around the left ventricle.

When Brad announced that we were flying to Jamaica for Christmas—just he and I—that sounded marvelous. Christmas fell on a long weekend. We could have three days and be back on Sunday. My mind neatly blocked out all the ramifications of such a holiday. I got together a wardrobe of resort clothes. If I wanted to go to Jamaica, I could. I earned my own living. I could pay my own way. I could choose my own companion. Whose business was it?

The very fact that I had to defend my action to myself must have had some sublimated source, but I never permitted it to rise to the surface. I was delighted at the thought of leaving behind the soiled snows of New York and the *Sturm und Drang* of merchandising. I looked forward to Jamaica. The usual seasonal hysteria was in progress. In addition to the store, I had to buy gifts, get them delivered, address the cards, cancel the brunch, mail off the packages, tip the unvarying queue that has to be tipped, get a permanent, have my teeth cleaned, fend off invitations, and show up at a few parties.

When I got home to pack the night before we were leaving, I was in a state of such advanced exhaustion that I couldn't eat and my mind didn't seem to be working. The packing was haphazard, and my bags were too small. At two o'clock in the morning, I was still wrestling with luggage, and there simply wasn't room. I got the stepladder, invaded the top shelf of my closet, and retrieved a cosmetic case I hadn't used in years.

It was a little pigskin fitted case, somewhat scuffed and disreputable, but it didn't look dangerous. I dusted it off and sat down on the bed to fiddle with the combination lock, which had been my first street number in New York. When I finally remembered that, the lock turned easily. I flung back the lid. Miss Mattie's pincushion looked up at me with bright and beady shoe-button eyes.

I was so startled that I swallowed a scream. If I *had* screamed and flung the frog in the wastebasket, I might never have taken it up and turned it over and over in my hands and read the old embroidered legend on the lily pad, now so dusty and frayed and faded.

And then I wouldn't have remembered.

What I remembered was not Miss Mattie or her impossible gifts or even my mother's determined gathering her in, but that circle of faces around the table in a more innocent time—the family whose love had been a roof over my head and always would be. It all washed over me in waves—the smell of spice and drying evergreens, the polished silver and the darn in the damask, the child perched on the three fat volumes—the unshakable solidarity. I heard again the mumbled grace, saw the light in my mother's eyes, and tasted happiness like a morsel on my tongue. A family has to stay together. I thought. Any family.

I didn't even try to work it out. I unpacked my resort clothes and hung them in the back of the closet and put the pincushion in the bottom drawer until somebody should need it.

I won't say that was a happy Christmas for me, in the

conventional sense, or that I can lay claim to one single shred of nobility, or even that I deserved to be saved by the gong. But it was curiously exciting, because something had really happened to me. I had learned something, and it had been an awfully long time since I had learned anything.

It becomes increasingly difficult for the cocksure to learn: but there is nothing like a continuing education. What I learned in that brief moment has had an invaluable effect on my entire life. The effect it has had on the lives of others may be considered extremely salubrious as well; but, actually, one can manage only his own life. What I learned was that Christmas outweighed all the busy, superficial knowledge of the world I had come to know.

The Gift

RAY BRADBURY

Ray Bradbury, one of America's more prolific literary imaginations who early put his money on space, chose a very simple topic for a Christmas Eve tale. What if there were no room for a tree on the rocket ship to Mars? Today's men, women, and children are hovering between the nearness and dearness of the familiar and the enchantment of the strange and faraway. In the nineteenth century, the Frenchman Jules Verne stretched his literary inventiveness to imagine what it might be like for regular earthlings to travel in space. Today, with so much more history under the bridge, the talent for illusion of countless film and television creators has flooded consumer dreams (in particular those of children) with what new forms we may expect in the way of friends and enemies, furniture and gadgets, and indeed, total environments, should we begin actually to live in space. But few creators have come up with answers more satisfying than Bradbury in this disarming little story.

There was no room for a tree on the rocket ship to Mars . . .

Ray Bradbury, "The Gift," in Norma Ainsworth, ed., *14 Favorite Christmas Stories* (New York: Scholastic Book Services, 1964), 153–56. Permission to reprint this story has been obtained from Mary Ann Flynn of Don Congdon Associates.

Tomorrow would be Christmas, and even while the three of them rode to the rocket port, the mother and father were worried. It was the boy's first flight into space, his very first time in a rocket, and they wanted everything to be perfect. And when, at the customs table, they were forced to leave behind the toy and the little tree with the lovely white candles, they felt themselves deprived of a great pleasure.

The boy was waiting for them in the Mars Rocket Terminal room. Walking toward him, after their unsuccessful clash with the Interplanetary Customs, the mother and father whispered to each other.

"What will we do?"

"Nothing, nothing. What *can* we do?"

"Silly rules!"

"And he was *so* much looking forward to the tree."

The siren gave a great scream, and people leaped up and pressed forward into the Mars Rocket, pushing the mother and father and their thin son along among the rumble and tussle.

"I'll think of something," said the father.

"What?" asked the boy.

But the rocket took off and they were flung immediately into dark space.

The rocket traveled at 29,000 miles an hour, leaving behind it Earth, on which the date was December 24, 2052, heading out into a place where there was no time at all, no month, no year, no hour. They slept away the first "day." Near midnight, by their Earth-time watches, the boy awoke and said, "I want to go look out the port window."

There was only one port, and that was up on another deck. "Not quite yet," said the father. "I'll take you up later."

"I want to see where we are and where we're going."

"There's plenty of time for that." The father had been thinking, lying awake, considering the problem of the toy and the wonderful tree and the white candles. And at last he had found a plan; he need only carry it out, and life would be very fine indeed.

"Son," he said, "in exactly one hour it will be Christmas."

"Oh," said the mother, dismayed that he mentioned it. She had rather hoped the boy would forget.

The boy's face grew pale and feverish. "I know, I know! Will I get a present? Will I have a tree?"

"Yes, all of that, but much more," said the father.

The mother started, "But—"

"I *mean* it." The father gave her a look.

He left their little cabin for ten minutes. When he came back he was smiling. "Almost time."

"Can I hold your watch?" asked the boy, and held his father's watch while the rest of the hour drifted by in fire and space and silent motion.

"It's Christmas *now!* Christmas! Where's my present?"

"Here we go," said the father, and took his boy by the shoulder and led him from the room, up several rampways through the rocket, his wife following.

"What . . . ?" she asked.

"Here we are," said the father.

"It's dark."

"I'll hold your hand. Come on, Mama."

They moved into the room and the door shut, and the room was very dark indeed. And before them loomed a great glass eye, the porthole, six feet high and ten feet wide, from which they could look out into space.

The boy gasped.

Behind him, the father and the mother gasped, also, and then in the dark room some people began to sing.

"Merry Christmas, Son," said the father.

And the voices in the room sang the old carols. And he moved forward slowly until his face was pressed against the cool glass of the port. And he stood there for a long, long time, just looking and looking out into space and the deep night at the burning and the burning of ten billion billion white and lovely candles. . . .

Epilogue

Christmas, in the five hundred years since the wreck of the *Santa Maria,* has become the most demanding of all American festivals. The holiday is now an epic event, celebrated from mid-October to mid-January, thanks in large measure to merchandising and advertising, two of the great opinion-making forces in American society.

Shop windows from hamlet to metropolis are decorated, and one enterprising retail chain sponsors a fall parade that has become synonymous with the beginning of Christmas. Not only are businesses aglow, but lighted trees inside and outside homes are standard, while many cities and towns use civic centers or official buildings as the hub of an elaborate scheme of holiday decor. Newspapers and periodicals stress the human interest themes, ranging from the president's lighting of the White House tree to seasonal emphasis on the poor and powerless, who live in slums or on the street. Radio and television broadcast popular and traditional music and drama on the Christmas theme. Mass media, someone said, have created public mania!

Pastor and priest alike seem at times to have given up on restoring Christmas as a purely religious occasion. In fact, their efforts often appear directed largely at competing for ways to keep the spiritual message going. Midnight masses are scheduled on Christmas Eve and other church services on Christmas Day, to share the good news in accommodation to the schedules of a maximum number of parishioners. The faithful may also attend organ and choral recitals and Sunday school pageants, and watch broadcasts of larger such events. But meager budgets and pulpit salaries cannot match the buying power or talent reserve of the national networks, where in general the sacred aspects of

Christmas have been overtaken by the secular. Still, in times of crisis, such as wars or depressions, there is often a more sober, even sombre tone that cuts into the reign of *Santa Claus Americanus*.

The legal state of Christmas is an interesting situation and one that is still being defined by courts across the land. Our national government, because of the principle of separation of church and state, has not made December 25th an official holiday. On the other hand, many of the states have elected to give the festival a legal or quasi-legal status. The latter development has spawned a variety of court tests, some of which were focused on getting at the character of Christmas and some that sought clarification of the government's role in the celebration. In 1926, for example, just one year after Scopes was tried for teaching evolution, Judge John H. Hatcher of the West Virginia Supreme Court of Appeals, anticipated real court challenges in a hypothetical case called *ex parte Santa Claus*. His opinion concluded: "Let the legislatures outlaw the law of evolution if they must; let the Constitution be amended until it looks like a patchwork quilt; but rob not childhood of its most intriguing mystery—Santa Claus."[1] The judge's colleagues on the bench unanimously agreed.

Twenty-one years later the nation was to become intrigued by a cinematic debate over Santa Claus. In 1947 Valentine Davis published a best seller called *Miracle on 34th Street*. The movie, produced later, featured child star Natalie Wood and two of the era's most popular stars: John Payne and Maureen O'Hara. A classic shown on television at holiday time, the film is about an employee of Macy's department store whom the state of New York wants to commit to a mental institution for insisting that he is the real Kris Kringle. The high point of the story is a trial in which Fred Gayley, Kris's attorney, wins the sanity plea by pointing out that the U.S. Post Office had forwarded mail to Kringle and that this deed, performed by an old and revered federal agency, should be accepted as proof of identity. Kringle is allowed to stay on as a Macy's employee to the relief of all concerned, including the judge and prosecutor, who had been getting into hot water with the public for bothering Santa Claus.

Not too much later, real court cases showed up. Sensitive to racial discrimination after World War II, the Jews became concerned with maintaining the separation of church and state. In particular, they scrutinized the issue of a national Christmas celebration. Many such Americans believed they had too long endured the pressures of Christmas on their children. Some worked to create "exchange" celebrations in the neighborhood so that families of different faiths learned something about the practices of each other. Some followed the old American axiom, "If you can't lick 'em, join 'em," advocating the substitution of Hanukkah in December for Christmas so that Jewish children could feel a sense of participation.

Sharpening of the social conscience led to outright challenge in the halls of justice. In New York State, Albert Vorspan, vice president of the Union of the American Hebrew Congregations, stated, "It is craven and irresponsible to allow one of New York City's unique resources—the park that belongs equally to everyone of us—to become a cockpit of religious conflict" by displaying a crèche on the lawn of Central Park.[2] The American Civil Liberties Union challenged an order by Chicago's mayor to exhibit a nativity scene at city hall and won removal of the scene. Judge Ann Diggs Taylor, a Michigan magistrate, prohibited a crèche display in Dearborn. Responding to such battles and not wishing to offend any American, the White House did not display a nativity scene on its lawn for eleven years. Subsequently, officials of the Community for Creative Non-violence sued Secretary of the Interior Donald P. Hodel and won; the crèche was restored to the president's lawn.

In the post-Vietnam era, state courts also began to seem more friendly toward public display of Christmas scenes. A tribunal in Pawtucket, Rhode Island, ruled that a crèche owned by the city and exhibited on private property was permissible because it was more cultural than Christian. The New York Court of Appeals voted to let stand a lower court decision protecting a nativity display from removal in Scarsdale in 1986.

Pollsters such as George Gallup tried to figure out what it all meant. Was the change in religious practices indicative of parallel change in other traditional American values? Gallup announced that 95 percent of Americans believed in God, and 68 percent belonged to churches; yet, infidelity and cheating on taxes were on the rise. This, he indicated, might suggest failure of "organized religion to make a difference in society in terms of morality and ethics."[3]

Public school Christmas practices are also being challenged. Keeping Christmas had been a matter of controversy just before and after World War I. But school administrators began to be more sensitive to the feelings of non-Christian minorities, and in the 1970s and 1980s, a number of new cases moved into court. Fairly typical was *Florey v. Sioux Falls School District Number 49–5*, in which some Sioux Falls citizens had complained about the illegality of including Christmas material in a 1977 school pageant. A South Dakota federal court heard the case and ruled that the First Amendment had not been violated by the programs, which were secular in purpose, did not promote one faith over another, did not foster excessive government entanglement, and were not illegal. With the Supreme Court's refusal to review, the decision held, and Christmas programs were continued.[4]

National and international events of consequence continued to color and shape our celebration of Christmas. In November 1963 the assassination of President John F. Kennedy caused many citizens to fly individual and institutional flags at halfmast until well after the holiday. In 1979 President Carter's daughter Amy pressed a button in Washington, D.C., that controlled lights on the White House Christmas tree and some fifty others on the lawn. To the surprise of onlookers, however, only the white star on the largest tree and tiny blue bulbs on the smaller ones began to glow. The president explained to the audience of 7,500, referring to the American hostages being held in Iran, "We will turn on the rest of the lights when the hostages come home."[5] In 1980 the White House tree was lit for only forty-seven seconds, one for each day of the hostages' captivity.

President-elect Reagan called the abductors criminals and kidnappers and lauded the thousands of Americans who tied yellow ribbons to their outdoor trees in further commemoration of their absent countrymen.

With the end of the hostage crisis, there seemed to be a new spirit of unity in families and some healing of a generational conflict that began when U.S. public support for the Vietnam War turned sour. Young married couples searched for a means of keeping Christmas with integrity in their homes. Anthropologist Margaret Mead phrased this trend succinctly: "How much of the past—which past—and whose past—shall we include in the Christmas we are preparing?"6

This quest for the most appropriate symbols and practices remains at the heart of American Christmas in our democratic and pluralistic society. Choices made along the way must be negotiated among all participants involved and those that allow diversity somehow seem the most historically American.

In this manner Christmas can be a bridge between past and present and a touchstone for renewal. At the very least, Christmas is and for most Americans will probably continue to be a reminder that humankind, hurtling through time and space, needs faith, hope, and charity.

Notes

1. Jim Comstock, ed., *West Virginia Heritage Encyclopedia*, Supplement, vol. 14 (Charleston, W. Va.: James Comstock, 1974), 201. I am indebted to Elizabeth Fraser of the Kanauka County Public Library for this citation.
2. *Christian Century* 102, no. 41 (16 January 1985): 16.
3. *America* 153 (21 December 1985): 434.
4. For a concise summary of this case, see Allen D. Schwartz, "Can Public Schools Celebrate Christmas?" *Education Digest* 47 (December 1981): 60–61.
5. *Time Magazine* 144 (14 December 1979): 8.
6. Margaret Mead, "Can Christmas Bring the Generations Together?" *Redbook* 142, no. 2 (December 1973): 27.

Acknowledgments

Keeping Christmas—that is, this particular book under that particular title—has been a long time being born. It was in the draft stage for almost ten years. Early in the 1980s, I joined forces with a bright young graduate student, Edward Daniel Kliska. Together we discussed the possibility of a book consisting of selected essays on all (or nearly all) of the American holidays. As do most projects, this one was to benefit enormously from a narrowing of scope. We soon concluded that our original project was far too massive, and we decided to focus on the American keeping of Christmas.

We thought our first organizational scheme was pure genius. We wanted to develop the manuscript around the rites of passage enumerated by Jacques in the "Seven Ages of Man" soliloquy from Shakespeare's *As You Like It*. We gathered stories and sorted them into seven stacks, beginning with the Infant and ending with the Old Man. This approach produced a confused chronology that muddled the historical intent of Shakespeare's design. Shortly thereafter, Edward and I abandoned the project as a joint venture, although working together has left us fast friends and it is a pleasure here to note his early contributions to the idea of a book on Christmas.

In 1985 I embarked once more, at the insistence of my wife, Annette, on the trail of Christmas in America. Two friends and colleagues from Tucson, Elizabeth Shaw and Becky Staples, agreed to look over my shoulder provided that I put aside my flirtation with social science and revert to the historical skills that have served me in writing ventures for more than twenty five years. So I proceeded, in a fairly solitary way, on an extended journey into the American past.

More and more I experienced Christmas as a fascinating topic. December 25 is a day that is indeed the best and worst of times, engendering complex blends of happiness and sadness, religion and superstition, euphoria and depression. The title for the final version came from Captain John Smith, who proclaimed in 1608 that, "Wherever an Englishman may be, and in whatever part of the world, he must keep Christmas with feasting and merriment!"

To piece together and tell this story, I have imposed on literally hundreds of authors, colleagues, editors, literati and their families, friends, librarians, permissions departments, politicians, publishers, reporters, and scholars in and out of Clio's domain. Among the greatest of my blessings was the splendid research assistance of Pamela Mendoza, Kellie Layton, James Haworth, Rebecca Patton, DeAnna Beachley, and Nancy Cannon. A colleague of two decades, Delno West, loaned me the text of the *La Navidad* document of Christopher Columbus. My largest debt is to Becky Staples for translating the Columbus document and for her insightful continuing advice. The publishing prescience of Elizabeth Shaw kept me on target for more than two years while essays were compiled and the narrative written for *Keeping Christmas*. Without them this manuscript might never have been exposed to printer's ink.

Documents and stories in this book come from many individuals and institutions: the former are identified in the credits accompanying many of the selections themselves; the latter are gratefully enumerated here. Appreciation is extended to the Northern Arizona University Library in Flagstaff; the Arizona State University Library in Tempe; the University of Arizona Library in Tucson; the Public Library, the Massachusetts Historical Society and the Athenaeum in Boston; the American Antiquarian Society in Worcester; the Houghton Library of Harvard; the John Carter Brown University Library in Providence; the William and Mary Library in Williamsburg, Virginia; the University of Virginia Library in Charlottesville; the Philadelphia Public Library; the Huntington Library in San Marino, California; and numerous small local libraries along the Hudson River and elsewhere in the states of New York and New Jersey, and, via interlibrary loans, from Hawaii to Florida. A very special "thank you" is extended to the staff of the Colonial Williamsburg Foundation, whose assistance finally unlocked the mysteries of Christmas in the colonial period.

Finally, I am most appreciative of the time and money provided by Kit Hinsley and Gene Hughes for research and writing. A mentor, Bill Seiler, and a colleague, George Lubick, read the next-to-the-last draft and each offered helpful suggestions. Margaret Cousins, who had returned to Texas after her career in New York by the time I met her, provided much insight into twentieth-century authors from her living room in San Antonio, Texas.

Suggested Readings

Books

Ainsworth, Norma Ruedi, ed. *14 Favorite Christmas Stories*. New York: Scholastic Book Services, 1964.

Alden, Raymond MacDonald. *Why The Chimes Rang and Other Stories*. Indianapolis, Ind.: Bobbs-Merrill Co., 1906.

Aldrich, Bess Streeter. *Journey into Christmas*. New York: Appleton-Century, 1949.

Auld, William Muir. *Christmas Traditions*. New York: Macmillan Co., 1931. Reprint. Detroit, Mich.: Gale Research Co., Book Tower, 1968.

Barnett, James. *The American Christmas: A Study in National Culture*. New York: Macmillan, 1954.

Baur, John E. *Christmas on the American Frontier 1800–1900*. Caldwell, Idaho: Caxton Printers, 1961.

Becker, May Lamberton, ed. *The Home Book of Christmas*. New York: Dodd, Mead and Co., 1941.

Brady, Cyrus Townsend. *A Little Book For Christmas*. Freeport, N.Y.: Books for Libraries Press, 1971.

Brentano, Francis, ed. *The Light of Christmas*. New York: E. P. Dutton and Co., 1964.

Buck, Pearl S. *Once Upon A Christmas*. New York: John Day Co., 1972.

Butcher, Fanny. *Christmas in Chicago*. Boston: Houghton Mifflin Co., 1926.

Cairns, Huntington, ed. *H. L. Mencken: The American Scene, A Reader*. New York: Alfred A. Knopf, 1965.

Capote, Truman. *Breakfast at Tiffany's. A Short Novel and Three Stories*. New York: Signet Books, 1958.

Carroll, Gladys Hasty. *Christmas Through The Years*. Boston: Little, Brown and Co., 1968.

Coffin, Robert P. Tristam. *Christmas in Maine*. Garden City, N.Y.: Doubleday, Doran and Co., 1942.

Coffin, Tristram P. *The Book of Christmas Folklore*. New York: Seabury Press, 1973.

Colonial Williamsburg Foundation. *A Williamsburg Christmas*. New York: Holt, Rinehart, and Winston, 1980.

Commager, Henry Steele, ed. *The St. Nicholas Anthology*. New York: Random House, 1948.

———. *The Second St. Nicholas Anthology*. New York: Random House, 1950.

Curtiss, Phebe A., ed. *Christmas Stories and Legends*. Indianapolis: Meigs Publishing Co., 1916.

Dawson, W. F. *Christmas: Its Origins and Associations*. London: Elliot Stock, 1902. Reprint. Detroit, Mich.: Gale Research Co., Book Tower, 1968.

DeGrazia, Ted. *Christmas Fantasies*. Tucson, Ariz.: DeGrazia Gallery in the Sun, 1977.

Del Re, Gerard and Patricia. *The Christmas Almanack*. Garden City, N.Y.: Doubleday and Co., 1979.

De Robeck, Nesta. *The Christmas Crib*. Milwaukee, Wis.: Bruce Publishing Co., 1956.

Dunphy, Hubert M. *Christmas Every Christmas*. Milwaukee, Wis.: The Bruce Publishing Co., 1960.

Emurian, Ernest K. *Stories of Christmas Carols*. Boston: W. A. Wilde Co., 1958.

Engle, Paul. *An Old Fashioned Christmas*. New York: Dial Press, 1964.

Field, Eugene. *The Holy Cross and Other Tales*. New York: Charles Scribner's Sons, 1905.

———. *A Little Book of Profitable Tales*. New York: Charles Scribner's Sons, 1924.

Foster, Helen. *Christmas in Desert Country*. Phoenix, Ariz.: Sims Printing Co., 1977.

Fremantle, Anne, ed. *Christmas Is Here: A Catholic Selection of Stories and Poems*. New York: Stephen Daye Press, 1955.

Frost, Lesley, ed. *Come Christmas*. New York: Coward-McCann, 1929.

Gabrilowitsch, Clara Clemens. *My Father, Mark Twain*. New York: Harper and Row, 1931.

Graham, Eleanor, ed. *Welcome Christmas!* New York: E. P. Dutton and Co., 1932.

Hale, Lucretia P. *The Complete Peterkin Papers*. Boston: Houghton Mifflin Co., 1960.

Harris, Joel Chandler, ed. *The World's Wit and Humor*. Vols. 3 and 4. New York: Review of Reviews Co., 1906.

Harte, Bret. *Mrs. Skagg's Husbands and Other Sketches*. New York: Garrett Press, 1969.

Haugan, Randolph E. *Christmas: An American Annual of Christmas Literature and Art*. Vols. 1–52. Minneapolis, Minn.: Augsburg Publishing House.

Hervey, Thomas K. *The Book of Christmas*. Chicago: Cuneo Press, 1951.

Hewitt, Edward Ringwood. *Those Were the Days: Tales of a Long Life*. New York: Duell, Sloan and Pearce, 1943.

Hughes, Langston. *Simple Takes a Wife*. New York: Simon and Schuster, 1953.

———, ed. *The Best Short Stories of Negro Writers*. Boston: Little, Brown and Co., 1967.

Lardner, Ring W. *Round Up*. New York: Charles Scribner's Sons, 1924.

Lewis, D. B. Wyndham, and G. C. Heseltine, eds. *A Christmas Book: An Anthology For Moderns*. London: J. M. Dent & Sons; New York: E. P. Dutton and Co., 1928.

Lewis, Taylor, Jr., and Joanne Young. *Christmas in the Southwest*. New York: Holt, Rinehart, and Winston, 1973.

Lexau, Joan. *The Christmas Secret*. New York: Scholastic Book Services, 1969.

Lohan, Robert and Maria, eds. *A New Christmas Treasury*. New York: Stephen Daye Press, 1954.

Love, W. DeLoss, Jr. *The Fast and Thanksgiving Days of New England*. Boston: Houghton Mifflin Co., 1895.

Lowance, Mason Ira, Jr. *Increase Mather*. New York: Twayne Publishers, 1974.

Mabie, Hamilton W., ed. *The Book of Christmas*. New York: Macmillan Co., 1909.

Mather, Increase. *A Testimony Against Several Prophane and Superstitious Customs*. London, 1687.

McKnight, George H. *St. Nicholas: His Legend and His Role in the Christmas Celebration and Other Popular Customs*. New York: G. P. Putnam's Sons, 1917.

McNaught, Rosamond Livingstone, ed. *Christmas Selections for Readings and Recitations*. Philadelphia, Penn.: Penn Publishing Co., 1917.

McSpadden, J. Walker. *The Book of Holidays*. New York: Thomas Y. Crowell Co., 1958.

Peterkin, Julia. *A Plantation Christmas*. Freeport, N.Y.: Books For Libraries Press, 1972.

Posselt, Eric, ed. *A Merry, Merry Christmas Book*. Englewood Cliffs, N.J.: Prentice-Hall, 1956.

The Reader's Digest Book of Christmas. Pleasantville, N.Y.: Reader's Digest Association, 1973.

Riis, Jacob A. *Children of the Tenements*. New York: Macmillan Co., 1905.

———. *Christmas Stories*. New York: Macmillan Co., 1923.

Rockwell, Molly, consulting ed. *Norman Rockwell's Christmas Book*. New York: Simon and Schuster, 1979.

Roehrenbeck, William, ed. *Christmastide: A Catholic Treasury for Young and Old*. New York: Stephen Daye Press, 1948.

Rollins, Charlemae, ed. *Christmas Gift*. Chicago: Follett Publishing Co., 1963.

Roosevelt, Eleanor, ed. *Eleanor Roosevelt's Christmas Book*. New York: Dodd, Mead and Co., 1963.

Sandoz, Mari. *The Christmas of the Phonograph Records: A Recollection*. Lincoln: University of Nebraska Press, 1966.

The Saturday Evening Post Christmas Stories. Indianapolis, Ind.: Curtis Publishing Co., 1980.

Sawyer, Ruth. *This Way to Christmas.* New York: Harper and Brothers, 1940.

Schauffler, Robert Haven. *Christmas.* New York: Dodd, Mead and Co., 1940.

————, ed. *The Days We Celebrate.* New York: Dodd, Mead and Co., 1946.

Sechrist, Elizabeth Hough, and Janette Woolsey, eds. *It's Time for Christmas.* Philadelphia, Penn.: Macrae Smith Co., 1959.

Shoemaker, Alfred L. *Christmas in Pennsylvania.* Kutztown: Pennsylvania Folklore Society, 1959.

Sibley, Celestine. *Christmas in Georgia.* New York: Doubleday, 1946.

Smith, Elva Sophronia, and Alice Isabel Hazeltine. *The Christmas Book of Legends and Stories.* New York: Lothrop, Lee and Shepard Co., 1944.

Steffens, Lincoln. *The Autobiography of Lincoln Steffens.* New York: Harcourt, Brace and Co., 1931.

Then, John N. *Christmas: A Collection of Christmaslore.* Milwaukee, Wis.:Bruce Publishing Co., 1934.

————. *Christmas Comes Again: A Second Book of Christmaslore.* Milwaukee, Wis.: Bruce Publishing Co., 1939.

Time Life Books. *The Glory and Pageantry of Christmas.* Maplewood, N.J.: Hammond, 1963.

Tittle, Walter, ed. *Colonial Holidays.* Garden City, N.Y.: Doubleday, Page and Co., 1910.

Townsend, Reginald T. *An Old-Fashioned Christmas.* New York: Doubleday, Doran and Co., 1902.

Traut, Elise. *Christmas in Heart and Home.* New York: Abbey Press, 1901.

Wagenknecht, Edward, ed. *The Fireside Book of Christmas Stories.* Indianapolis, Ind.: Bobbs-Merrill Co., 1945.

Wallenchinsky, David, and Irving Wallace. *The People's Almanac.* Garden City, N.Y.: Doubleday and Co., 1975.

Wallower, Lucille. *The Morning Star.* New York: David McKay Co., 1957.

Watts, Franklin, ed. *The Complete Christmas Book.* New York: Franklin Watts, 1961.

Weiser, Francis X. *The Christmas Book.* New York: Harcourt, Brace and Co., 1952.

Wernecke, Herbert H., ed. *Tales of Christmas From Near and Far.* Phliadelphia, Penn.: Westminster Press, 1963.

Wiggin, Kate Douglas. *The Romance of a Christmas Card.* Boston: Houghton Mifflin Co., 1915.

Wilder, Thornton. *The Long Christmas Dinner and Other Plays in One Act.* New York: Harper and Row, 1963.

Wilson, Dorothy, ed. *The Family Christmas Book.* Englewood Cliffs, N.J.: Prentice-Hall, 1957.

Woollcott, Alexander. *The Portable Woollcott.* Westport, Conn.: Greenwood Press, 1972.

Short Stories

Adams, Bill. "God Rest You, Merry Gentlemen." *Atlantic*, December 1938, 758–66.

Alden, Raymond MacDonald. "Why the Chimes Rang." *Coronet*, December 1950, 46–54.

"Americans Wander, But They Get Home for Christmas." *Saturday Evening Post*, 22 December 1956, 6.

Bach, Marcus. "One Town's Christmas." *Christian Century*, 18 December 1940, 1581–82.

"Bah and Humbug to Dr. Spock." *Life*, 10 December 1965, 4.

Bailey, Temple. "The Candle in the Forest." *Collier's*, 23 December 1950, 15.

———. "Three Who Stole at Christmas Time." *Good Housekeeping*, December 1923, 18.

Baldwin, Faith. "Christmas Has Taught Me This." *Good Housekeeping*, December 1952, 39.

Barbour, Ralph Henry. "A Christmas Surrender." *Cosmopolitan*, December 1903, 169–75.

Barnhouse, Donald Grey. "Let's Put Christ Back into Christmas!" *American Mercury*, December 1955, 153–58.

Baum, L. Frank. "Kidnapped Santa Claus." *Delineator*, December 1904, 986–89.

Beatty, Jerome, Jr. "Yes, Virginia, There Is a South Pole Santa Claus." *Collier's*, 70–74.

Becket, Jean C. "Brand-New World." *Saturday Evening Post*, 20 December 1941, 16.

———. "Deck The Halls." *New Yorker*, 25 December 1948, 17–24.

Benchley, Nathaniel. "A Pig for Christmas." *New Yorker*, 24 December 1949, 40–48.

Benchley, Robert. "In Pursuit of an Old-Fashioned Christmas." *Today's Health*, December 1974, 48–51.

Benjamin, Herbert S. "Dr. McDowell's Christmas Gamble." *Coronet*, December 1959, 142–43.

Bernoudy, Jane. "Jane Bernoudy Tells Here of an Alaskan Christmas." *Sunset*, December 1929, 31.

Bittle, Camilla. "Miracle at Midnight." *McCall's*, December 1957.

Blair, Virginia. "The Adventure of the Merry Heart." *Good Housekeeping*, December 1915, 747–51.

Blank, Joseph P. "Santa and the Sister." *Reader's Digest*, December 1978, 81–84.

Bloomingdale, Teresa. "My Life As Mrs. Santa Claus." *McCall's*, December 1979.

Boltwood, Edward. "The Heart of the Mistletoe." *Harper's Weekly*, 14 December 1901, 1250–61.

Booth, Charles E. "Behind Our Christmas Customs." *American Mercury*, December 1955, 96–99.

Bosworth, Jim and Allan. "The Christmas Racket." *Saturday Evening Post*, 10 December 1949, 31.

Bracken, Peg. "Husbands vs. Wifes vs. Christmas." *Ladies' Home Journal*, December 1965, 46.

Brooks, Helen Fislar. "Papa's Disappearing Christmas Tree." *Today's Health*, December 1963, 30.

Brown, Gary. "About 37 miles of track—A Christmas reminiscence." *Arizona Republic* (Phoenix), 20 December 1981, Arizona section, 8.

Brown, Harold O. J. "'Tis the Season to Be Surly." *National Review*, 26 December 1967, 1424–27.

Brown, Margery Finn. "The Night of the Magic." *McCall's*, December 1973, 69.

———. "A String of Popcorn." *McCall's*, December 1968, 79.

Buchwald, Art. "Joyeux Noel at Our Maison." *Coronet*, December 1960, 103–7.

Buck, Pearl S. "All the Days of Love and Courage." *Good Housekeeping*, December 1969, 73.

———. "Christmas Day in the Morning." *Collier's*, 23 December 1955, 10–12.

Burns, Eugene. "The Helpers of Hollywood." *Coronet*, December 1948, 93–97.

Calisher, Hortense. "A Christmas Carillon." *Harper's*, December 1953, 32–41.

Call, Hughie. "Always Listen for the Bells." *Redbook*, December 1965, 42.

Carr, Constance. "Christmas-card Winter." *American Mercury*, December 1961, 111–15.

Carter, Hodding. "A Street in Our Town." *Ladies' Home Journal*, December 1949, 51.

Carter, Judy Langford. "A Christmas Letter to My Children." *Redbook*, December 1979, 47.

———. "The Gift My Grandmother Gave Me." *Redbook*, December 1980, 31–33.

Case, Robert Ormond. "Christmas at Whitman's Mission." *Ladies' Home Journal*, December 1948, 56.

Cavanaugh, Arthur. "The Nights Before Christmas." *McCall's*, December 1964, 100.

Chase, Mary Ellen. "Old-Time Christmases in Maine." *Ladies' Home Journal*, December 1937, 28.

Cheever, John. "Christmas Is a Sad Season for the Poor." *New Yorker*, 24 December 1949, 19–22.

"Chicago's Christmas-Tree Ship." *The Literary Digest*, 20 December 1924, 36–38.

"Christmas at the Nixons'." *Time*, 26 December 1969, 6–7.

"Christmas in Wartime." *Journal of Home Economics*, December 1917, 576.

"Christmas Locket." *Old and New: The People's Magazine*, 25 December 1871, 1–96.

"Christmas Made in America." *Scientific American*, 18 October 1919, 393.

Coffey, Ivy M. "Mrs. Santa Claus—Personal Shopper to 3,000 Children." *Independent Woman*, December 1950, 368–70.

Cole, John N. "Taking the Tree." *Reader's Digest*, December 1978, 85–91.

Collins, Gary R. "'Tis the Season to Be Jolly—or Melancholy." *Christianity Today*, 7 December 1973, 5–6.

Coolidge, Mrs. Calvin. "What Christmas Means to Me." *Delineator*, December 1929, 8–9.

Cousins, Margaret. "The Homemade Miracle." *Good Housekeeping*, December 1941, 40.

———. "The Rockefeller Center Romance." *McCall's*, December 1960, 86.

———. "Virginia's Madness." *Woman's Home Companion*, December 1952, 30.

———. "A Visit to Aunt Adeline." *McCall's*, December 1977, 119.

Coyne, Patricia S. "Christmas at Sixty Below." *National Review*, 29 December 1970, 1405.

Craig, Robert. "Maggie's Christmas Tree." *Ladies' Home Journal*, December 1950, 40.

Crothers, Samuel McCloud. "Christmas and the Spirit of Democracy." *Everybody's Magazine*, December 1907, 794–99.

Crowell, Marnie Reed. "Our Farmhouse Christmas." *Reader's Digest*, December 1973, 61–64.

Dale, Virginia. "Christmas Secret." *Ladies' Home Journal*, December 1931, 23.

Dalmas, Herbert. "Santa's Last Trip." *American Magazine*, December 1952, 18–19.

D'Aloise, Lawrence. "Message of the Beads." *Seventeen*, December 1975, 91.

"Dear Mom." *House Beautiful*, December 1943, 58.

De Forest, Lockwood and Elizabeth. "Christmas in a Santa Barbara Garden." *Sunset*, December 1929, 20–21.

Devoe, Alan. "Natural History of Christmas." *American Mercury*, December 1948, 730–34.

DeVoto, Bernard. "Seed Corn and Mistletoe." *Harper's*, December 1936, 109–12.

DeZouche, Dorothy. "All Is Calm, All Is Bright." *Ladies' Home Journal*, December 1949, 50.

Dickson, Alex. "Why a Tree for Christmas?" *American Christmas Tree Growers' Journal*, November 1963, 5.

Didion, Joan. "The Big Rock Candy Figgy Pudding Pitfall." *Saturday Evening Post*, 3 December 1966, 22.

Donnell, Annie Hamilton. "Her First Christmas Party." *Country Life*, December 1906, 193–98.

Dreiser, Theodore. "Christmas in the Tenements." *Harper's Weekly*, 6 December 1902, 52–53.

Duncan, Vera. "The Gift of Memory at Christmas." *Hobbies*, December 1964, 28.

Dunne, F. P. "Mr. Dooley on the Christmas Spirit." *American Magazine*, December 1906, 172–74.

————. "Mr. Dooley's Christmas Scheme." *Ladies' Home Journal*, December 1902, 14.

Dunne, Irene. "Christmas in Hollywood." *Good Housekeeping*, December 1954, 13.

Edmondson, Vera. "The Steig Bear." *Good Housekeeping*, December 1915, 737–46.

Egan, James. "The Boyhood Joys of Christmas." *Good Housekeeping*, December 1971, 44.

Ellis, Carlyle. "We Decorate For a Desert Christmas." *Christian Science Monitor*, 14 December 1940.

Evans, Nell Womack. "If I Had a Child This Christmas." *American Mercury*, December 1956, 25–28.

Fante, John. "Papa Christmas Tree." *Woman's Home Companion*, December 1946, 18.

Farnum, William. "The Bowery Sees a Christmas Miracle." *Coronet*, December 1951, 21–25.

Fick, Alvin S. "Christmas on Bitter Creek." *Conservationist*, December 1973-January 1974, 3–5.

Forbes, Kathryn. "Mama and the Christmas Tradition." *Good Housekeeping*, December 1945.

Ford, Corey. "The Boy Who Was Born Again." *Collier's*, 25 December 1952, 94–97.

————. "'Twas the Night *After* Christmas." *Reader's Digest*, January 1960, 177–79.

Fosdick, Harry Emerson. "Christmas and the Family." *Pictorial Review*, January 1931, 1.

Frank, Gerold. "The Littlest Tree." *Coronet*, December 1954, 71–78.

Gallico, Paul. "Silent Night." *Saturday Evening Post*, 15 December 1962, 22–25.

"A Garland of Christmases Past." *McCall's*, December 1967, 96.

Gibbs, Sir Philip. "This Is Station XMAS." *Reader's Digest*, December 1934, 1–3.

Gilbert, Halpin O'Reilly. "A Christmas Pilgrimage." *Catholic World*, January 1940, 402–6.

Gill, Brendan. "A Little Rain." *New Yorker*, 27 December 1941, 36–37.

Gilligan, E. "Long Charles Has His Christmas." *Collier's* 30 December 1950, 12.

Gillis, J. M. "Christmas in War Time." *The Catholic World*, January 1942, 385–88.

Godden, Rumer. "The Fairy Doll." *Ladies' Home Journal*, December 1955, 58.

Gross, Amy. "A Christmas Memory." *Mademoiselle*, December 1973, 124.

Hale, Edward Everett. "The Same Christmas in Old England and New." *The Galaxy*, 1868, 47–59.

Hartt, Susan L. "Christmas in Miami." *McCall's*, December 1977, 32.

Hastings, Mary. "A Forbidden Christmas." *Good Housekeeping*, December 1909, 650–59.

Hayes, Helen. "The Happiest Holiday I Ever Spent." *House Beautiful*, January 1943, 13.

Heath, Aloise Buckley. "A Trapp Family Christmas." *National Review*, 30 December 1969, 1317–19.

Heath, Pam, et al. "The True Spirit of Christmas." *National Review*, 4 January 1974, 24.

Henderson, Robert. "The Circular Tent." *New Yorker*, 20 December 1952, 30–35.

———. "The Spectre of the Fir Tree." *New Yorker*, 21 September 1957, 38–41.

Herrmann, Helen Markel. "Carmel Christmas." *House Beautiful*, December 1945, 99.

Herrod, Virginia. "Our First Christmas . . . Without You." *American Home*, December 1944, 26.

Hill, Elizabeth Starr. "A Young Girl's Gift." *Reader's Digest*, December 1966, 49–52.

Hiltner, Seward. "Sadnesses of Christmas." *Christian Century*, 19 December 1973, 1262.

Hilton, James. "To Whom It May Concern." *Good Housekeeping*, December 1938, 107.

Hoban, Russell. "Emmet Otter's Jug-Band Christmas." *Parents*, December 1973, 42–45.

Hoffman, J. E. "The Mountain Comes to Mohomet." *Recreation*, November 1941, 497.

Hoffman, Paul. "Country Christmas." *Atlantic*, December 1935, 712–17.

Hoover, Herbert. "Peace on Earth, Good Will to Men." *The Independent*, 25 December 1920, 419–20.

Hoover, J. Edgar. "My Most Memorable Christmas." *Coronet*, December 1952, 37.

Hoyt, Eleanor. "The Black Sheep's Christmas." *Ladies' Home Journal*, December 1904.

Hughes, Carol. "Lady Santa to Lonely Children." *Coronet*, December 1948, 45–48.

Hutcheson, Maud MacDonald. "Into the Byways." *Nature*, December 1938, 581–83.

"I Remember A Christmas—Stories from the Lives of Four Celebrities." *Delineator*, December 1923, 10–11.

Iversen, William. "The Dooley Miracle." *Good Housekeeping*, December 1959, 58.

Jackson, Margaret Weymouth. "Anthony Scarlet's Christmas Eve." *Good Housekeeping*, December 1935, 42.

Johnson, Mrs. Lyndon B. "Christmas Memories from the White House." *McCall's*, December 1968, 81.

Kane, Harnett T. "Christmas Deferred." *Collier's*, 23 March 1946, 72.

Kantor, MacKinley. "The Legend of Jones City." *McCall's*, December 1963, 63.

Kavanaugh, James. "Christmas Doesn't Mean Much Anymore." *Saturday Evening Post*, 16 December 1967, 10–12.

Keller, James. "God's Finger on a Man's Shoulder." *Good Housekeeping*, December 1952, 30.

Kent, Louise Andrews. "Mrs. Appelyard Almost Forgets *Which* Christmas This Is." *House Beautiful*, December 1943, 62.

Keyes, Frances Parkinson. "*Under the Eaves.*" *St. Nicholas*, December 1937, 24–26.

King, Grace. "A War-Time Santa Claus." *Collier's*, 11 December 1909, 12.

Kirkland, Winifred. "A Christmas City of the Old South." *North American Review*, December 1923.

Klein, Norma. "Sunshine Christmas." *Ladies' Home Journal*, December 1977, 125.

Knott, Desmond. "Miracle on the Roof." *Woman's Home Companion*, December 1949, 20.

LaFarge, Oliver. "The Snow Too Deep." *New Yorker*, 26 December 1953, 22–26.

Laughton, Charles. "The Charles Laughton Christmas Reader." *Good Housekeeping*, December 1960, 49–55.

Lawrence, Mary Preston. "Christmas Down Yonder." *Ladies' Home Journal*, December 1946, 49.

L'Engle, Madeleine. "A Full House." *McCall's*, December 1980, 98.

Levien, Sonya. "Sentimental New York." *The Survey*, 4 January 1913, 415–16.

Lew, Marion. "Santa Santa." *Ladies' Home Journal*, December 1977, 88.

Lockwood, Sarah M. "'Round Robin's Red Barn." *Country Life*, December 1925, 66–67.

Luce, Clare Booth. "Christmas in the White House." *McCall's*, December 1966, 48.

Lyons, Ruth. "Trim a Tree for Mary." *American Magazine*, January 1942, 26–28.

MacKay, Constance D'Arcy. "The Miracle of Saint Nicholas." *Woman's Home Companion*, December 1928, 28.

Mahlo, Jery. "A Christmas Eve to Remember." *Parents*, January 1940, 15.

"Man Who Saved Christmas for the Children." *American History Illustrated*, December 1980, 43.

March, Fredric. "Papa Christmas." *American Magazine*, December 1955, 88.

Marshall, Jim. "Canyon Christmas." *Collier's*, 20 December 1941, 13.

Martin, Edward S. "Christmas Again." *Harper's*, December 1923, 36–37.

Martin, Mary. "A Family Christmas with Mary Martin." *Harper's Bazaar*, December 1978, 52.

Marx, Joseph and Adeline. "The Gift That Mattered." *Ladies' Home Journal*, December 1948, 38.

McCarthy, Joe. "The Tall, Attractive Blonde." *Good Housekeeping*, December 1952, 56.

———. "The Undiscourage Fiancè." *Good Housekeeping*, December 1956, 80.

McCarthy, Marianne. "Broken Tradition." *Seventeen*, December 1977, 112–13.

McCay, Winsor. ". . . And a Merry Christmas from Little Nemo." *Redbook*, December 1965, 70–71.

McFarlane, Margaret and Arthur E. "An Enganglement of Ties." *McClure's*, December 1909, 221–30.

McInerny, Ralph. "The Pain of Possession." *Redbook*, December 1966, 46.

McLean, Margharite Fisher. "The Lonesome Christmas-Tree." *Scribner's*, December 1926, 646–55.

McNair, Kate. "A Tale for Christmas Eve." *McCall's*, December 1980.

McWhirter, Millie. "The Day Santa Rode the Caboose." *Coronet*, January 1959, 25–28.

Mead, Margaret. "At Christmas I Remember . . ." *Redbook*, December 1969, 66–71.

———. "Can Christmas Bring the Generations Together?" *Redbook*, December 1973, 27–28.

———. "The Gift of Celebrating Christmas." *Redbook*, December 1974, 4.

Melick, Weldon. "A Merry Secondhand Christmas." *Reader's Digest*, December 1936, 96–98.

Melton, Jeanne. "The Night My Father Came Home." *Saturday Evening Post*, 12 December 1953, 23.

"Memory Lane." *Good Housekeeping*, December 1953, 4.

Mooney, Philip. "Lindbergh and the Quiet of Christmas." *Commonweal*, 17 December 1976, 818–20.

Murdock, Henrietta. "Christmas at the Smiths'." *Ladies' Home Journal*, December 1942, 104.

Nelson, Kay Shaw. "A Moravian Christmas." *Americana*, November-December 1979, 54.

Norris, Kathleen. "Christmas." *Pictorial Review*, December 1929, 1.

Odell, Joseph H. "A Santa Claus on the Western Front." *Ladies' Home Journal*, December 1918.

O'Flaherty, Shane. "The Man Who Scorned Christmas." *Saturday Evening Post*, 19 December 1959, 29.

O'Hare, Joseph A. "A Season for Stories." *America*, 25 December 1976, 457.

Oliver, Owen. "Sparrows: A Christmas Story." *Lippincott*, December 1909, 675–83.

O'Roark, Mary Ann. "Christmas with the Crosbys." *McCall's*, December 1976, 78.

———. "The Star at the Top of My Tree Is Moi." *McCall's*, December 1980, 10.

Orr, Clifford. "The Death of Santa Claus." *New Yorker*, 23 December 1933, 14–16.

Overton, Gwendolen. "Esther's Christmas." *St. Nicholas*, January 1910, 227–31.

Paine, Albert Bigelow. "Christmas Luck." *Harper's Weekly*, 6 December 1902, 28–29.

Pauli, Hertha. "Our First Christmas Tree." *Reader's Digest*, December 1944, 31–34.

Pearson, Roy M. "Simon's Christmas." *Christian Century*, 23 December 1953, 1496–98.

Peeples, Edwin A. "Roadhouse Christmas." *Saturday Evening Post*, 25 December 1954, 28.

Petracca, Joseph. "Practically Christmas." *Collier's*, 1 January 1949, 17.

Phillips, Ethel Calvert. "The Brownies' Christmas Eve." *Ladies' Home Journal*, December 1928, 163–67.

———. "The Brownie Who Found Christmas." *Ladies' Home Journal*, December 1927, 6.

Phillips, H. I. "Christmas Ain't What It Used to Be." *Collier's*, 25 December 1926, 10–11.

Pickett, La Salle Corbert. "An Old-Time Virginia Christmas." *Harper's Bazaar*, January 1907, 48–54.

Pillsbury, Dorothy L. "Drums of Christmas." *Christian Science Monitor*, 20 December 1947, 5.

Pinkerton, Anne. "Cluck-Cluck and Christmas." *Coronet*, December 1956, 36–38.

Portor, Laura Spencer. "The Christmas Dance at 'Old Oaks.' " *Ladies' Home Journal*, December 1903, 11.

Powers, J. F. "A Couple of Nights Before Christmas." *New Yorker*, 21 December 1957, 30–38.

Rabin, Arnold. "The Runaway Christmas Stockings." *Ladies' Home Journal*, December 1963, 138a–138d.

Rodgers, Mary Augusta. "Two-Gun Holiday." *American Magazine*, December 1950, 38.

Roosevelt, Eleanor. "A Christmas-Spirited Housekeeping." *Reader's Digest*, December 1937, 1.

———. "If You Ask Me." *McCall's*, December 1959, 48.

———. "The Right To Give." *Woman's Home Companion*, December 1934, 21.

Roselund, Ruth G. "Christmas in the Sky." *American Mercury*, December 1954, 15–17.

Ruark, Robert C. "The Old Man and the Boy." *Field & Stream*, January 1955, 6–8.

Ruhen, Olaf. "Barren Christmas." *Saturday Evening Post*, December 1955, 26.

Rutledge, Archibald. "Carolina Festival." *Coronet*, December 1949, 117–19.

Saroyan, William. "Christmas." *Good Housekeeping*, December 1943, 21.

Savage, Elizabeth. "Bitter Christmas." *Saturday Evening Post*, November 29, 1952.

Sawyer, Ruth. "The Boy Who Saved Christmas." *Coronet*, December 1951, 44.

Schaefer, Jack. "The Raiders of Saint Nicholas, A Story of Christmas Eve at the Slash Y." *Saturday Evening Post*, 17 December 1960, 16.

Scheffauer, Herman. "The Man Who Hated Christmas." *Harper's Weekly*, 21 December 1912, 14–15.

Scott, Vernon. "Grandpa Sinatra." *Ladies' Home Journal*, December 1975, 71.

Scott, William R. "The Skinflint." *Collier's*, 16 December 1950, 21.

Scroggs, William O. "Christmas and the Payroll." *Outlook*, 18 December 1929, 621.

Sergeant, Elizabeth Shepley. "Christmas in the Pueblos." *Survey*, 1 December 1923, 252.

Shafer, Elizabeth. "Santa Discovers Christmas." *Harvest Years*, December 1968, 14–17.

Sheard, Virna. "The Christmas Peacemaker." *New England Magazine*, December 1900, 438–46.

Siddons, Anne River. "Christmas Country." *House Beautiful*, December 1968, 65–67.

Smith, Lillian. "Memories of Christmas." *McCall's*, December 1979, 121–25.

Soman, Florence Jane. "The Surprising Stranger." *Good Housekeeping*, December 1971, 71.

Sowder, Arthur M. "Christmas Trees: The Tradition and the Trade." *U.S. Department of Agriculture Bulletin No. 94*, 1966.

Spock, Benjamin. "Christmas When I Was a Boy." *Redbook*, December 1980, 40.

———. "Making the Holidays Pleasant for Children—and Their Parents." *Redbook*, December 1965, 20.

Spofford, Harriet Prescott. "Nancy's Southern Christmas." *St. Nicholas*, December 1912, 161–64.

Stanton, Will. "The Trail of Ernestine." *McCall's*, December 1975, 71.

Stapleton, Ruth Carter. "Christmas with the Carters." *Ladies' Home Journal*, December 1977, 74.

Steun, Richard Martin. "The Cherishing Kind." *Good Housekeeping*, December 1963.

Stong, Phil. "Christmas in Iowa." *Holiday*, December 1952, 83–84.

Streeter, Edward. "You Can't Run Away from Christmas." *McCall's*, December 1964, 112.

Swett-Sommers, Naomi. "Memories of Early Oregon Christmases." *Sunset*, December 1929, 29–30.

Swigget, Geoffrey Palamore. "The Exegesis of St. Nick." *New Yorker*, 24 December 1966, 28–29.

Taber, Gladys. "Diary of Domesticity." *Ladies' Home Journal*, 218–20.

Taylor, Theodore. "The Christmas Parade." *McCall's*, December 1975, 104.

Tazewell, Charles. "The Bells of Christmas." *Coronet*, December 1953, 37–46.

———. "The Littlest Angel." *Coronet*, December 1949, 53–68.

———. "The Littlest Snowman Rescues Christmas." *Coronet*, December 1956, 94–106.

———. "The Littlest Stork." *Coronet*, December 1952, 46–54.

Temple, Shirley. "Shirley Temple Tells a Christmas Story." *American Home*, December 1958, 23.

Temple, Willard. "Cherub in Black." *Good Housekeeping*, December 1960, 86.

Thomas, Dorothy. "The Christmas Lie." *Saturday Evening Post*, 21 December 1957, 18.

———. "The Home Place: Christmas Morning." *Harper's*, January 1936, 210–24.

Tigner, High Stevenson. "Christians Had a Hard Christmas." *Christian Century*, 17 January 1940, 77–78.

Truman, Harry S. "The Love of Our Fellow Man." *Vital Speeches*, 1 January 1950.

———. "The Spirit of Peace." *Vital Speeches*, 1 January 1946, 162.

"U.S. Troops Bring Their Christmas to the World . . ." *Newsweek*, 29 December 1952, 24–27.

Van Horne, Harriet. "The Christmas Syndrome or Must We Hang Mother on the Christmas Tree?" *Redbook*, December 1967, 38–44.

Viorst, Judith. "Dear TWIMC: A Holiday Letter." *Redbook*, December 1978, 56.

Warwick, Loy. "How the Willopus-Wallopus Came to Sour Apple Cove." *Coronet*, December 1958, 109–28.

Weaver, Philip. "Christmases and Christmases." *Overland Monthly*, January 1893, 32–44.

Webb, Walter Prescott. "Christmas and New Year in Texas." *Southwestern Historical Quarterly* 44 (July 1940-April 1941): 357–79.

Weeks, Edward. "Christmas on 25 Cents a Week." *Reader's Digest*, December 1964, 95–96.

Wertkin, Gerard C. "Christmas at the Shakers." *Horizon*, December 1978, 27–29.

Wheeler, A. C. "Going Home for Christmas." *Harper's Weekly*, 8 December 1900, 1153.

White, Agnes Frances. "The Night of the Angels." *McCall's*, December 1974, 92.

"Why Take Christ out of Christmas?" *American Mercury*, December 1957, 114–16.

Wiesner, Alma. "Christmas Candy." *New Republic*, 28 December 1918, 246–48.

Wiley, Harvey W. "Christmas—As It Seems to Me." *Good Housekeeping*, December 1922, 32.

Woodrum, Lon. "Dark Counsel at Christmas." *Christianity Today*, 20 December 1968, 12.

Wright, Katharine O. "Mountain Christmas." *Atlantic*, December 1940, 727–31.

Wyatt, Edith. "A Beggar's Christmas." *Atlantic*, December 1908, 848–50.

Wylie, Philip. "Company for Christmas Dinner." *Saturday Evening Post*, 23 December 1950, 18.

394.26
RUL

Rulon, Philip Reed.

Keeping Christmas.

$27.50

DATE			

MAR 1991

© THE BAKER & TAYLOR CO.